THE AMERICAN WEST 1840–1895

The Struggle for the Plains

a study in depth

THE SCHOOLS HISTORY PROJECT · OFFICIAL TEXT · S·H·P

DISCOVERING THE PAST FOR GCSE

Dave Martin
Colin Shephard

Series Editor:
Colin Shephard

Hodder Murray
A MEMBER OF THE HODDER HEADLINE GROUP

The Schools History Project

This project was set up by the Schools Council in 1972. Its main aim was to suggest suitable aims for History teachers, and to promote the use of appropriate materials and teaching methods for their realisation. This involved a reconsideration of the nature of history and its relevance in secondary schools, the design of a syllabus framework which shows the uses of history in the education of adolescents, and the setting up of appropriate examinations.

Since 1978 the project has been based at Trinity and All Saints' College, Leeds. It is now self-funding and with the advent of the National Curriculum it has expanded its publications to provide courses for Key Stage 3, and for a range of GCSE and A level syllabuses. The project provides INSET for all aspects of National Curriculum, GCSE and A level history.

Series consultants
Terry Fiehn
Tim Lomas
Martin and Jenny Tucker

© Dave Martin and Colin Shephard 1998

First published in 1998
by Hodder Murray, a member of the Hodder Headline Group
338 Euston Road
London NW1 3BH

Reprinted 1999 (twice) 2001, 2002 (twice), 2003, 2004, 2005 (twice)

All rights reserved. No part of this publication may be reproduced in any material form (including photocopying or storing in any medium by electronic means and whether or not transiently or incidentally to some other use of this publication) without the written permission of the publisher, except in accordance with provisions of the Copyright, Designs and Patents Act 1988 or under the terms of a licence issued by the Copyright Licensing Agency.

Layouts by Liz Rowe
Artwork by Barking Dog Art and Steve Smith
Typeset in 10.5/12pt Walbaum Book
Colour separations by Colourscript, Mildenhall, Suffolk.
Printed and bound in Spain by Bookprint S.L., Barcelona

A catalogue entry for this title is available from the British Library.

ISBN - 10: 0 7195 5181 1
ISBN - 13: 978 0 719 55181 9
Teachers' Resource Book ISBN 0 7195 5182 X

Note: The wording and sentence structure of some written sources have been adapted and simplified to make them accessible to all students, while faithfully preserving the sense of the original.

Words printed in SMALL CAPITALS are defined in the Glossary on page 163.

Contents

Introduction — 2
The struggle for the Plains — 2
Outlaws and savages: was that the real West? — 6

Section 1: The Plains Indians

Chapter 1: Introduction — 12
The 'Great American Desert'? — 12
Who were the Plains Indians? — 14

Chapter 2: How did the Indians solve the problems of living on the Great Plains? — 16
The daily life of the Sioux — 16
How important was the buffalo to the Plains Indians? — 22
How warlike were the Sioux? — 28
How important were horses to the Plains Indians? — 32
How religious were the Sioux? — 34
Who treated the sick in Plains Indian nations? — 38
Living on the Plains — 40
Not a Sioux village! — 42

Chapter 3: The attitudes of outsiders towards the Plains Indians — 44
The witnesses of Plains Indian life — 44
Plains Indian life as outsiders saw it — 46
Land – the big issue — 48
Manifest Destiny — 50

Section 2: The settlers

Chapter 4: The early pioneers – why did they cross the Plains? — 54
The mountain men lead the way west — 54
Wagons west! — 58
What was it like to travel west? — 60
The California Gold Rush — 68
Why were the Mormons so unpopular in the East? — 72
Why did the Mormons succeed in the West? — 76

Chapter 5: How did the homesteaders and ranchers settle the Plains? — 82
The homesteaders: why did so many people want to settle on the Plains? — 83
Did all the homesteaders go west for the same motives? — 84
How did homesteaders survive on the Plains? — 86
How important was the role of women in homesteading? — 90
How did the cattle industry develop? — 94
The development of ranching on the Plains — 98
Who were the cowboys and what was their life like? — 100
Why was there conflict between cattle ranchers and homesteaders? — 104
Case study: the Johnson County War — 106

Chapter 6: How wild was the West? — 108
Why was there lawlessness or violence in the West? — 110
Billy the Kid: hero or killer? — 116
Abilene: law and order in a cow town — 120

Section 3: Why did the Indians lose the struggle for the Plains?

Conflict on the Plains: a chronology — 124

Chapter 7: What role did the US army play in the defeat of the Plains Indians? — 126
Negotiate or exterminate? — 126
Why did the Sioux go to war? — 128
Was the US army well equipped for war with the Plains Indians? — 134
Was Custer responsible for the defeat of the US army at the Battle of the Little Bighorn? — 138
Was Crazy Horse a great American hero? — 146

Chapter 8: How did the USA destroy the Indian way of life? — 148
The destruction of the buffalo herds — 148
How were reservations used to control the Plains Indians? — 152

Chapter 9: Conclusion — 157
Review: why did the Indians lose, or the settlers gain, control of the Great Plains? — 157
Why study the American West? — 159

Glossary — 163
Index — 164
Acknowledgements — 166

INTRODUCTION

The struggle for the Plains

IN THIS BOOK you will be investigating the history of the American West during a period of dramatic change.

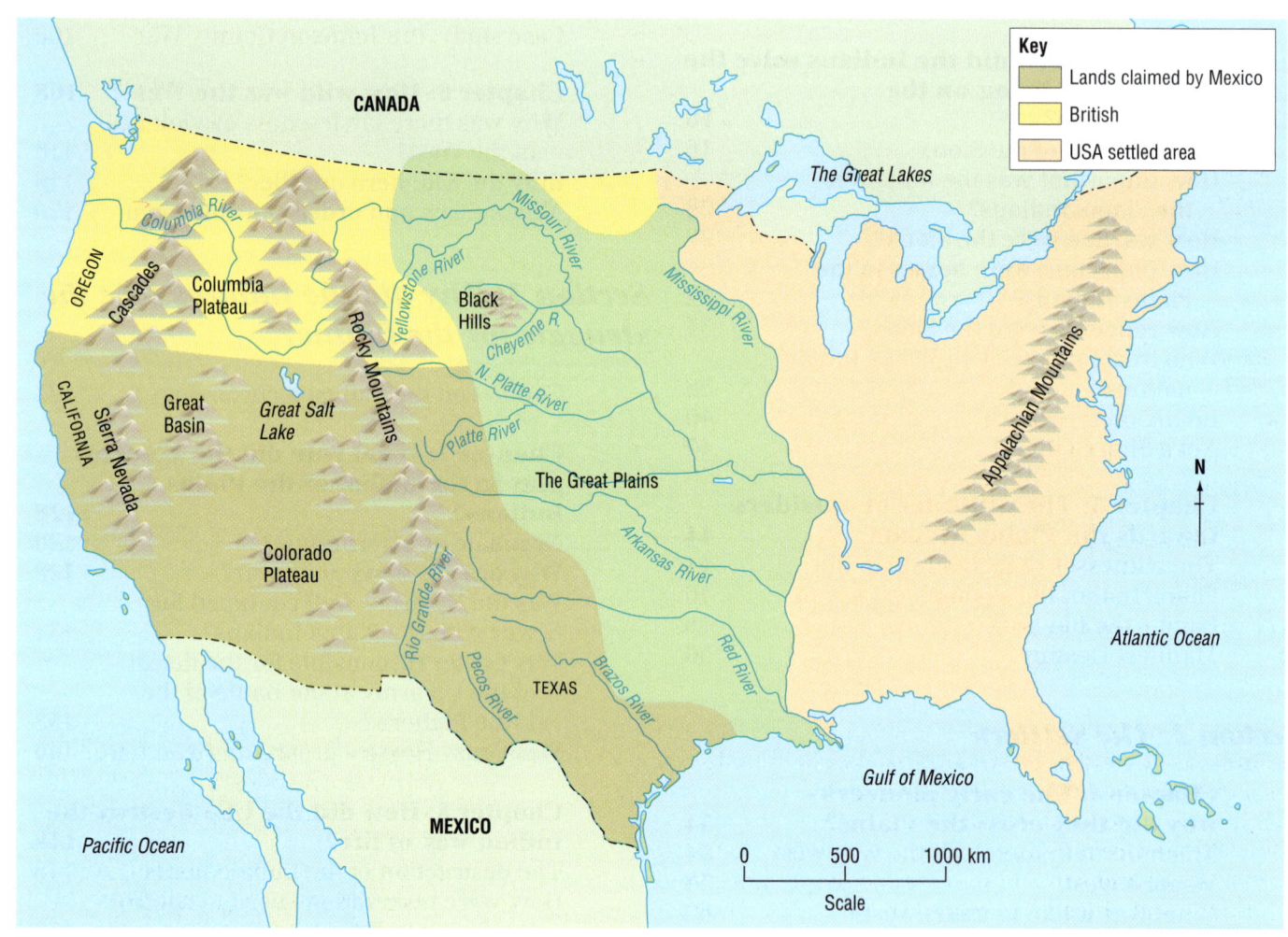

SOURCE 1 North America in 1840

THE STRUGGLE FOR THE PLAINS

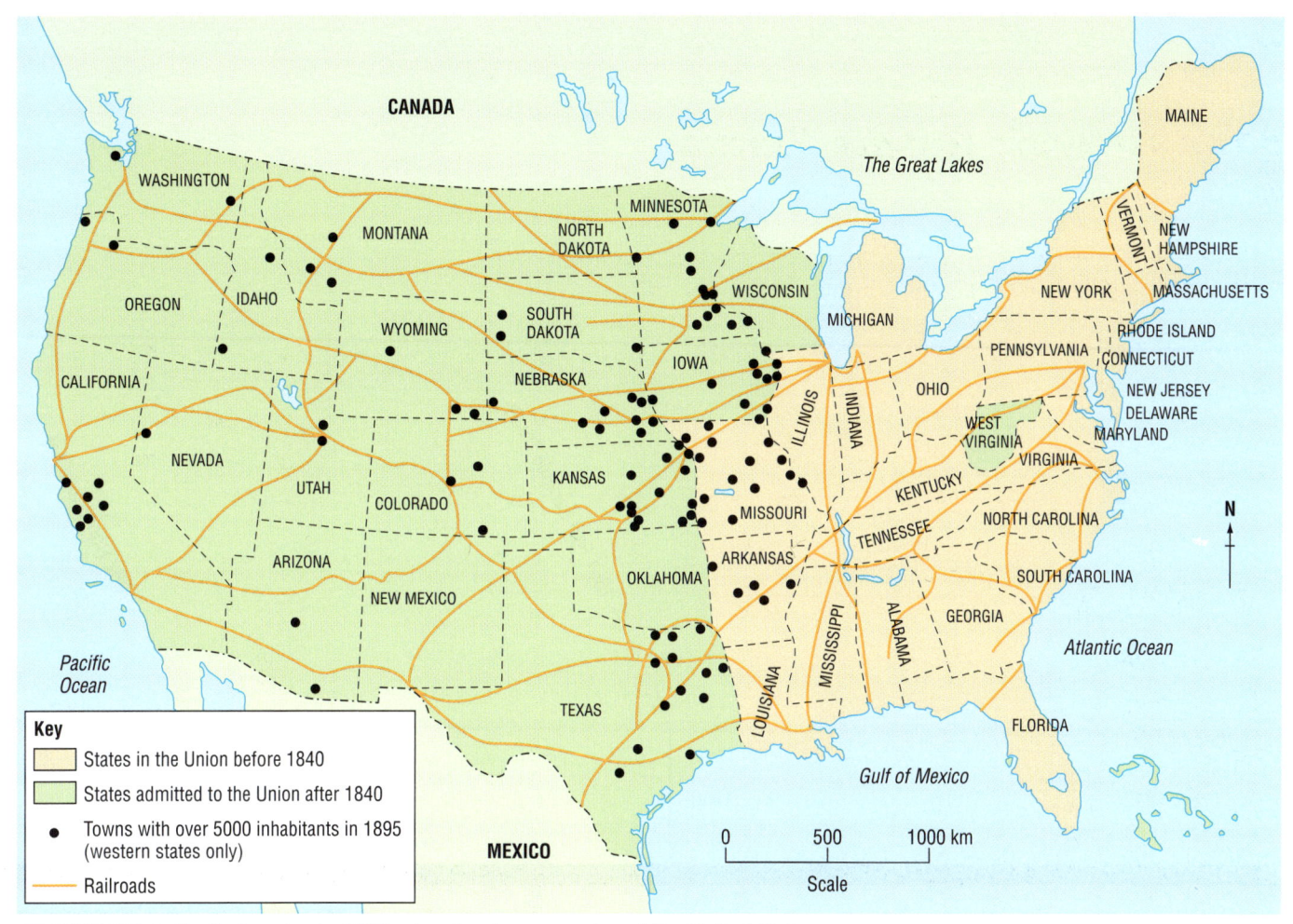

SOURCE 2 North America in 1895, showing the expansion of the United States

In 1840 the Great Plains were sparsely inhabited by the Plains Indians. The Indians depended upon the huge herds of buffalo that roamed the grasslands. To the few non-Indians who travelled across them, the Great Plains were a useless desert.

By 1895 the Great Plains were populated by thousands of HOMESTEADERS and ranchers. The once-empty grasslands were dotted with towns and cities and crossed by railroads. Those Plains Indians who still survived were confined to RESERVATIONS and the buffalo had all been slaughtered.

Why was it that, by 1895, settlers had taken over the Plains from the Indians? In this book you will consider a number of issues which will help you answer that question:

- How did the Plains Indians survive on the Great Plains?
- Why did the settlers want to move out on to the Great Plains?
- How did they get there?
- How did they survive on the Great Plains?
- What happened when the Indians and settlers met?
- Why did they come into conflict?
- What were the results of that conflict?

Plains Indians is the term used in this book to cover the many different nations such as the Sioux and the Cheyenne who lived in this region. It is a name that foreign explorers gave to the indigenous peoples of North America, but it is not a name that many of these people would use to describe themselves today.

THE STRUGGLE FOR THE PLAINS

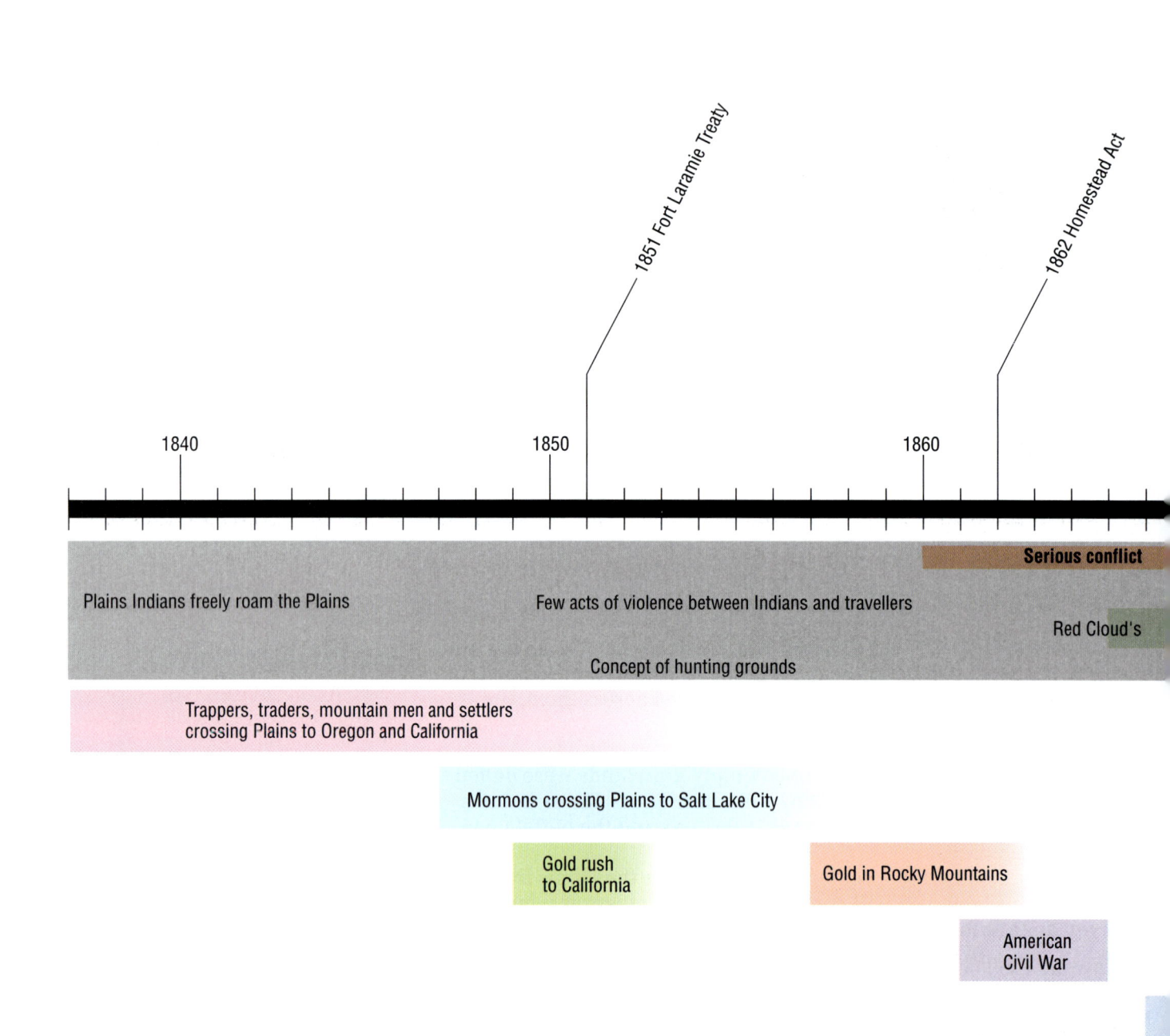

1840	1850	1860	

1851 Fort Laramie Treaty

1862 Homestead Act

Serious conflict

Plains Indians freely roam the Plains   Few acts of violence between Indians and travellers

Red Cloud's

Concept of hunting grounds

Trappers, traders, mountain men and settlers crossing Plains to Oregon and California

Mormons crossing Plains to Salt Lake City

Gold rush to California

Gold in Rocky Mountains

American Civil War

THE STRUGGLE FOR THE PLAINS

SOURCE 3 Timeline of the American West 1840–95

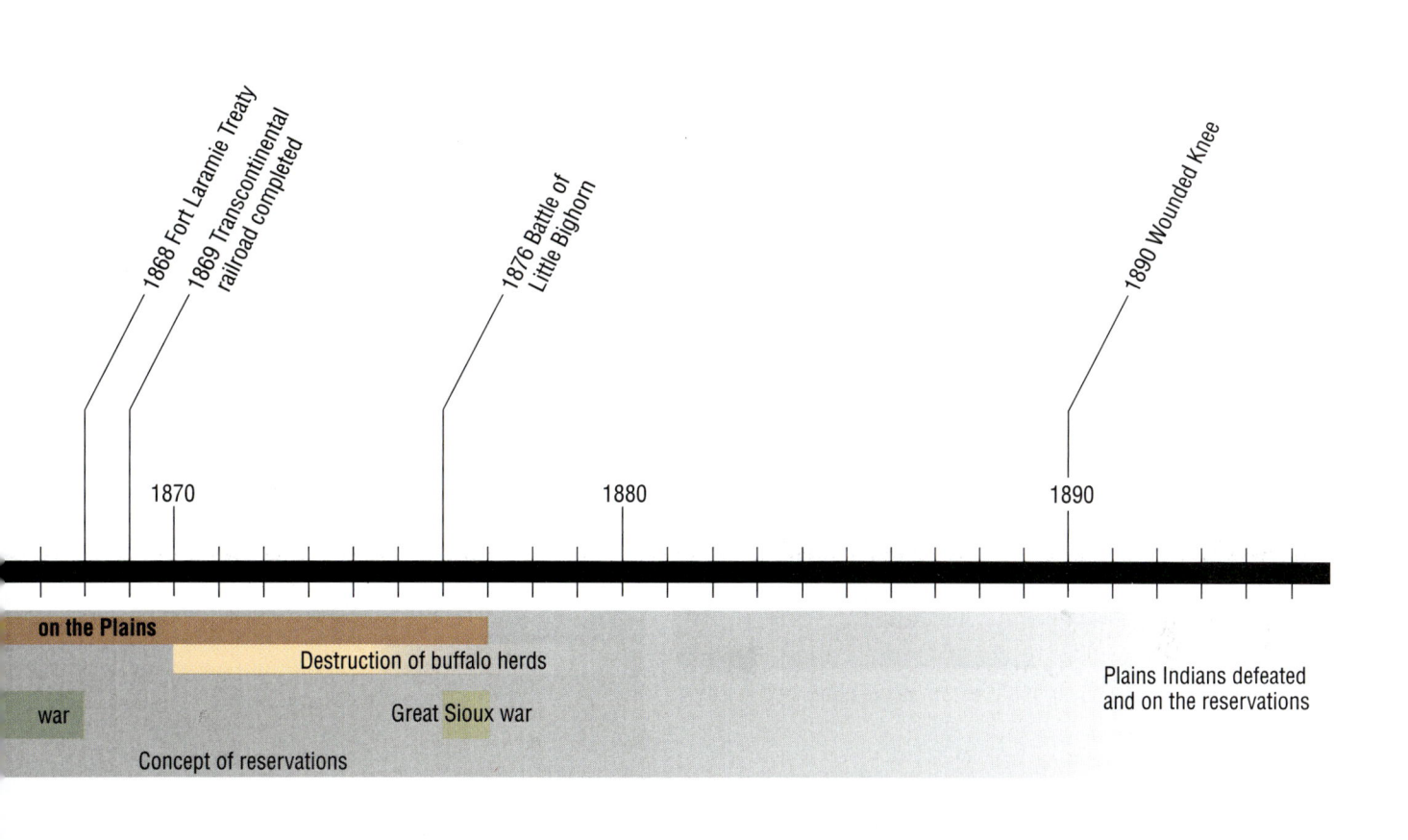

- 1868 Fort Laramie Treaty
- 1869 Transcontinental railroad completed
- 1876 Battle of Little Bighorn
- 1890 Wounded Knee

1870 — 1880 — 1890

on the Plains
Destruction of buffalo herds
war
Great Sioux war
Concept of reservations
Plains Indians defeated and on the reservations

Gold in Black Hills
Transcontinental railroad
Cattle drives from Texas
Cattle ranching on Plains
Homesteaders settle the Plains

Outlaws and savages: was that the real West?

SOURCE 1 The cover of a Western novel published in 1996

SOURCE 2 Comanche Indians attacking a wagon train

SOURCE 3 An Indian scalping a dead cavalryman, an engraving from 1892

SOURCE 4 *A dash for the Timber,* a painting by Frederic Remington, 1889

OUTLAWS AND SAVAGES: WAS THAT THE REAL WEST?

SOURCE 5 An engraving showing railroad passengers shooting buffalo in the 1870s

SOURCE 6 A still from a film based on the life of Wild Bill Hickok, made in 1995

■ TASK

Sources 1–7 show various aspects of the American West.

1. What is happening in each source?
2. What impression of the American West do they give?

Now turn over to look at Sources 8–14.

SOURCE 7 Victims of a VIGILANTE hanging in Kansas

7

OUTLAWS AND SAVAGES: WAS THAT THE REAL WEST?

SOURCE 8 The reconstructed town of Silver City at the 'American Adventure' Theme Park in Derbyshire, England

SOURCE 9 A grocery store in the town of Sparks, Nevada

SOURCE 10 The mining town of Helena, Montana, in the 1870s

SOURCE 11 Cowboy CHUCK WAGON exhibit in the American Museum, Bath, England

■ **TASK**

Sources 8–14 show various aspects of the American West.

1. What is happening in each source?
2. What impression of the American West do they give?
3. Is this impression different from the one you got from Sources 1–7?

8

OUTLAWS AND SAVAGES: WAS THAT THE REAL WEST?

SOURCE 12 The Shores family, homesteaders, in Custer County, Nebraska, 1887

SOURCE 13 A Kiowa Indian village, a painting by Baldwin Mollhausen

SOURCE 14 *American Express Train*, painted by Fanny Palmer, 1864

At the end of this depth study you should return to these pages and make your selection of seven picture sources that, in your opinion, give a balanced view of the American West. You will need to justify your choice.

section 1

THE PLAINS INDIANS

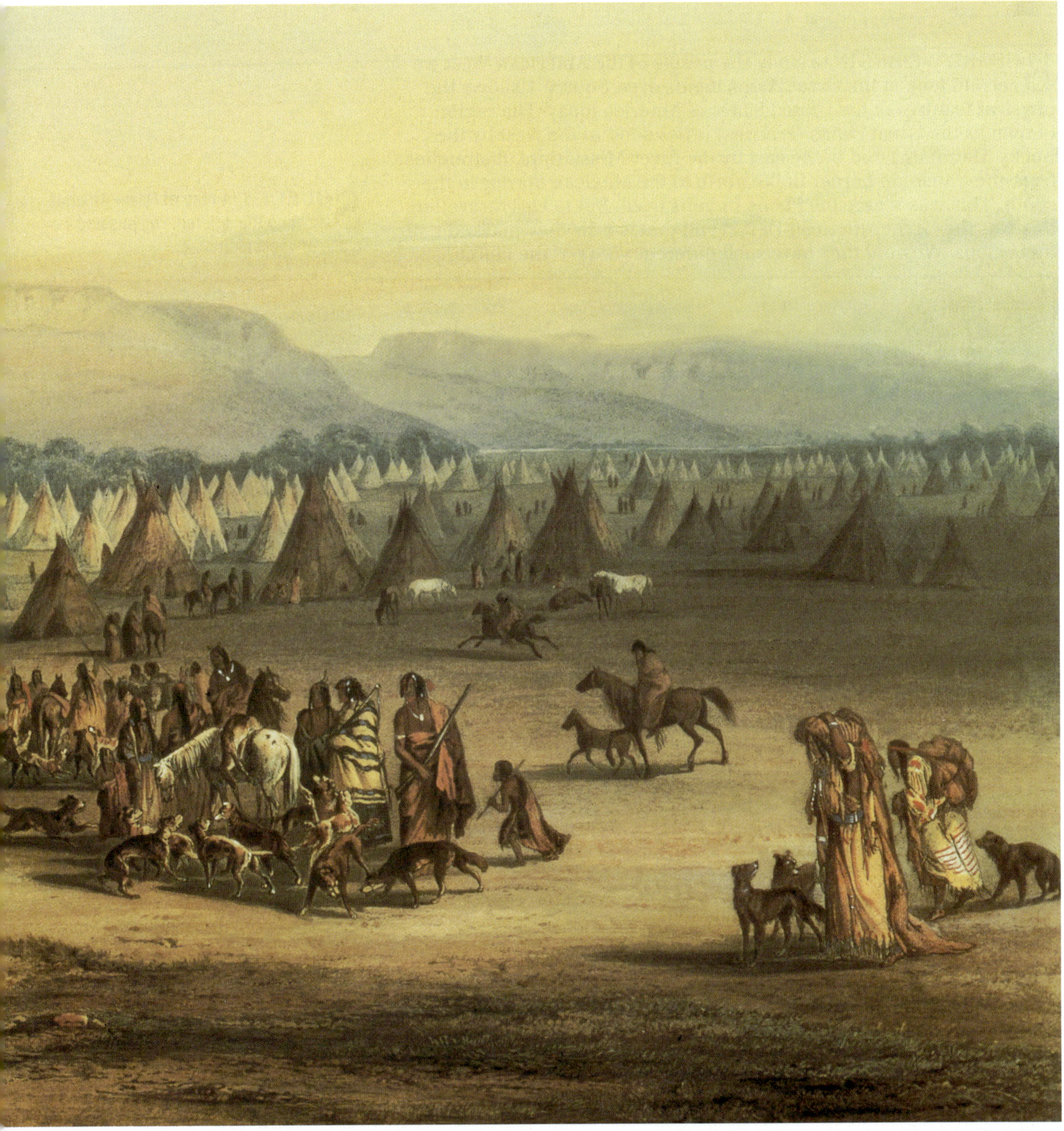

chapter 1

INTRODUCTION

The 'Great American Desert'?

BEFORE WE BEGIN to study the people of the American West we need to look at the Great Plains themselves. Source 1 shows the physical features of the United States of America today. The region known as the Great Plains (Prairies) is bounded in the west by the Rocky Mountains and in the east by the River Mississippi. It stretches from the Canadian border in the north to the Mexican border in the south. This was where the Plains Indians lived. But to early travellers this was the Great American Desert and that is how they marked it on their maps. Why did they have such different views of the Plains?

SOURCE 1 A map of North America showing the different regions and types of vegetation

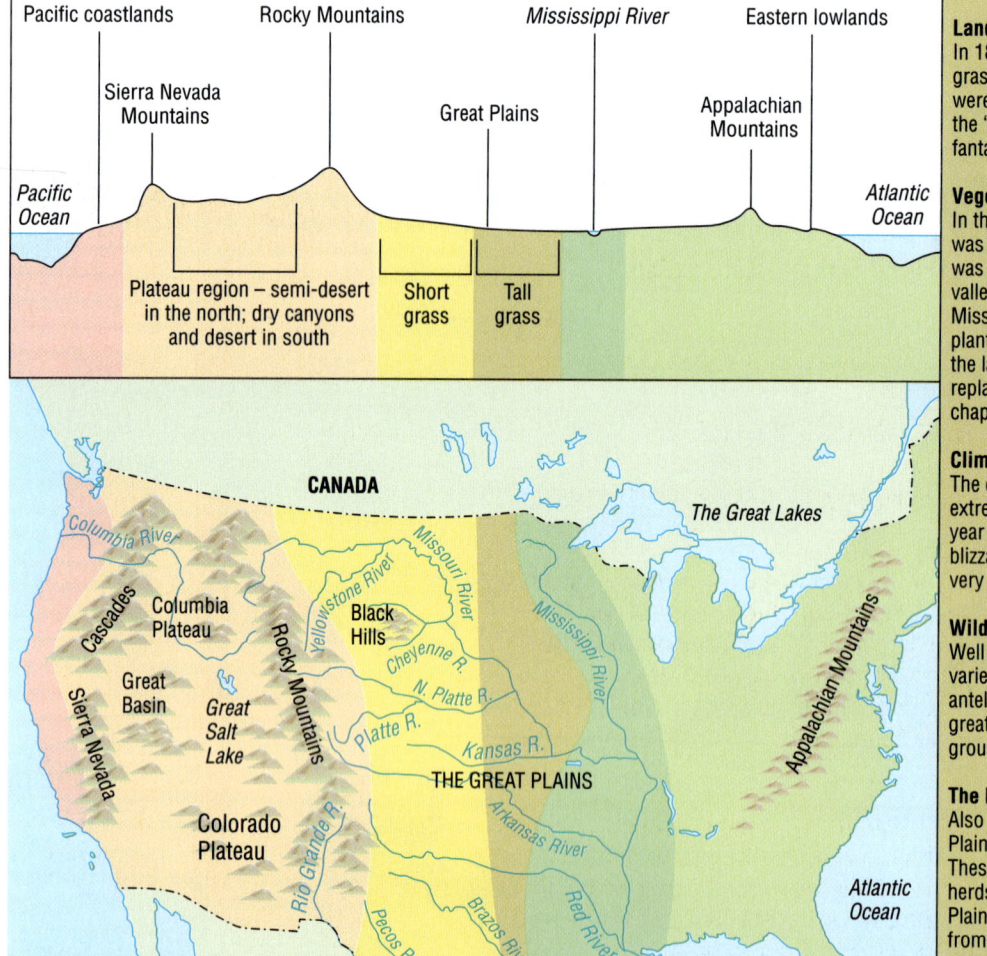

The Great Plains

Landscape
In 1840 this was a region of gently rolling grasslands and slow-flowing rivers. In the north were the Black Hills, wooded hills surrounded by the 'Badlands', where soft rock was eroded into fantastic shapes.

Vegetation
In the west, near the Rocky Mountains, the grass was short. Towards the east it grew taller; this was the prairie grass. In some of the river valleys, and in the area closest to the River Mississippi, there was woodland. Berries, root plants and wild fruit grew in places. In the south the land became much drier. The grass was replaced by semi-desert plants such as black chaparral and mesquite.

Climate
The climate of the region was, and still is, one of extremes of temperature with strong winds all year round. In winter these winds brought blizzards and freezing cold. In summer they were very hot, drying up the land and rivers.

Wildlife
Well adapted to living in this region were a wide variety of animals and birds. These included antelope, coyote, deer, gophers, rabbits and the great herds of buffalo (bison), plus eagles, grouse and hawks.

The Plains Indians
Also well adapted to living in this region were the Plains Indians. To them it was not a desert. These Indians were hunters who followed the herds of buffalo as they moved across the Great Plains. In summer they moved northwards away from the scorching heat and in winter they camped in the foothills of the Rocky Mountains, sheltered from the wind-driven blizzards. To outsiders they were nomads, people who did not live settled in one place. But the Plains Indians would disagree. They did live in one place: the Great Plains.

THE 'GREAT AMERICAN DESERT'?

SOURCE 2 A photograph of the Great Plains, Badlands National Park, South Dakota

1. Read Source 3. Why might scarcity of wood and water be such an obstacle to settlement?
2. Why might travellers call the Great Plains a desert?

SOURCE 3 Major Stephen Long's description of the Great Plains, 1819–20

In regard to this extensive section of country, I do not hesitate in giving the opinion that it is almost wholly unfit for cultivation, and of course uninhabitable by a people depending upon agriculture for their SUBSISTENCE. Large areas of fertile land are occasionally to be found, but the scarcity of wood and water will prove an impossible obstacle in the way of settling the country.

Attitudes to the Plains were greatly influenced by early travellers such as Long. It would be many years before outsiders began to see the farming potential of the Plains. In the 1830s they could only see the problems – the harsh weather, the lack of trees, the wind, the absence of water. The Indians of course had a very different view. They were not farmers but hunters, and the Plains were perfect for a hunter's way of life.

3. Who do you think would find it easier to live on the Great Plains, farmers or hunters?

Who were the Plains Indians?

THE ORIGINAL INDIANS came from the plains of north Asia, as you can see from Source 1. They spread throughout North America.

The different Indian NATIONS adapted their lifestyle to the different environments in which they lived. Nations like the Cherokee, who lived in the fertile eastern woodlands, were farmers growing maize, squash and beans, whilst the Utes, who lived in the semi-desert Plateau region, were mainly gatherers of berries, roots, seeds, insects and nuts.

The nations which we know as the Plains Indians did not originally settle on the Great Plains. Instead they lived in the river valleys to the east. In the eighteenth century they began to move on to the Plains. Source 2 shows where the different Plains Indians lived by 1840.

SOURCE 1 Migration to the Americas

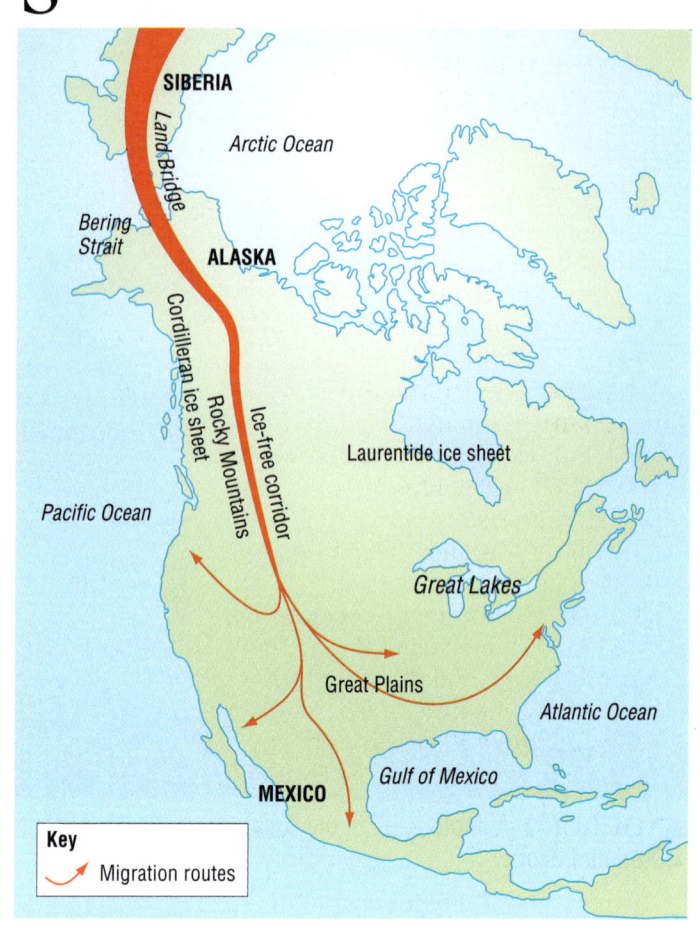

SOURCE 2 A map of the Great Plains showing the locations of the main Indian nations by 1840

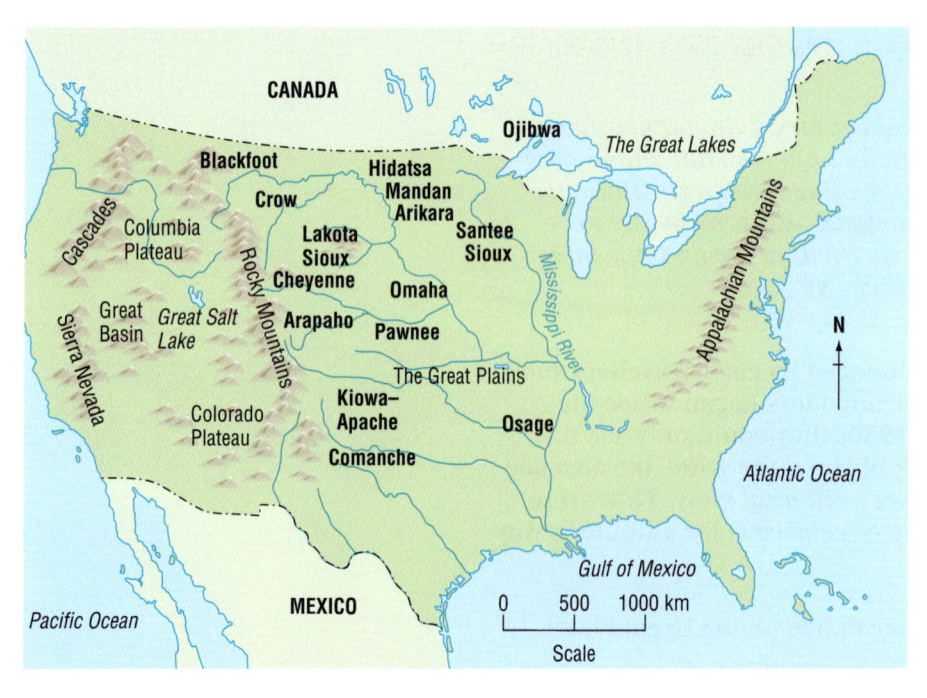

WHO WERE THE PLAINS INDIANS?

Why did nations like the Sioux and Cheyenne move to the Great Plains?

Horses
Originally there were no horses in America. Spanish invaders in the sixteenth century brought the first horses to the continent. These horses were not given to the Indians. In 1640 the Pueblo Indians of Mexico revolted against the Spanish and captured many of their horses. From then on horses were bred and traded between the Indian nations.

By the 1680s and 1690s Indian nations like the Sioux and Cheyenne had horses. Once they had horses they were able to move out on to the Great Plains to live and to hunt the buffalo far more easily. As you will see from pages 32–33, the horse transformed their way of life. They were able to give up farming in the river valley and rely upon hunting on the Plains instead. There is evidence of this in the legends of the Cheyenne which recall the time when they 'lost the corn' (see Source 3). The horse was so important to their way of life that they counted wealth in horses.

Diseases
The Europeans who came to America also brought with them new diseases such as cholera and smallpox. These diseases had a disastrous impact on the Indians, who had no resistance to them. In 1795, for example, a smallpox epidemic wiped out 30 of the 32 Arikara villages, killing approximately 3500 of their 4000 warriors. Historians estimate that in the smallpox epidemic of 1830 half the Indian population of the Mississippi valley area died. The Sioux, Cheyenne and others moved west on to the Great Plains to escape from these diseases.

SOURCE 3 An account by Iron Teeth, a Cheyenne woman

"My grandmother told me that when she was young... the people themselves had to walk. In those times they did not travel far nor often. But when they got horses, they could move more easily from place to place. Then they could kill more of the buffalo and other animals, and so they got more meat for food and gathered more skins for lodges and clothing."

Trade goods
The goods brought by traders also had an important impact on Indian life. Guns changed the balance of power in Indian warfare. The guns in the hands of their enemies, the Ojibwa, were a factor that helped to drive the Sioux out on to the Great Plains.

■ TASK
These drawings show some of the reasons why the Sioux moved on to the Plains. Use them to explain in your own words why they moved.

15

chapter 2

HOW DID THE INDIANS SOLVE THE PROBLEMS OF LIVING ON THE GREAT PLAINS?

THE LIFE OF the Plains Indians differed from nation to nation. We cannot look at all Plains Indians, so we are going to focus upon one nation: the Sioux. You will use them to examine the way of life of the Plains Indians.

We use the name 'Sioux' since this is the most familiar term. However, 'Sioux' is, in fact, the name given to them by their enemies. It covers several groups spread out over a wide area, the main ones being the Lakota, Yankton and Santee. The different groups still argue about names.

The daily life of the Sioux

Homes

The *tipi* (also referred to as a lodge or tepee) was the home of each Indian family. It was made from ten to twenty buffalo skins sewn together and supported by a frame of wooden poles arranged in a circle. It was the responsibility of the women. They made it, owned it, put it up and moved it. It could be taken down and packed for transport in ten minutes. This made it an ideal home for people who were frequently on the move.

At the top of the *tipi* there were two 'ears' or flaps that could be moved to direct the wind so that the smoke from the fire inside could escape. In summer the *tipi* bottom could be rolled up to let air in. In winter it could be banked with earth to keep the *tipi* warm. The *tipi*'s conical shape made it strong enough to resist the strong winds on the Great Plains. Sioux *tipis* were decorated by the men with geometric patterns and scenes recording their bravery in the hunt and in battle.

Inside, a fire would always be burning at the centre to provide heat and for cooking. The floor was covered with furs.

Everybody had their place in the *tipi*. Because the space was small there were strict rules about behaviour. For example, it was rude to pass between another person and the fire.

- Poles support the tipi and can be used to make a travois for moving
- Ears/flaps
- Paintings
- Scalps hanging as trophies on lodge poles
- Wooden pegs holding skins together
- Doorway facing east towards the rising sun
- Buffalo skins

SOURCE 1 A modern artist's drawing of a *tipi*

THE DAILY LIFE OF THE SIOUX

SOURCE 2 A Sioux proverb

" A beautiful tipi is like a good mother. She hugs her children to her and protects them from heat and cold, snow and rain. "

SOURCE 3 George Catlin, *Manners, Customs and Condition of the North American Indian,* 1841. Catlin's writings and the hundreds of paintings he made of scenes from Indian life have had a great influence on the way people think about the Plains Indians. You can find out more about Catlin on page 44

" The lodges are taken down in a few minutes by the women and easily transported to any part of the country where they wish to camp. They generally move six to eight times in the summer, following the immense herds of buffalo. The manner in which a camp of Indians strike [take down] their tents and move them is curious. I saw a camp of Sioux, consisting of six hundred lodges, struck and everything packed and on the move in a very few minutes. "

SOURCE 4 A model from the Blackfoot Museum at Browning, Montana, showing Blackfoot Indians moving camp. The lodge poles have been used to form a *travois*, a sled pulled by a horse, on which all the family's belongings are carried. This allowed the Indians to move home quickly and easily. The Sioux used the same method

■ TASK

1. On your own picture of a *tipi* label the following:
   - Scalps hanging as trophies on lodge poles
   - Ears or flaps
   - Poles supporting the tipi
   - Wooden pegs
   - Buffalo skins
   - Doorway
   - Paintings

2. Make brief notes on how *tipi* design solved the following problems facing Indians living on the Plains:
   - the lack of wood
   - the strong winds
   - the extremes of temperature
   - the need to move frequently.

3. Now use all your notes to help you write an answer to this question: why did the Sioux live in *tipis*?

THE DAILY LIFE OF THE SIOUX

SOURCE 5 Colonel Dodge, writing in his book *Hunting Grounds of the Great West*, 1877. Colonel Dodge was a US army officer who had served on the Great Plains in the 1830s. He was a very influential writer. You can find out more about him on page 45

The home or lodge of the Plains Indians is from twelve to twenty feet in diameter, and about fifteen feet high. The fire is built in the centre, and the smoke escapes through an opening at the top. The draught is, however, not effective, and the lodge is usually in cold weather too full of smoke to be bearable to anyone but an Indian. It is, however, well adapted to their needs. Its shape secures it from the danger of being overturned by windstorms, and with very little fuel it can be kept warm and comfortable even in the coldest weather.

The beds are piles of buffalo robes and blankets, spread on the ground as close to the outer circumference as possible. They serve as sleeping places by night, and seats by day. In this small space are often crowded eight or ten persons, possibly of three or four different families. Since the cooking, eating, living and sleeping are all done in the one room, it soon becomes unbelievably filthy.

SOURCE 6 Flying Hawk, a Sioux chief quoted in a history published in 1947, compares the *tipi* to the settlers' houses

The white man builds big house, cost much money, like big cage, shut out sun, can never move. The tipi is much better to live in: always clean, warm in winter, cool in summer; easy to move.

1. Compare Colonel Dodge's description of a *tipi* (Source 5) to Flying Hawk's description (Source 6). What points do they agree on?
2. List the points they disagree about.
3. Why do you think they disagree?

Family life

Men and women

Indians spent most of the year travelling, hunting and camping with their band. This would consist of between ten and fifty families, each living in their own *tipi*. Within the family there were different roles for men and women. The men were responsible for hunting, looking after the horses and protecting the band. They were judged by their skills as hunters, warriors and horsemen. Women were responsible for the *tipi*, for preparing food and fetching water, and for making clothing and other items. They were judged by their skill at crafts and as home-makers. Women were highly valued as the bearers of children.

■ TASK

You have seen how the *tipi* was an ideal home for people living on the Great Plains. As you read the following pages, fill in a chart like the one below to provide evidence that the lifestyle of the Sioux was well suited to the environment of the Great Plains.

	Evidence
Family life and marriage	
Children	
Old people	
Custom and tradition	
Decision-making by councils and chiefs	
The role of warrior societies	

THE DAILY LIFE OF THE SIOUX

Arranged marriages took place in some Indian nations but in most cases marriages were love matches. A young man would have to impress the young woman with his bravery, whilst a gift of horses or buffalo skins would convince her parents of his ability to support a wife. The horses did not mean that the bride had been sold. Instead it was proof of her husband's love for her and the high esteem in which her family held her. When they were married, men went to live with their wife's family. Indian descent was matrilineal, meaning that they traced their descent through their mother, her mother and so on, not through their father.

Most men had one wife but rich men could have several wives (POLYGAMY). Polygamy made sense in a situation where there were more women than men, and this was often the case because of the dangers of hunting and warfare. Polygamy was a way of making sure that all the women were cared for and that the band had as many children as possible. If a woman's husband was killed in warfare or while hunting then she would marry again. Divorce was not unknown. Either partner could declare a marriage over but the woman kept the *tipi*.

Children

Children were highly valued. They were the future of the band. They did not go to school but learned the skills they would need from their parents and other relatives. They were taught to ride at an early age. Boys were taught how to hunt using bows and arrows whilst girls were taught how to maintain a home. Above all, children had to learn how to survive on the Great Plains. Early travellers such as Francis Parkman commented on the way children were treated.

SOURCE 7 Pretty Shield, a Crow woman describes how a Crow woman drove off some Sioux attackers. There were a few famous women warriors

> *Now I shall have to tell you about the fighting, because it was a woman's fight. A woman won it. The men never tell about it... I saw Strikes Two, a woman sixty years old, riding around the camp on a grey horse. She carried her root digger, and she was singing her medicine song as though Sioux bullets and arrows were not flying around her... She rode out straight at the Sioux, waving her root digger and singing that song. I saw her, and my heart swelled because she was a woman.*

4. In Source 7, why do 'The men never tell about it'?

SOURCE 8 Francis Parkman (see page 45) describes how the Sioux chief Big Crow and his wife treated their children

> *Both he and his wife, like most other Indians, were very fond of their children, whom they indulged to excess and never punished, except in extreme cases, when they threw a bowl of cold water over them. Their children became wild, disrespectful and disobedient under this system, which tended to foster the idea that there was no need for restraint; something which lies at the heart of the Indian character.*

Old people

Old people had an important part to play in the life of the band. They were able to give advice in council and pass on the history of the people. They were involved in helping to bring up children. However, when they became too old and weak to keep up they might have to be left behind. The survival of the band was of greater importance than any individual.

SOURCE 9 George Catlin (see page 44) describes an incident he witnessed

> *When we were about to start on our way from the village, my attention was directed to a very aged and emaciated man, who was to be exposed... a man who had once been a chief, and a man of distinction in his tribe, who was now too old to travel. 'My children,' he said, 'our nation is poor, and it is necessary that you should all go to the country where you can get meat... My strength is no more, my days are nearly all numbered, and I am a burden to my children. I cannot go and wish to die.'*
>
> *This cruel custom of exposing their aged people belongs I think to all the tribes who roam about the prairies...*

5. Catlin called the custom in Source 9 cruel. How would the Indians justify it?

THE DAILY LIFE OF THE SIOUX

How was Indian life organised?

In order to survive on the Great Plains the members of an Indian band had to co-operate and work closely together. They had to be well organised. Throughout the year the band would have to move across the Great Plains. From time to time bands would meet up to camp and hunt together. Once a year, and sometimes more often, the bands would meet together as a nation. Indian society was organised in a way that reflected the need for co-operation.

Custom and tradition

There was a very strong sense of custom and tradition. If individual Indians did wrong and broke the 'rules' – by stealing, for example – then they would be shamed or humiliated in the eyes of the rest of the band. These were the people with whom they lived and hunted all year round; many of them were their relations. So to be shamed would be a very effective punishment. In extreme cases, such as murder, some bands banished the wrongdoer. This was because a murder damaged the whole band.

Chiefs

Indian chiefs were not elected, nor did they inherit power. They became chiefs for a number of reasons – because of their wisdom, their spiritual power or 'medicine', and their skills as hunters and warriors. They might not remain a chief for life (see Source 9 on page 19). Only great chiefs like Red Cloud and Sitting Bull were able to persuade the warriors of many bands and even of different nations to follow them. When he was older, Red Cloud made peace with the settlers and agreed to live on a reservation. From then on, many Sioux no longer followed him, choosing instead to follow younger chiefs such as Crazy Horse.

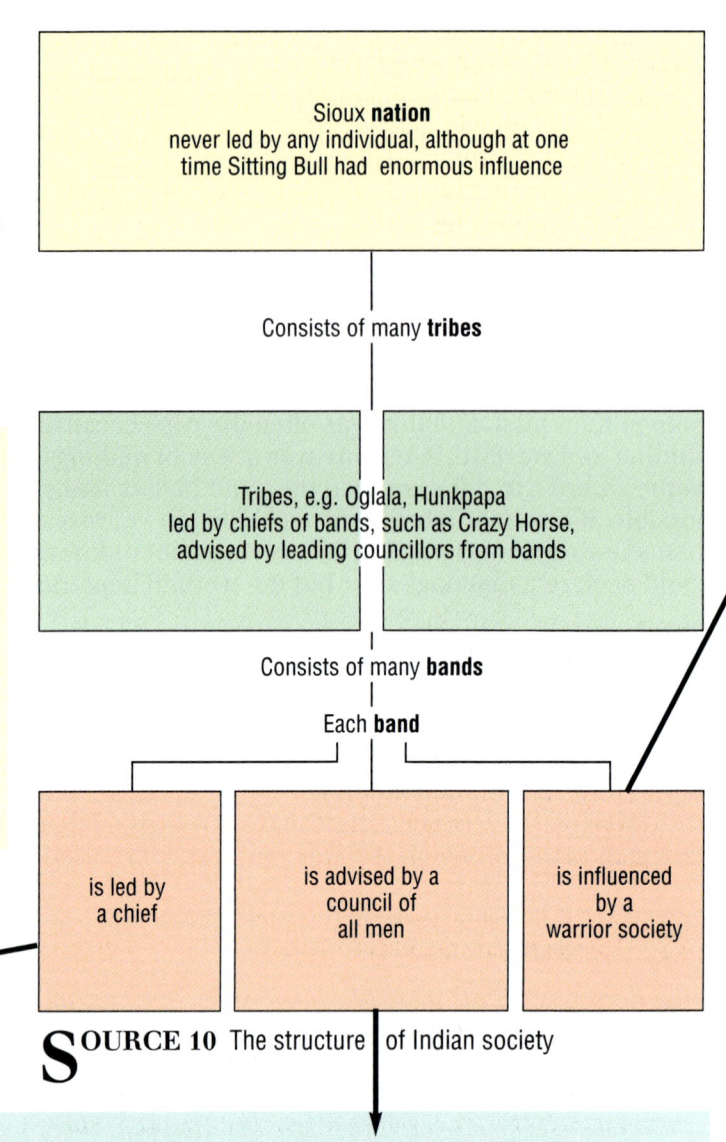

Sioux nation
never led by any individual, although at one time Sitting Bull had enormous influence

Consists of many **tribes**

Tribes, e.g. Oglala, Hunkpapa
led by chiefs of bands, such as Crazy Horse, advised by leading councillors from bands

Consists of many **bands**

Each **band**:
- is led by a chief
- is advised by a council of all men
- is influenced by a warrior society

SOURCE 10 The structure of Indian society

Councils

Important decisions were taken in council, where the men of the band would discuss what to do. The advice of the MEDICINE MAN, chiefs and elders (old men) would be listened to, carefully and with respect, but these men would not tell the others what to do. Normally, the council members would keep talking until everyone had agreed. While they talked, they would smoke a ceremonial pipe. The Indians believed that the smoke would inform the spirit world and help them to make good decisions. Sometimes councils were made up of all the men of the band; at other times only the important men would meet.

When bands met together the council of the nation would meet. This was made up of representatives from each band. The council of the nation could take important decisions, such as deciding to go to war, but the bands were not bound to agree with the council's decision. As a result, some bands might be at war whilst others were at peace. Later this was a source of confusion for the settlers when conflict broke out. Was a band at war or not? Were all its members peaceful, or just some of them?

THE DAILY LIFE OF THE SIOUX

The role of warrior societies
All the men of a band belonged to a warrior society, such as the Kit Foxes of the Sioux. They were responsible for supervising hunting and travelling, and for protecting the village from attack. Their opinions were always important when decisions had to be taken.

SOURCE 11 *A Sioux Council*, a painting by George Catlin, 1847

SOURCE 12 Colonel Dodge's (see page 45) comments on government

" I cannot say exactly how these powers and duties of these three governmental forms [i.e. chiefs, councils and warrior societies] blend and concur... and I have never met an Indian or white man who could satisfactorily explain them. The result, however, is fairly good, and seems well suited to the character, needs and peculiarities of the life of the Plains Indians. "

SOURCE 13 *Indian Council*, a painting by Seth Eastman, 1849. Eastman was a US army officer who served in the West from the 1820s to the 1850s. He made over 300 paintings of Indians

SOURCE 14 Colonel Dodge's comments on warrior societies

" Whatever the power of the chief and the council there is another power to which both have to yield. This power is the hunters of the tribe, who form a sort of guild. Among the Cheyenne these men are called 'dog soldiers'. This 'guild' comprises the whole working force of the band. It is they who protect and supply the women and children. From them come all orders for marches. By them the camps are selected. They supply the guards for the camp and choose the hunting parties. One of the most important functions of the dog soldiers is the protection of the game. Except when laying in the supply of meat for winter, only enough buffalo are killed for the current needs of the camp. Great care is taken not to alarm the herds, which will feed for days in the vicinity of an Indian camp of a thousand souls, while a half a dozen white men would have driven them away in a day. "

■ TASK

Sources 11 and 13 both show Indian councils. Catlin and Eastman were both attempting to record Indian life. The two men had the same ambition: to create an Indian gallery. Use these two sources to describe the main features of an Indian council. You should comment on the setting, the people, what they are wearing, what objects they are holding and how they are acting.

21

How important was the buffalo to the Plains Indians?

SOURCE 1 A Plains Indian village. These two modern illustrations of a Plains Indian village are based upon an original illustration by George Catlin (see page 44).

HOW IMPORTANT WAS THE BUFFALO TO THE PLAINS INDIANS?

■ TASK

Compare the two villages.

1. Record all the things that are missing from the second village.
2. What do you think the missing items have in common?

HOW IMPORTANT WAS THE BUFFALO TO THE PLAINS INDIANS?

Hunting the buffalo

Everything missing from Source 1 picture 2 was made from the buffalo. You can see how the buffalo was vitally important to the lives of the Indians.

Buffalo Dances

The Plains Indians did not farm the buffalo; they hunted them. Before setting out to hunt, they would hold a ceremonial Buffalo Dance which could last for many days (see Source 2). They would dress as buffalo and copy their movements. The purpose of the dance was to call upon the spirit world for help in their hunting and to call the buffalo herd closer to them. Plains Indians believed this would bring them good luck and ensure a successful hunt. The Buffalo Dance was as important as the sending of scouts to find the buffalo herd.

How did Plains Indians hunt the buffalo?

Before the introduction of the horse, Plains Indians hunted the buffalo in two ways. The first method was for warriors to creep up on the grazing buffalo and shoot them with arrows. Buffalo herds would allow wolves to approach quite close to them, so Indians would sometimes disguise themselves in wolf skins (see Source 3). The second method of hunting was to STAMPEDE a buffalo herd into 'buffalo jumps' so that the animals were trapped in narrow valleys or driven over a cliff and killed.

Once they had horses, Plains Indians were able to kill greater numbers of buffalo. The hunt was carefully organised and policed by the members of warrior societies. They did this to make sure that the buffalo were not scared away before all was ready, and to ensure that not too many animals were killed in the excitement of the chase. Two or three successful buffalo hunts a year were sufficient to feed and shelter the band. Some modern historians have, however, suggested that the Indians were careless in their slaughter of the buffalo.

SOURCE 2 *Buffalo Dance of the Sioux*, painted by George Catlin

1. What are the men in Source 2 dressed as?
2. Find the bows. What are they re-enacting?
3. Find the drum and the rattle. Why are they using these?

SOURCE 3 Sioux Indians disguised in wolf skins approach a herd of buffalo, painted by George Catlin

When the hunt began, the warriors would surround or stampede the buffalo and kill them by firing arrows at the running animals. Each warrior marked his arrows so that the buffalo he killed could be identified. Besides ensuring the survival of the tribe, the warriors would also gain honour and prestige from their skill in hunting. In order to get close enough to kill the animal, the hunter had to put himself and his horse in considerable danger.

HOW IMPORTANT WAS THE BUFFALO TO THE PLAINS INDIANS?

SOURCE 4 George Catlin, writing in May 1832

When I first arrived at this place, on my way up the river, and had taken up my lodgings in the Fur Company's fort, Mr Laidlaw, his chief clerk, Mr Halsey, and many of their men, as well as the chiefs of the Sioux, told me that only a few days before I arrived, an immense herd of buffaloes had showed themselves on the opposite bank of the Teton river, almost blackening the plains for a great distance. A party of five or six hundred Sioux Indians on horseback forded the river about midday, and spending a few hours amongst the buffalo, recrossed the river at sun-down and came into the Fort with fourteen hundred fresh buffalo tongues, which were thrown down in a mass, and for which they required but a few gallons of whiskey, which was soon demolished, indulging them in a little, harmless drinking spree.

[Buffalo tongue was a delicacy.]

SOURCE 5 *Buffalo Chase, A Surround by the Hidatsa*, painted by George Catlin, 1832–33

SOURCE 6 *The Buffalo Hunt*, a painting by John Mix Stanley, 1855

ACTIVITY

Imagine you are a newspaper reporter for the *New York Times* visiting the West in 1860. Your task is to describe buffalo hunting for your readers, who have never seen a buffalo or the Sioux. Use the text and Sources 1–7. Think about whether the sources are accurate representations. You will need to describe how the Plains Indians found the buffalo, and what weapons and tactics they used to kill buffalo. You should also explain the dangers of buffalo hunting, and say why young Sioux warriors were keen to take part in the buffalo hunt, despite these dangers.

SOURCE 7 Black Elk, a Sioux Indian, born CIRCA 1863, describes the preparations for a hunt

Then the crier shouted, 'Your knives shall be sharpened. Make ready, make haste; your horses make ready! We shall go forth with arrows. Plenty of meat we shall make!'

Then the head man went around picking out the best hunters with the fastest horses, and to these he said, 'Young warriors, your work I know is good; so today you will feed the helpless. You shall help the old and the young and whatever you kill shall be theirs.' This was a great honour for young men.

SOURCE 8 A still from the film *Dances with Wolves*, 1990

25

HOW IMPORTANT WAS THE BUFFALO TO THE PLAINS INDIANS?

After the hunt

Once the buffalo was dead, it was butchered by the women and children. Some of the body parts, such as the liver and kidneys, were immediately eaten raw as delicacies. Other parts were boiled or roasted, and the rest cut into strips to be smoked, or dried in the sun. This dried meat would keep for a long time. It could be pounded into a pulp and mixed with wild berries, such as cherries, to make pemmican.

The hides were worked by the women. First, the hides were pegged out to dry and scraped to remove all the flesh. This made RAWHIDE. Some hides were then TANNED, using the animals' brains, and worked to make them soft and pliable. They were then ready to be made into clothing or *tipi* covers. The preparation of buffalo hides was another important role performed by women in Plains Indian society.

Horns were used for arrow-straighteners, cups, fire-carriers, head-dress ornaments, ladles, spoons, toys and quill-flatteners.

The **skull** was used in religious ceremonies. The **brain** was used for tanning the hides.

The **tongue** was used as a hairbrush and also eaten raw as a delicacy.

The **heart** was cut from the body and left on the ground to give new life to the herd. The buffalo was sacred, man's relative who gave his life so that the people could live. The heart might also be eaten raw so that the warrior could take the strength and power of the buffalo.

Fat was used for cooking, to make soap and as hair grease.

Gall was used to make yellow paint. The liver was eaten raw as a delicacy.

Bones were used for arrowheads, dice, game counters, jewellery, knives, needles, paint brushes, saddle frames, shovels, sledge runners, tools and war clubs.

SOURCE 9 A hundred uses? How the Plains Indians used every part of the buffalo

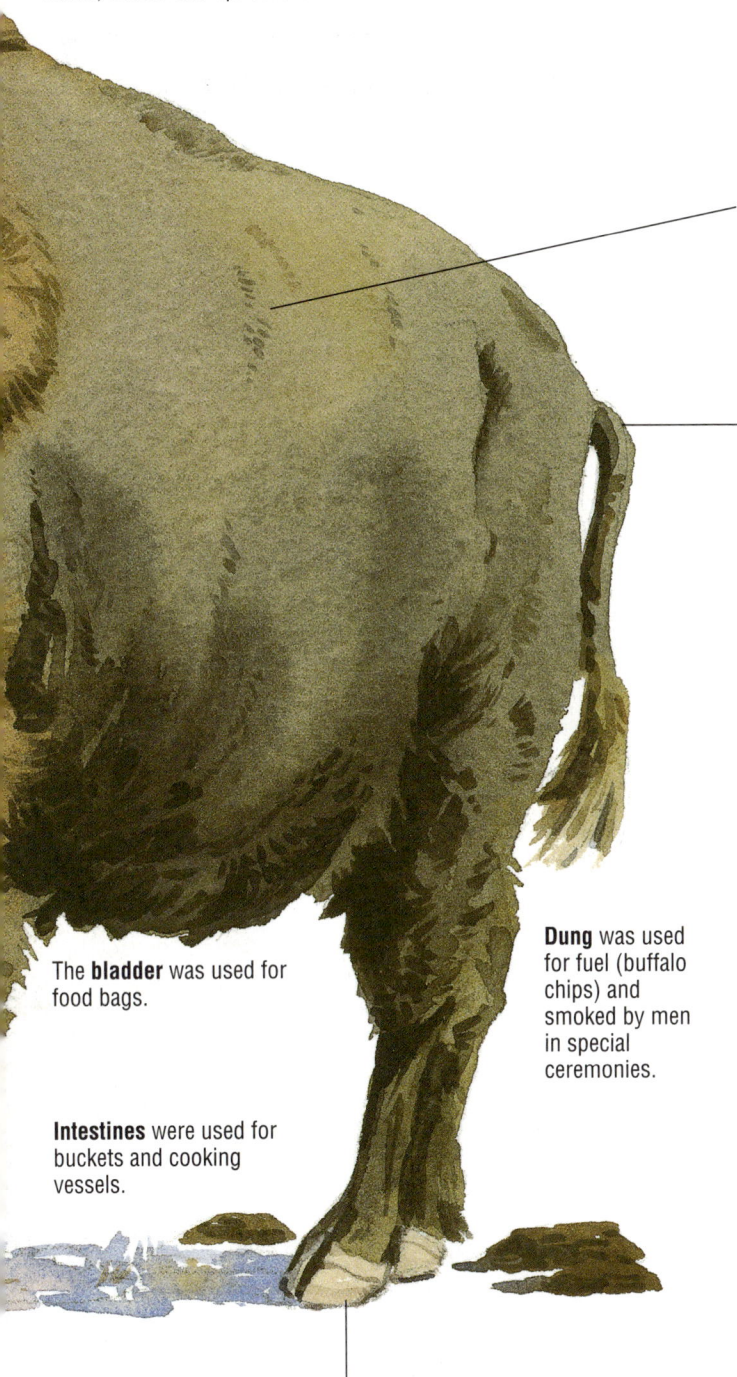

HOW IMPORTANT WAS THE BUFFALO TO THE PLAINS INDIANS?

Rawhide was used for bags, belts, containers, horse harnesses, lashings, masks, PARFLECHES, sheaths, shields, snow-shoes, string and travois lashings.

Tanned hide was used for bags, bedding, blankets, BULL BOATS, clothes, dolls, dresses, drums, leggings, mittens, moccasins, pouches, robes, saddle and tipi covers.

The **flesh** was cooked, or dried and mixed with fat and wild cherries to preserve it as pemmican.

Sinews were used for bowstrings and thread.

Fur was used for decoration on clothes, as stuffing for saddles and pillows, and to make mittens and rope.

The **tail** was used for fly swats, ornaments and whips.

The **bladder** was used for food bags.

Dung was used for fuel (buffalo chips) and smoked by men in special ceremonies.

Intestines were used for buckets and cooking vessels.

Hooves were used to make glue and also to make rattles and tools.

■ TASK

1. Copy out the chart below. Fill in how the buffalo was important for each of the four aspects of Plains Indian life and add one of your own. Use Sources 1 and 9 to help you complete the chart.

Aspect of Indian life	Buffalo part	Used for
Clothing		
Homes		
Religion		
Warfare		

2. George Catlin commented upon life on the Great Plains. He saw how the Plains Indians depended upon the buffalo. At that time people could already see that the numbers of buffalo were falling. Catlin wrote, 'The buffalo's doom is sealed, and with their extinction, the Indians must surely sink into despair and starvation. The Plains offer them no other means of living.' Do you agree with him? If you took away the buffalo, could the Plains Indians survive?

Use the chart and the sources on pages 22–27 to help you write your answer to the question.

How warlike were the Sioux?

YOU ARE A SIOUX WARRIOR. Your name is White Cloud. You have decided to join a war party to go and fight against the Crow. Your war leader has had a vision. In it, he saw a Crow village nearby with many horses. He is a good war leader who brings back many horses and loses very few warriors, so you have decided to go with him. You think this will be a good chance to show your skill in war and to impress the older warriors and the young woman you admire. Your brother is not going. In his dream he saw a bad omen.

You have already taken part in a war dance to draw upon the spirit world for help and guidance. Now you and your companions, Little Bear and Running Horse, are ready to set out.

The picture and notes around it show how you and your friends have prepared for the battle.

■ ACTIVITY

Imagine that the picture in Source 1 is the first of a series of story boards. Film directors use these pictures to plan film storylines. This one shows the three friends ready to set out on a raid. Your task is to complete the story of the raid with another five pictures. You should use the information on pages 29–31 to help you.

Your film story recipe is simple. It must be filmed in only two locations, White Cloud's village and a Crow village. You can have only three main actors, White Cloud and two others. One of these must be a woman. Lastly, it must include a heroic deed. You decide what that deed is and who performs it.

Remember that your film story needs to be historically accurate as well as exciting!

Feathers
These are important as they show your previous acts of bravery. They show that you have killed three enemies and taken two scalps. (Killed enemy = black tip and red spot; scalped enemy = notch in black tip.)

Bow and arrow quiver
Your wooden bow is reinforced with sinew glued to the back. Your bowstring is made from twisted buffalo sinew. The quiver holds roughly twenty arrows tipped with stone or iron. It is decorated with quill work.

Amulet
You always wear this around your neck. Its strong medicine (spiritual power) protects you.

Body painting
You are painted in magical colours to protect you in battle.

Lance
Your lance is four to five metres in length with a blade of polished steel. You have decorated it with beadwork, buffalo fur and feathers.

Horse
Your prized possession. This is the best of your three ponies. The lines encourage speed in your horse. The handprint is the mark of your warrior society. This helps the warriors to recognise you in battle.

SOURCE 1 A story board showing Sioux warriors ready to go to war

HOW WARLIKE WERE THE SIOUX?

Coup stick
Little Bear carries this to touch his enemies in battle. It is decorated with buffalo fur and feathers. It is braver to touch an enemy in the fighting with a coup stick, or to get even closer and touch him with a hand, than it is to kill him.

Rifle
Your friend Running Horse's prized possession. He took this from a dead Pawnee warrior. Rifles were introduced to the Great Plains by travellers and settlers from the East. Your band got them by trading, as well as in fights with non-Indians and other nations like the Pawnee.

Little Bear

Running Horse

Shield
Little Bear wears his shield on his left arm. It is made from the skin of the buffalo's neck, hardened by steam, smoke and buffalo hoof glue. It is arrow-proof. He has decorated it with magical symbols of powerful animals which will protect him in battle.

War shirt
Running Horse's war shirt is made from deerskin. It is decorated with feathers and hair from enemy scalps. It has scenes painted on it, showing his previous brave deeds.

Indian warfare

Warfare to the Sioux was not a matter of long campaigns fought by large numbers of men. There were no formal declarations of war and fighting did not continue until one side had won or a peace treaty was signed. Instead, it was a series of raids by relatively small groups of warriors. Raiding parties would typically set out from a village three or four times a year.

Plains Indians went on these raids for a number of reasons: to steal horses, to seek revenge or to destroy their enemies. They did not want to conquer land in the way that the settlers did later on. Plains Indians did not believe that anyone could own land. But there was rivalry for hunting and living space. So before the arrival of the settlers on the Great Plains, the Sioux had driven the Crow from the Powder River country.

These wars did not happen in the cold winter months, when snow covered the Great Plains. Wars happened in the summer, when the Plains Indians had built up their food supplies by hunting the buffalo. Some modern historians have argued that the warfare between the Plains nations helped to keep the bands together. Certainly, by 1840 the Sioux nation had traditional enemies, such as the Crow and the Pawnee, and traditional allies, such as the Cheyenne.

Later, wars were fought to defend the Plains Indians' way of life against the threat from settlers and soldiers. In some of these, such as Red Cloud's War, the Sioux were forced to fight in winter as well as in summer.

HOW WARLIKE WERE THE SIOUX?

Why did individual warriors fight?

Individual warriors took part in warfare for a number of reasons. It was an opportunity to prove their bravery and to gain personal glory. This might enable them to enter a warrior society or to gain a wife. By capturing horses and weapons they could also become wealthy. For leaders, chiefs like Crazy Horse and Sitting Bull, it was a way to test their spiritual power, their 'medicine', and to increase their standing in the tribe. A successful leader was one who brought back horses and captives and did not lose many warriors. If chiefs were not successful, warriors would not follow them. Plains Indians did not consider it heroic to die in battle. It was more important to stay alive as a provider for their family and their tribe, and to avoid losing their scalp.

SOURCE 3 A speech made by Little Crow, Santee Sioux leader, as remembered by his son

" Little Crow (Ta-oya-te-duta) is not a coward, and he is not a fool. When did he run away from his enemies? When did he leave his braves behind him on the warpath and turn back to his tipi? ... Is Little Crow without scalps? Look at his war feathers! Behold the scalp locks of your enemies hanging there on his lodge poles! "

SOURCE 2 War songs by Plains Indians, first written down in the nineteenth century

*" See them prancing.
They come neighing,
They come a Horse Nation.
See them prancing,
They come neighing,
They come. "*

*" Crow Indian
You must watch your horses.
A horse thief,
Often,
Am I. "*

Kit Fox war song
*" I am a Fox.
I am supposed to die.
If there is anything difficult,
If there is anything dangerous,
That is mine to do. "*

*" Black face paint,
and a feather,
I seek.
So
I have done this. "*

[Returning warriors who had taken a scalp could paint their face black.]

Counting coup

The arrival of the gun on the Great Plains could have made war far more destructive. Yet it did not, because war was made into a ritual with the idea of 'counting coup'. It was considered braver to touch an enemy, to count coup, than to kill him. Warriors were usually members of one of the warrior societies, such as the sash-wearing Kit Foxes. During a fight a Kit Fox warrior might peg the end of his sash to the ground. This meant that he would not move until the fight had been won, until he was rescued by another warrior pulling out the peg, or until he was killed. Casualties were relatively low. Between 1835 and 1845 the Sioux were at war with their eastern neighbours, the Ojibwa. In that decade the Sioux lost 88 people, their enemies 129. Roughly half of these were women and children. So the Sioux lost fewer than four warriors a year. More men were probably lost as a result of hunting accidents than through fighting.

SOURCE 4 Extract from *Native Americans: the Sioux* by Richard Erdoes, 1982

" For young braves the main purpose of making war was to 'count coup', that is, to gain war honors, which was the way to fame and advancement. There was comparatively little prestige in killing an enemy. After all, a coward could shoot a man from ambush without any danger to himself. But to ride or walk up to a foe while he was still alive and armed, touching him with one's hand or one's special coup stick brought great honours, because a man risked his life doing it. Stealing horses right under the enemy's nose was also counted as a fine 'coup'. "

SOURCE 5 Plenty Coups, Crow chief, describing a raid

" We soon reached the timber ... and drove the enemy back easily. Three days later, we rode back into our village singing of victory, and our chiefs ... came out to us singing praise songs. My heart rejoiced when I heard them speak my name ... I shall never forget it, or how happy I felt because I had counted my first coup. "

HOW WARLIKE WERE THE SIOUX?

Why did Plains Indians take scalps?

Plains Indians took scalps as evidence of their successes in battle. The scalps were dried and hung as trophies outside their *tipis*. They were also used to decorate their war gear – shirts, lances and shields. The Plains Indians believed that if a warrior lost his scalp he could not go into the afterlife. So you scalped your enemy so that he would not be there to fight you in the afterlife. This was also the reason for the mutilation of dead enemies: to leave them disabled in the afterlife. Mutilation happened less frequently, as Plains Indians rarely captured the bodies of their fallen enemies. Plains Indians also wore eagle feathers, marked in various ways, to show their success in warfare.

SOURCE 6 *Indian Scalp Dance*, a contemporary engraving

1. What weapons can you see in Source 6?
2. What else are the warriors dancing with?
3. What impression of the Indians might this dance have given to non-Indian observers?

■ TASK

1. What were the most important reasons why Indian nations fought each other?

   Copy the table below and give each reason a score from 1–5. The higher the score, the more important the reason.

Reason	Score
To keep the tribe together	
To protect their hunting grounds	
To capture slaves, women and children	
To increase their wealth by capturing horses	
To keep the young warriors contented	
To destroy their traditional enemies	
To maintain the honour of the tribe	

2. Make a list of the reasons why individual Indian warriors took part in warfare.
3. Now use your answers to questions 1 and 2 to help you write your answer to this question: how warlike were the Sioux?

You should start with an introductory paragraph describing the weapons they used:
Sioux warriors were well armed. They fought using . . .

Your second paragraph should explain the reasons for fighting:
Individual Sioux warriors took part in warfare for a number of reasons. These were . . .

Your third paragraph should explain how warfare was controlled so that casualties were limited:
Warfare was fought according to certain rules. The bravest deed was to . . .

Your fourth paragraph should explain why the Sioux as a nation fought wars:
The Sioux fought against their traditional enemies, the Crow and Pawnee, for a number of reasons. The most important was . . .

Your conclusion should include your judgement about how warlike the Sioux were. You need to think about the savage images, scalping, war dances and war paint on the one hand, and on the other hand about the low casualties and 'rules'.

31

How important were horses to the Plains Indians?

OVER THE PAST few pages you have read about the many different roles of the horse in Indian life – as a means of transport for home and family (see page 17); its use in hunting (see page 24); and its role in warfare. The horse changed the nature of warfare. It enabled warriors to raid over much longer distances and gave a new reason for warfare – stealing horses. It also changed the way that individuals actually fought. It led to war skills and horsemanship becoming an important measure of bravery and status in Plains society.

The horse was so vital to life on the Plains that individuals counted their wealth by the number of horses they owned. Their status and prestige was partly measured by the number of horses they could give away to those who were needy and to those to whom they owed gifts.

SOURCE 1 *Comanche Feats of Horsemanship*, a painting by George Catlin, 1834

HOW IMPORTANT WERE HORSES TO THE PLAINS INDIANS?

> **SOURCE 2** Plenty Coups, Crow chief
>
> *"My horse fights with me and fasts with me, because if he is to carry me in battle he must know my heart and I must know his or we shall never become brothers. I have been told that the white man, who is almost a god, and yet a great fool, does not believe that the horse has a spirit. This cannot be true. I have many times seen my horse's soul in his eyes."*

1. Why did Plenty Coups (Source 2) think that the 'white men' were fools?

> **SOURCE 3** George Catlin, describing the horsemanship of the Comanche
>
> *"Amongst their feats of riding, there is one that astonished me more than anything of the kind I have seen, or expect to see, in my life, a stratagem of war learned and practised by every young man in the tribe. By this he is able to drop his body upon the side of his horse and he is screened from his enemies' weapons as he lies in a horizontal position behind the body of his horse. With his heel hanging over the horse's back he has the power to change to the other side of the horse if necessary. In this wonderful condition, he will hang whilst his horse is at full speed, carrying with him his bow and shield, and also his long lance of fourteen feet in length, all of which he will use against his enemy as he passes, rising and firing his arrows over the horse's back, or with equal ease and equal success under the horse's neck."*

SOURCE 4 The estimated distribution of horses across the Great Plains

Nation	Date	Lodges	Population	Horses	Ratio of horses to lodges	Ratio of horses to people
Sioux: Oglala/Brule	1871	600	5000	2000	3.3	0.4
Sioux: Hunkpapa/Miniconjou	1878	360	2900	3500	9.7	1.2
Cheyenne (part of)	1868	51	400	700	13.7	1.7
Arikara	1871	180	1650	350	1.9	0.2
Blackfoot	1860	300	2400	2400	8.0	1.0
Comanche	1869	300	2538	7614	25.4	3.0
Crow	1871	460	4000	9500	20.6	2.4
Omaha	1871	120	984	650	5.4	0.7
Pawnee	1871	260	2364	1050	4.0	0.4

2. As Plains Indians measured their wealth in horses, which Indian nation was the richest?

3. How important were their horses to Plains Indians?

How religious were the Sioux?

The spirit world

The Sioux believed in Wakan Tanka, the Great Spirit. He had created the world and all that lived. All living things had spirits of their own. This included animals, birds, fish and plants, as well as human beings. Even the rocks, trees and streams had spirits. These spirits were very important to the Sioux, and they believed that the spirits could influence their lives. These beliefs help to explain some of the things that the Sioux did.

Source 1 is the Sioux story of creation.

> **SOURCE 1** The Sioux story of creation, as told by by Lame Deer, South Dakota in 1969
>
> *Wakan Tanka was angry with us for some reason. Maybe he let Unktehi, the water monster, win because he wanted to make a better kind of human being. Well, the waters got higher and higher. Finally everything was flooded and the people died except one girl, a beautiful girl. When the water swept over the land a big spotted eagle, Wanblee Galeshka, flew down and let her grab his feet. He took her to the top of a tall tree which stood on the highest stone pinnacle of the Black Hills. It was the only place not covered with water.*
>
> *Wanblee kept the girl with him and made her his wife. There was a closer connection between people and animals then, so he could do it. She became pregnant and bore him twins, a boy and a girl. She was happy, and said, 'Now we will have people again. It is good.'*
>
> *When the waters subsided Wanblee helped the children and their mother down from his rock. 'Be a nation, become a great nation – the Lakota,' he told them. The boy and girl grew up. He was the only man on earth, she was the only woman of child-bearing age. They married, had children, a nation was born.*
>
> *So we are descended from the eagle. That is good because the eagle is the wisest of birds, a great warrior and the Great Spirit's messenger. That is why we wear the eagle plume.*

> **SOURCE 2** Goodbird, a Hidatsa Indian
>
> *We Hidatsas believed that this world and everything in it was alive and had spirits, and our faith in those spirits and our worship of them made our religion. My father explained this to me. 'All things in the world,' he said, 'have souls or spirits. The sky has a spirit, the clouds have spirits, the sun and moon have spirits: so have animals, trees, grass, water, stones, everything. These spirits are our gods: and we pray to them and give them offerings, that they may help us in our need. Anyone could pray to the spirits, receiving answer usually in a dream . . .'*

Circles

The Sioux believed in the circle of nature. They were physically surrounded by the circle of the horizon, the circle of their village, the circle of their councils, the circle of their *tipi*, the circle of their shield. They looked up at the circle of the sky, the circle of the sun and the circle of the moon. They lived through the circle of birth, childhood, adulthood, old age, second childhood and death.

> **SOURCE 3** Black Elk describes the importance of the circle in Indian beliefs
>
> *Everything an Indian does is a circle, and that is because the power of the world works in circles, even the seasons form a great circle, and come back to where they were before. Our* tipis *are round, like birds' nests, and they are set in a circle, the nation's hoop, a nest of many nests, where the Great Spirit meant us to raise our children.*

Sacred land

The religion of the Sioux also affected their attitude to land. They believed that they came from the earth, just like the plants and animals. When they died, they believed they returned to the land. They were part of the land, and such land could not be owned by one individual, or even one nation. The land was part of life itself. They called the land their mother, and they said that ploughing the land was like ripping their mother's breast.

Some land was particularly sacred, especially high places that were close to the spirit world. For the Sioux, the Black Hills were sacred. This was where the first Sioux were saved from the great flood. It was the place where they took their dead for burial. It was there that their holy men went to seek guidance when the nation had an important decision to make.

Outside observers of Indian religion misunderstood many aspects of the Sioux's beliefs. The Sioux's attitude to land was one of the most misunderstood. It was also the greatest source of conflict, as the ownership of land became an increasingly tense issue over the period 1840–70. The Sioux were prepared to fight to the death over their sacred lands. You will return to this issue on page 48.

Visions

One way to contact the spirits was through visions. Every Indian, male and female, wanted to have a vision. Young boys were expected to go in search of theirs. First, they might use the SWEAT LODGE to clean their body. Then they would pray and go without food. Finally, they would receive their vision. This would be interpreted for them by the shaman (medicine man) and their adult name would be given, often based upon their vision. That is how Sitting Bull got his name.

Women could easily make contact with the spirit world, another reason for their importance in Sioux society. They developed this ability when they reached puberty and menstruated for the first time. They received training from a medicine woman on how to control their contacts with the spirit world. Then, just as boys did, they received their adult name.

These visions would help the Sioux throughout their lives. Before the Battle of the Little Bighorn, Sitting Bull dreamed that he saw US army soldiers on horseback, riding just below the rim of the sun. They were upside down, and they were falling into the Sioux camp. He believed that this meant that the soldiers would die in the battle with the Sioux.

SOURCE 4 The vision of Crazy Horse. He believed that the world men lived in was a shadow of the real world

" A man on horseback rode out of a lake. The horse kept changing colours, and it floated above the ground, so light was it, the man too, who sat well forward on the horse. He wore plain leggings and a simple shirt. His face was unpainted and he had only a single feather in his long brown hair. He had a small brown stone tied behind his ear. He did not seem to speak, but Crazy Horse heard him clearly nonetheless.

The man told Crazy Horse never to wear a war bonnet, nor to tie up his horse's tail. He said that before going into battle Crazy Horse should pass some dust over his horse in lines and streaks, but should not paint the pony. And he should rub some of the dirt over his own hair and body. Then he would never be killed by a bullet or an enemy. But he should never take anything for himself. "

SOURCE 5 George Catlin, in his book *North American Indians*, 1844

" I fearlessly say to the world that the North American Indian is everywhere, in his native state, a highly moral and religious being. "

HOW RELIGIOUS WERE THE SIOUX?

Dances and ceremonies

These were used when the whole tribe needed to contact the spirits. Before hunting, they would dance a Buffalo Dance to get the spirit world to call the buffalo to them (see page 24). After a victory in war they would dance the Scalp Dance to celebrate, and to thank the spirits for their help (see page 31).

The most famous ceremony was the Sun Dance. The Sun Dance was used to get help or guidance from the spirit world. Sitting Bull had taken part in one for four days before his great vision of victory came. He had hoped for guidance from the spirit world in his war against the US army. On other occasions individuals might dance the Sun Dance to get help from the spirit world, perhaps for someone who was ill in their family.

SOURCE 6 *Funeral Scaffold of a Sioux Chief near Fort Pierre*, by Karl Bodmer, 1834. After the body of the chief had dried out the bones would be carefully collected for burial in a cleft in the rocks. The artist travelled in the West in 1833–34

1. Why is the scaffold in Source 6 built off the ground?
2. Why is the body covered by a framework of branches?
3. 'People who care for their dead are not savages.' Do you agree?

SOURCE 7 *The Sun Dance Ceremony of the Mandan Indians*, painted by George Catlin, 1835. Catlin observed the Sun Dance himself

4. Sources 6 and 7 were exhibited in the East of the USA to people who had never seen an Indian village. Explain what view of the Indians these pictures would give them.

HOW RELIGIOUS WERE THE SIOUX?

SOURCE 8 *Sun Dance*, a painting by Short Bull

5. Compare Sources 7 and 8. What differences can you find between them?
6. Catlin is a non-Indian artist, Short Bull is a Sioux artist. Do you think this makes either painting more reliable?

SOURCE 9 Luther Standing Bear, writing in his book *My Family the Lakota*, 1975. He is describing the start of the Sun Dance ceremony for one young warrior

"The medicine men would lift the young man and lay him under the pole. An old man would then come forward with a very sharp pointed knife. He would take hold of the breast of the young brave, pull the skin forward and pierce it through with the knife. Then he would insert a wooden pin ... through the slit and tie a strong buckskin thong to this pin.

From the pole two rawhide ropes were suspended. The candidate would now be lifted up ... and was hanging from his breast ... Although the blood would be running down from the knife incision, the candidate would smile, although everyone knew he must be suffering intense pain."

■ **TASK**

1. Study Sources 7–9. In many religions the ceremonies share common features:
   ■ a congregation
   ■ priest(s)
   ■ music
   ■ special places/special buildings
   ■ holy objects
   ■ individual participants.

   Can you find evidence of these features in the Sun Dance ceremonies shown and described in Sources 7–9?

2. Some non-Indians believed Indians to be savages. A savage is someone who is wild, cruel and uncivilised. How might different features of Indian religion lead observers to see Indians as savages?

3. Copy the chart below. Then complete each box with an example to show how religion affected every aspect of the daily life of the Sioux. Some have already been completed for you. You need to try to decide how important an effect religion has in each example.

Aspect	How was it affected by religion?
Name	Your name has come from your spiritual guardian, whom you saw in a vision (see page 41).
Visions	
War	
Village life	Your *tipi* is round and your band always pitch their *tipis* in a circle with the doorway facing east.
Hunting	
Chiefs	You follow a man who has strength and power from his visions – a man like Crazy Horse.
Ceremonies	
Councils	
Medicine	You believe that evil spirits cause disease and call on the spirit world for help and healing (see pages 38–39).
Land	

4. Now write your answer to this question: how religious were the Sioux?

Who treated the sick in Plains Indian nations?

IN 1846 FRANCIS PARKMAN travelled amongst the Plains Indians and recorded his experiences. One incident concerned White Shield, an Indian who was suffering from 'an inflammation of the throat and much shivering'.

> **SOURCE 1** Francis Parkman's description of the treatment of White Shield
>
> *" He went to one of the medicine men in the village. This old impostor thumped White Shield for some time with his fists, howled and yelled over him, and beat a drum by his ear to drive out the evil spirit that he said was lodged there. This failed to have any effect, and White Shield returned to his lodge, certain he was possessed of an evil spirit. "*

1. What does Parkman (Source 1) think about White Shield's and the medicine man's idea of the cause of the illness?

The medicine man

'Medicine man' was the name given by non-Indians to an Indian SHAMAN because he carried herbs. To the Plains Indians there was a connection between religion and every aspect of their lives, including their health. For them, all spirit power was 'medicine'. They believed that the medicine man could cure sickness because he could use the power of the spirits. If a man like White Shield was ill it was because he was possessed by an evil spirit. The medicine man would try to drive out the spirit. As the patient believed in the power of spirits he or she would be relieved if the medicine man said that the evil spirit was gone, and so might well get better.

SOURCE 2 A medicine man of the Blackfoot, painted by George Catlin

2. What creatures can you see in the medicine man's clothing in Source 2?
3. Why is he wearing them?

WHO TREATED THE SICK IN PLAINS INDIAN NATIONS?

Medicine men also used practical remedies, such as ointments and potions made from herbs, to treat sickness. Plains Indians knew the medicinal properties of more than 2000 plants.

The medicine men were consulted not only about medical matters but also about every aspect of tribal life, from where to hunt the buffalo to when to go to war. They charged high fees, normally paid in ponies, and were known to return their fees if their treatments had been unsuccessful.

SOURCE 3 Herbal cures used by Plains Indians

Black cohosh	used for pain relief, especially nerve and muscle pains.
Skunk-cabbage root	used for asthma
White willow bark	used for pain relief (the extract is used today in aspirin)
Witch hazel	used to help the healing of bleeding, bruising and burns
Yarrow	used for minor wounds

Charms

When a child was born women acted as midwives. The baby's umbilical cord was dried and saved. It was kept in a case decorated with quill work or bead work, and shaped like a turtle for a girl, or like a lizard or rattlesnake for a boy. It was used as a plaything and then presented to the child when he or she was older. The Plains Indians believed that the cord that had given them life would also have great protective power for the rest of their life.

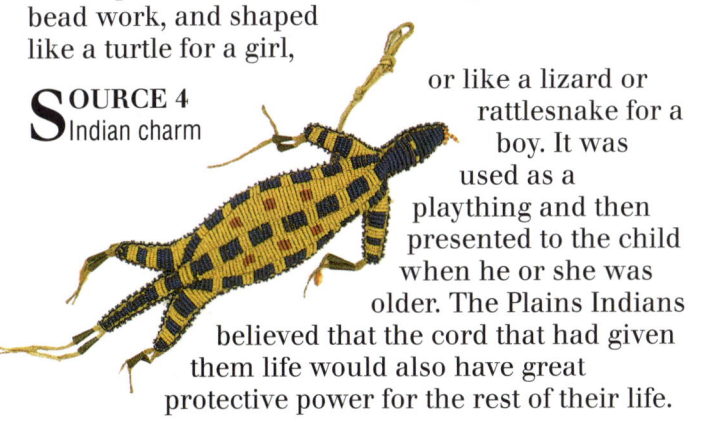

SOURCE 4 Indian charm

Way of life

Their active way of life made sure that Plains Indians were very fit. The most likely causes of death were warfare, hunting accidents, food shortages and old age. The fact that they lived in small family groups, or bands, and frequently moved their villages meant that they did not suffer from public health problems, such as pollution of the water supply by sewage.

SOURCE 5 A stomach pusher, used by Plains Indians to deal with indigestion or stomach pains. The patient lay down and the curved end of the wooden instrument was rubbed against his or her stomach

■ ACTIVITY

Try to put yourself into the moccasins of an Indian medicine man or woman. You need to think about their beliefs and the types of practical remedy that they used. During one week you have to treat three patients.

1. For each patient choose the treatment that you think will be the most effective. Remember that you can choose more than one treatment.
2. Record your choices and the reasons for them.

Patient 1
A young woman, Crystal Stone, comes to you complaining of stomach pains. Do you:

a) make a tea from black cohosh for her to drink?
b) massage her stomach with a stomach pusher?
c) perform a ceremonial dance with rattles and drum to drive out the evil spirit?

Patient 2
A warrior, Dull Knife, is brought to you with a knife cut on his arm. Do you:

a) tie a thong around his arm above the cut?
b) sit and put yourself into a trance so that you can ask the spirits for help?
c) make a poultice of witch hazel and place it over the cut?

Patient 3
You go to visit a child, Full Moon, who is suffering from a fever. Do you:

a) dance and sing over her body and change her name?
b) make a potion from white willow bark for her to drink?
c) tell her parents to bathe her with cool water?

To find out how well you did, ask your teacher for a score sheet.

Living on the Plains

1	Male	Your uncle teaches you how to break (train for riding) a pony.
2	Female	Your period starts. You now have the power to talk to the spirits. Your adult name is...
3	Male	You receive your first vision after a three-day fast. Your adult name is...
4	Female	Your mother teaches you how to do porcupine quill embroidery.
5	Life or death	Your village is raided by the Pawnee. Are you killed in the fighting?
6	All	In the Moon when Wolves Run Together, the snow is so deep that the men cannot hunt. The story telling is good.
7	All	In the Moon When Green Grass is Up, the buffalo hunting is good. No one will go hungry in your village this year.
8	All	Your father, Little Bear, leads a successful raid against the Crow. The people have many horses.
9	Female	You are invited to join the quilling society as your skill is admired.
10	Male	You go on your first raid against the Crow. You look after the horses.
11	Life or death	The white man's sickness (smallpox) comes to your village. Many of the people die. It is a time of great sorrow. Do you survive?
12	Female	You pick berries with Three Bears. He plans to ask your parents for permission to marry you.
13	Male	You are invited to join the Kit Fox society as your bravery is admired.
14	Male	You count coup for the first time on a Crow warrior.
15	Female	Your first child is born.
16	Male	Your offer of marriage is accepted by Little Moon's parents.
17	Female	Your husband takes a second wife, your sister. You are pleased as now you can share the work.
18	Male	You are selected by the medicine man to hunt the buffalo for the tribe, the old, young, the helpless. A great honour.
19	Female	You gain a reputation as a skilled healer. People come to you for help.
20	All	You camp with the Oglala, Crazy Horse's Sioux band. It is a happy time with horse racing and other games.
21	Male	You lose all five of your horses in a bet on a ball game.
22	Female	Your husband is gored and killed during the buffalo hunt.
23	Life or death	Bluecoats attack your village. Many of the people are killed. Are you?
24	Life or death	The buffalo hunting is poor. There is little food for the people. Many people die. Do you?
25	All	You have lived for many moons. Now it is time for you to record your life for the people who are to come.

LIVING ON THE PLAINS

■ **ACTIVITY**

You and your partner should start by choosing whether to be male or female and giving yourselves Indian names (see panel below). You need to roll a dice to move around the board. Make notes of what happens to you as you move around the board. Keep this as a diary. If you land on a life-or-death square you must roll the dice again. If you throw two or less, you die. If you do die, take a new name and begin again.

Indian names

In your life as an Indian you would probably have more than one name. Soon after your birth, a person chosen by your parents would give you a name such as Kicking Bird or Running Fox. This name would come from a vision. Later, if you were a boy, you might take a new name, such as Red Cloud, given to you by your own spiritual guardian in a vision. If you became unwell the medicine man might give you a new name to fool the evil spirit into leaving you. Finally, you might be given a nickname because of something remarkable that you had done, such as Man Afraid of his Horses. All of these names were linked closely to the spirit world.

■ **ACTIVITY**

Study Source 1. Use it and the diary you made during the board game to help you to draw a pictogram history of your life.

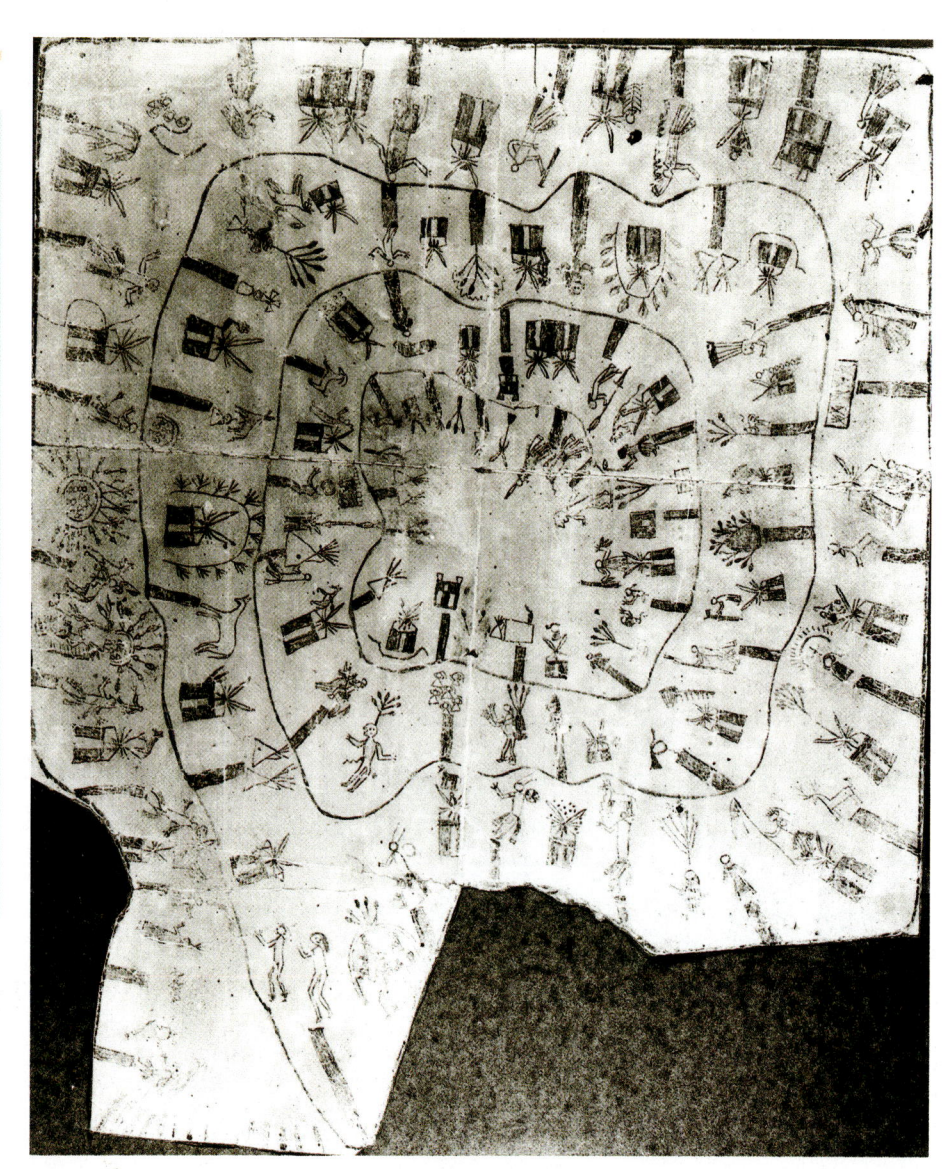

SOURCE 1 A pictogram history of the Kiowa tribe. It was drawn by Little Mountain to record the events between 1833 and 1892. It was copied each time it wore out through use. This photograph shows the last surviving copy

41

Not a Sioux village!

■ **SOURCE INVESTIGATION**

Not all Indians lived like the Sioux. How well do you know the Sioux now? To help you revise, analyse these three pictures. They show aspects of the life of a different Indian nation – the Mandans. What can you learn from these pictures about these people and the way that they lived? Record your information in a table like the one on the right, to show how their lives were similar to or different from the lives of the Sioux. Remember, it is not just a case of what **is** in the pictures. You also need to think about what is **missing** from the pictures. You may need to look back at the rest of this chapter to help with this.

Similar to the Sioux	Different to the Sioux

SOURCE 1 *Bird's-eye View of a Mandan Village*, painted by George Catlin, 1832

This village is surrounded by a fence.

The dead are placed on platforms.

There are scalps hanging on poles.

There is a boat on a roof.

The lodges are made of earth.

There are buffalo skulls on a roof. They hunt buffalo.

The men are wearing feathers.

42

The Mandans

Sources 1–3 show a Mandan village. The Mandans lived on the edge of the Great Plains by the River Missouri. They occupied two great walled towns. In 1804 theirs was the largest community west of the Mississippi.

What made them different from the Sioux was where they lived. The river valley was a good place for farming. They grew corn, enough to provide a good supply of food for themselves and a surplus which they could trade. So the Mandans could build permanent towns and villages. They didn't need to follow the buffalo. Once the riverboats came up the Missouri they were also well placed to trade with the settlers. All of this made them rich, so they had to build fences around their villages and towns to protect them from attack.

There were other Indian nations who lived by farming like the Mandan, nations such as the Pawnee and the Hidatsa. Similarly, there were nations whose lives were more like those of the Sioux.

SOURCE 2 *A Mandan Village*, a painting by Karl Bodmer, 1834–35

SOURCE 3 *Interior of a Mandan Earth Lodge*, a painting by Karl Bodmer, 1834–35

Chapter 3: THE ATTITUDES OF OUTSIDERS TOWARDS THE PLAINS INDIANS

The witnesses of Plains Indian life

OUR IMPRESSION OF THE Plains Indians is greatly affected by the pictures and descriptions of non-Indian witnesses. The three men below are particularly influential.

George Catlin (1796–1872)

Catlin was born on 26 July 1796, in Wilkes-Barre, Pennsylvania, the fifth of fourteen children. He was an artist and entrepreneur of great vision and energy. He travelled widely in the West in the 1830s. His purpose was to make a collection of drawings and paintings to form an Indian Gallery. This would be a record of the Plains Indian society that he knew would soon disappear. He wrote at the time, 'Nothing short of the loss of my life shall prevent me from visiting their country and becoming their historian.'

The exhibition, his completed masterpiece, contained over 500 drawings and paintings which he exhibited around America and Europe. It was based upon his wide experience of Indian life, gained in eight years of travel, and he was obviously sympathetic towards the Indians. He also published his writings, *Manners, Customs and Condition of the North American Indians*, in 1841. The power of his visual images gave him a great influence on the way other Americans thought about the Indians, but his images can be used to portray Indians in a negative way – as savages – as well as in a positive way.

SOURCE 1 *Comanche Meeting the Dragoons*, painted by George Catlin, 1834–35

SOURCE 2 George Catlin's opinion of the Indians, from his book *Manners, Customs and Condition of the North American Indians*, 1841

> From what I have seen of these people I say there is nothing very strange in their character. It is a simple one, and easy to understand if we take the time and care to familiarise ourselves with it. The North American Indian in his native state is an honest, faithful, brave, warlike, cruel, revengeful, relentless – yet honourable, thoughtful and religious being. From the very many acts of their hospitality and kindness, I pronounce them, by nature, a kind and hospitable people.

■ TASK

Study Sources 1–5. Then look back at the sources you have used earlier in this book which were produced by these three men.

1. Which of these three men do you think was most sympathetic towards the Plains Indians?
2. Which was most prejudiced against them?
3. Which of these three men has been of most help to you in your study of Plains Indians?

THE WITNESSES OF PLAINS INDIAN LIFE

Francis Parkman (1823–1893)

Francis Parkman came from a rich Boston family. He was expensively educated at a private school and went on to Harvard University. He was always interested in the 'primitive' Indians.

In 1846 he and his friend Quincy Adams Shaw set off to explore the frontier, something many wealthy people did at this time. Parkman wanted to find out about the Indians, to help his health, and to gather material to write a book. The two men travelled from April until October. On the trip Parkman was frequently ill and his health broke down completely on his return to Boston. He spent several months bedridden, and during this time he dictated his book *The Oregon Trail* (1849), which was first published as a series of articles.

In the short time he spent with the Sioux, Parkman gained some understanding of them but essentially he saw them through the eyes of a wealthy, educated Easterner. He was interested in writing a romantic history, based upon a very limited experience of a few bands of this one nation.

Nevertheless, he is important because he *did* write his book, *The Oregon Trail*. This book informed the wider American public and influenced their view of Indians. It was also used as a source by later writers. So Parkman's views, based upon a limited experience and coloured by his own prejudices, had a great influence on how other Americans saw the Plains Indians.

SOURCE 3 Extract from Francis Parkman's book, *The Oregon Trail*, 1849

" I came across Mene-Seela, seated alone, as still as a statue. His eyes were fixed on the gently swaying top of a pine tree. He was obviously engaged in some religious ritual, for the Indian sees all of nature as having a mystic influence; he watches the nature around him as an astrologer watches the stars. So closely is he linked with it that his guardian spirit is often in the form of a living creature, or even such a living thing as a pine tree. I did not disturb him, but crept away back into the mountains. "

SOURCE 4 Extract from *The Oregon Trail*, 1849

" Having lived among the Sioux I could observe them. They were savages. Neither their manners nor their ideas were in the slightest way changed by their contact with civilization. Their religion, superstitions and prejudices were handed down to them from time immemorial. They fought with the weapons that their fathers used and wore the same clothes made of skins. They were living representations of the 'stone age'. "

Colonel Richard I Dodge

Dodge was a colonel of a cavalry regiment of the US army, who served in the West. In the summer of 1834 he led a campaign to establish friendly contacts with the Comanche and Pawnee of the southern Plains. He was accompanied by the artist George Catlin on this campaign and Catlin painted him meeting the Comanche, as shown in Source 1. He later wrote a book based upon his experiences, called *Hunting Grounds of the Great West*, which was published in 1877.

In the time he spent with the Indians Dodge learned a lot about them. He certainly had more experience of them than Parkman but he did not wholly understand them. What he wrote was influenced by his military background and his role as a soldier trying to keep the peace between Indians and settlers. Like Parkman, he is important because he wrote a book that influenced the attitudes of other Americans to the Plains Indians.

SOURCE 5 Extracts from Colonel Dodge's book, *Hunting Grounds of the Great West*

" ... The first impulse of the Indian, on being surprised in his camp, is that natural to most animals. To run away as fast as his legs will carry him.

... Where all are such magnificent thieves, it is difficult to decide which of the Plains tribes deserves the prize for stealing. The Indians themselves give it to the Comanches, whose sign in the sign language of the Plains is a forward, wriggling motion of the forefinger, meaning a snake.

... Kill every buffalo you can. Every buffalo dead is an Indian gone. "

45

Plains Indian life as outsiders saw it

THE SETTLERS WOULD come into conflict with the Plains Indians for two reasons. Firstly, they wanted the land the Plains Indians occupied. Secondly, they failed to understand Indian culture, and so labelled the Plains Indians as primitive savages. Source 1 is a summary of their prejudices.

SOURCE 1 *Tipi Village of Comanche Tribe in Texas*, a painting by George Catlin, 1834

The Indian *tipis* are decorated with scalps and scenes of hunting and warfare. The Indians believe that if they paint a scene showing them killing the buffalo then the spirits will help their hunting. Indians are pagans.

The Indian men are lounging around. Indians are lazy. They are almost naked except for feathers in their hair. These feathers record their war exploits. Indians are savages.

PLAINS INDIAN LIFE AS OUTSIDERS SAW IT

Look at all this land. These wide open spaces are good for cattle grazing. This stream valley would be good for farming. The Indians refuse to sell their land and yet they waste it. They believe that no one can own land. Indians are wasteful and uncivilised.

This *tipi* village may be an ideal way for nomads to live but these Indians are wasting the vast area they travel in.

Buffalo flesh drying in the sun. What a primitive way to preserve food! Food is plentiful on the Plains so the Indians do not have to work hard to live. This encourages them to be lazy.

The Indian women are working on buffalo skins using bone scrapers. Indians are primitive.

The Indian children are playing. They are not sent to school and are not punished. They are allowed to run wild. Indians are uncivilised.

Women do all the work. Indians do not treat women with proper respect. Indian men can have several wives (polygamy). This is sinful.

■ **TASK**

Discuss with a partner how a Plains Indian might counter each of these prejudices.

Land – the big issue

OF ALL THE attitudes described on the previous page, the most important for future events was the attitude to land. The Indians and the settlers had very different attitudes to land.

The Indians

To the Plains Indians, the land was part of the circle of nature, part of the circle of life and death. They came from the earth, just like the plants and animals, and when they died they returned to the earth. They believed that they were part of the land and that no one could own it. They lived and thought as a community, and their land was the land of the whole nation. That was the only way their lifestyle on the Plains could be successful. This made it very difficult for them to understand how non-Indians could buy and sell land.

The Plains Indians also believed that some places were sacred, particularly high places that were close to the spirit world. The Black Hills were sacred for the Sioux (see page 35). When miners invaded the Black Hills and dug their mines they were violating the Sioux's most sacred place. (It was as though they were drilling for oil in a great cathedral or religious shrine today. How would we feel?)

1. What would be the reaction of a Sioux to the mining in Source 1?
2. What would be the reaction of a settler or miner to Curley's words in Source 2?

SOURCE 2 Curley, a Crow warrior

"The Great Father in Washington sent you here about this land. The soil you see is not ordinary soil. It is the dust of the blood, flesh and bones of our ancestors. We fought and bled and died to keep other Indians from taking it, and we fought and bled and died helping the whites. You will have to dig down through the surface before you can find nature's earth, as the upper portion is Crow. The land, as it is, is my blood and my dead; it is consecrated, and I do not want to give up any portion of it."

SOURCE 1 Miners looking for gold in the Black Hills in the 1880s

LAND – THE BIG ISSUE

The settlers

For the settlers and miners, land was the very reason why they had moved west. They thought and acted as individuals. They wanted their own land. Each person wanted to establish ownership: their claim to a mine, their title to a farm. They needed to dig mine shafts, plough the soil and fence off their plot of land. They found it difficult to understand the attitude of the Indians. In fact they made little effort to understand the Indians, dismissing them as savages and their religious beliefs as superstition. They saw the Indians as an obstacle in their way and were quite prepared to use force to remove them.

The US army frequently found itelf called in to try to keep the peace between the two groups. When they tried to negotiate with the Indians, they were frustrated by the Indians' refusal even to talk about selling land or making treaties. When the government did persuade some Indian chiefs to sign treaties giving up Indian land, they failed to understand that to other Indians those treaties were meaningless.

With two groups competing for the same land and having such different views about it, conflict on the Plains was inevitable.

SOURCE 3 Crowfoot, a Blackfoot Indian

" Our land is more valuable than your money. It will last forever. As long as the sun shines and the waters flow, this land will be here to give life to men and animals. We cannot sell the lives of men and animals. It was put here by the Great Spirit and we cannot sell it because it does not belong to us. "

3. What would be the reaction of a government treaty negotiator to Crowfoot's words in Source 3?

SOURCE 4 A Plains Indian

" You ask me to plough the ground! Shall I take a knife and tear my mother's bosom? Then when I die she will not take me to her bosom to rest. You ask me to cut grass and make hay and sell it and be rich like white men. But how dare I cut off my mother's hair? "

SOURCE 5 An extract from the diary of Major Howard, US army, describing his treaty talks with Plains Indians

" Toohoolhoolzote had the usual long discussion about the earth being his mother, that she should not be disturbed by hoe or plough, etc. etc. We answered, 'We do not wish to interfere with your religion, but you must talk about practical things. Twenty times over you repeat that the earth is your mother. Let us hear it no more, but come to business at once.' "

4. What do Sources 1–4 tell you about Indian attitudes to land?
5. Study Source 5. Does Major Howard understand the Indians' attitude?
6. Think about the attitude to land of people in your local area. Would they understand the Indians' attitude?

Manifest Destiny

IN 1845 JOHN L. O'SULLIVAN, editor of the New York newspaper *The Morning Post*, first used the phrase 'Manifest Destiny':

[It is] our manifest destiny to overspread and to possess the whole of the continent which Providence has given us for the development of the great experiment of liberty.

This phrase had a ring to it and it soon caught on. Soon newspapers all over the country had taken up the cry and were telling the people of the United States to fulfil their 'Manifest Destiny'. So what does the phrase mean? The explanation is simple enough – it means that the United States was destined to dominate the entire continent!

The people of the United States saw their country as a shining example to freedom-loving people everywhere. Their government was the perfect form of government. It must therefore be the God-given duty of the United States to spread these blessings across the whole of the continent of North America. As it was the will of God, anyone carrying it out was doing God's will, and anyone who opposed it was a traitor to the United States and to God.

SOURCE 1 Horace Greeley, writing in his book *New York to San Francisco*, 1859. Greeley was a journalist who travelled across the Plains

" The average Indian of the prairies is a being who does little credit to human nature. As I passed over those magnificent bottoms of Kansas which form the reservations of the Delaware, Potawatomies, [East Indian nations who had been forcibly moved to the Great Plains] – the very best cornlands on earth – and saw their owners sitting around the doors of their lodges at the height of the planting season and I could not help saying, 'These people must die out – there is no help for them. God has given the earth to those who will tame and cultivate it.' "

SOURCE 2 An engraving called *Westward the Course of Empire Takes Its Way*, 1868. It has appeared in more history books in the USA than any other image, and has shaped the way generations of Americans have viewed westward expansion. It shows the artist's optimistic view of 'Manifest Destiny' – the locomotive puffing along the endless tracks, the hard-working men and women building their community, the covered wagons heading for further frontiers, and the vast open spaces of yet-to-be-settled America

MANIFEST DESTINY

In the 1840s there were four areas into which the USA wanted to spread:

- Texas, in the south, which was taken over by the USA in 1845
- Oregon, in the north-west, which was taken over in 1846
- California, in the south-west, which the USA won from Mexico in 1846 after winning the war between them.
- the vast prairies in the centre of the continent, which were home to the Plains Indian nations you have studied in Chapter 2.

SOURCE 3 *Emigrants Crossing the Plains,* by Alfred Bierstadt

The way to gain control of these areas was to settle them, to fill them with people from the United States. The emigrants who went west on the wagon trains therefore knew that they were doing something for their country and that they were doing God's will. With them, they would bring Christianity and liberty. And there was no need to worry about the 'savage' Indians. They had no right to the land because they wasted it. And in any case, the settlers would be bringing civilisation to the Indians.

It might be necessary to fight for these lands and in fact they did have to fight for control of California and the Plains. But in doing this, the people of the United States knew that they were in the right, because they were fulfilling their 'Manifest Destiny'!

1. In what different ways do these three artists show their attitudes towards 'Manifest Destiny'?

SOURCE 4 *Westward the Course of Empire Takes Its Way,* painted in 1861 by Emanuel Leutze

MANIFEST DESTINY

■ TASK

In the chapters that follow we are going to look at the arrival of the settlers on the Great Plains. As they came in increasing numbers they inevitably affected the lives of Plains Indians. You will need to think about the Indians and record what these effects were as you work through Section 2. The table below will help you to do this. You should particularly consider their effect on the Indians'

- food supply
- ability to roam freely
- right to live in peace
- desire to live in harmony with nature
- respect for their holy places, such as the Black Hills.

Group	What effect did they have on the lives of Plains Indians?
Mountain men	
Travellers	
Gold miners	
MORMONS	
Homesteaders	
Cattlemen	
Railway builders	
Buffalo hunters	
US army	

section 2

THE SETTLERS

Chapter 4: THE EARLY PIONEERS – WHY DID THEY CROSS THE PLAINS?

THE FIRST WAVE of people moving west regarded the Plains simply as a useless desert which they had to cross. None of them had any intention of settling there. They were on their way to somewhere or something much better, further west.

We are going to look at four groups of people who travelled across the Plains. First, there were the mountain men. They were followed by settlers in California or Oregon. Then there were the Mormons, who settled by the Great Salt Lake, and, finally, there were the 'FORTY-NINERS' attracted by the discovery of gold in California.

Each of these groups had their own reasons for going west, and all faced enormous difficulties. As you study this part of the book, keep in mind the following questions.

- Did they all go west for the same reasons?
- Did they all face the same problems and difficulties?
- What effect, if any, did they have on the Plains Indians?

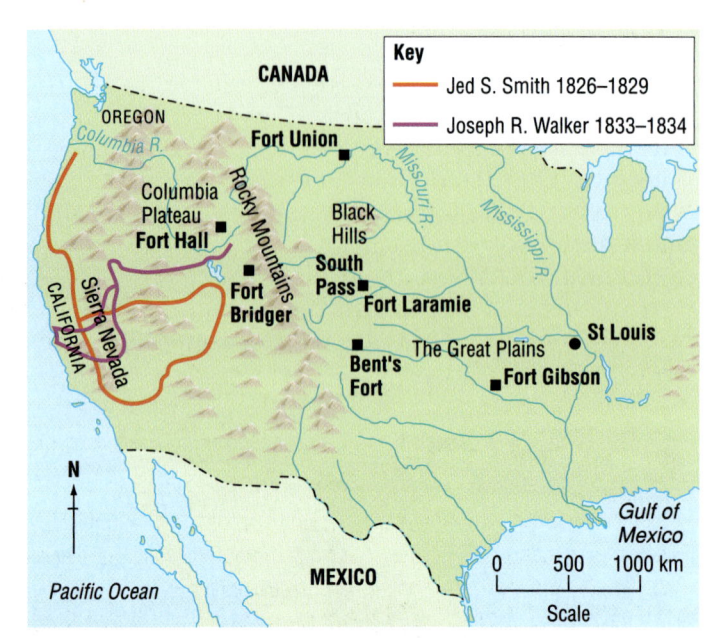

SOURCE 2 A map showing routes through the West established by the fur traders

SOURCE 1 A painting from 1837, showing the inside of Fort Laramie, which was built in 1832 on the Oregon Trail. The big companies, such as the American Fur Company, built trading posts where trappers, Indians and merchants could meet and trade. The trading posts were called forts because they could be defended against attack

The mountain men lead the way west

SOME OF THE first non-Indians to travel west across the Plains and over the Rockies were the fur trappers. Fur hats were all the fashion in cities such as New York and Paris, and the fur trade flourished from the 1820s to the 1840s. The trappers blazed trails into the heartlands of the far West. They roamed the Rocky Mountains, trapping beavers and hunting other animals for their fur.

General William Henry Ashley made his fortune from the fur trade by sending hundreds of trappers into the mountains. It was one of his men, Jed Smith, who in 1823 found the important South Pass route through the Rockies. Wagons could now travel not just from St Louis to the Rockies, but *through* the Rockies. In 1832 the fur companies found a second way of travelling west when a steamboat got as far as Fort Pierre on the River Missouri.

THE MOUNTAIN MEN LEAD THE WAY WEST

Not all trappers worked for companies like Ashley's. Many were independent, working for themselves. They called themselves 'mountain men', and often spent their entire lives in the mountains.

The rendezvous

Once a year, from 1825 to 1840, all the trappers gathered at an agreed spot to trade their year's catch. This was called the rendezvous. As many as 600 trappers would arrive with their pack mules loaded down with furs. They would meet merchants from St Louis, who brought with them rifles, powder, knives, beaver traps, coffee and sugar, blankets, tobacco and whisky. The mountain men would tell the merchants about the rich fertile lands to the west of the Rockies, and news of these wonderful lands would eventually get back to the East. Friendly Indians would also be present at the rendezvous, as the description in Source 5 shows.

SOURCE 3 A description of a rendezvous by a visitor from the East

> The whole rendezvous was a military camp. Every little camp had its own guards to protect [the possessions of] its occupants from being stolen by its neighbour. The arrow or the gun decided disputes. The only law for horse-stealing was death to the thief.

1. Do Sources 3–5 all give the same impression of the rendezvous?

SOURCE 4 *The 1837 Rendezvous on the Green River*, a painting by Alfred Jacob Miller

The mountain men spent some of the money they earned from the sale of their furs on essential equipment but often squandered the rest on drink and gambling. The evenings at the rendezvous would quite often end in drunken orgies. Many of the men were quite happy to spend an entire year's earnings in a few hours of fun.

SOURCE 5 Joseph Meek, who spent ten years as a mountain man

> The lonely mountain valley was populated with the different camps. The Rocky Mountain and American Companies with their separate camps; the Nez Percés and Flatheads . . . friends of the whites, had their lodges all along the streams; so that altogether there could not have been less than one thousand souls, and two or three thousand horses and mules.
>
> It was always chosen in some valley where there was grass for the animals and game for the camp. The waving grass of the plain with patches of wild flowers; the clear summer heavens flecked with white clouds that threw soft shadows; laughter and the murmuring of Indians voices, all made up a most enchanting picture.

THE MOUNTAIN MEN LEAD THE WAY WEST

The struggle for survival

The life of the mountain men was hard and dangerous. The climate was harsh, and the men could easily freeze to death after wading waist-deep in the icy mountain streams while setting their traps. The Rockies were full of grizzly bears – it was not unusual to see 50 or 60 in a day. These bears were as tall as men and able to cut to the bone with their claws. Jed Smith had to have his ear sewn back on after a grizzly had ripped it off.

And then there were the Indians. The relationship between mountain men and the Indians was a mixed one. Some Indian nations, such as the Blackfoot, were dangerous enemies. Others were more friendly, and about half the mountain men married Indian women. This gave them family ties and somewhere to live in the winter. The repayment the Indians received was not so beneficial. The mountain men introduced them to firearms and alcohol, which made the Indians less self-sufficient and more dependent on outsiders. In some ways, this was the beginning of the destruction of the Indian way of life.

The only way the mountain men could survive was to adapt themselves to the wilderness. In many ways they lived like the Indians and even looked like Indians. Their skins were tanned by their outdoor life, they wore buckskin hunting shirts decorated with coloured porcupine quills, and their unkempt hair reached to their shoulders. In their belt they wore a tomahawk or a pistol. Their trousers were made of leather and on their heads they wore a cap of skins decorated with animals' tails. These clothes were best appreciated from a distance because they were never removed – except when they were laid across an ant hill to allow the ants to eat some of the lice!

Many mountain men turned savage to survive. A man called Cannibal Phil went off into the mountains with an Indian on a hunting trip. The weather was terrible, with howling winds sweeping the countryside. He eventually returned, alone. As he unpacked his mule he pulled out a shrivelled human leg, threw it to the ground and said, 'There, damn you, I won't have to gnaw on you any more.' Cut off by a snowstorm on another journey, he survived by eating his Indian wife. The mountain men were brutal towards unfriendly Indians. Their method of scalping was to make two semi-circular cuts into the scalp, loosen the skin with the point of a knife, and pull with their feet against the dead man's shoulders until the scalp came loose.

SOURCE 6 *The Trapper's Bride*, by Alfred Jacob Miller, painted in 1837. It shows a mountain man being accepted into the band of his new Indian wife

■ CONNECTIONS

How similar was the mountain men's way of life to the life of the Plains Indians?

THE MOUNTAIN MEN LEAD THE WAY WEST

SOURCE 7 A drawing of a fur trapper by Frederic Remington

By 1840 the mountain men had moved on. Most of the beavers had been wiped out and fewer and fewer skins were traded at the rendezvous. In 1836 there were only 120 trappers. Back in the East and in Europe beaver hats were no longer in fashion. Finally, in 1837, a steamboat arriving at Fort Union brought smallpox with it. The friendly Indians went down like flies and those who escaped carried the virus to their villages. Thousands died, and the trappers were no longer welcome.

A mountain man named Jim Bridger and several others earned a living by guiding wagon trains across the West. Their knowledge of the West was unrivalled.

SOURCE 8 George Ruxton, an Englishman who lived among some of the last mountain men in 1847, summed up their contribution to the eventual settlement of the West

" Not a hole or corner in the vast wilderness of the 'Far West' but has been ransacked by these hardy men. From the Mississippi to the mouth of the Colorado in the West, from the frozen regions of the North to Mexico in the South, the beaver-hunter has set his traps in every creek and stream. All this vast country, but for the daring enterprise of these men, would even now be an unknown land to geographers, as indeed a great portion still is in 1849. "

2. Now that you know more about the mountain men, which of Sources 3–5 on page 55 do you think is the most accurate description of a rendezvous?
3. What effect did the mountain men have on the Indians – was it good or harmful?
4. In what ways were the mountain men important to the later settling of the West?

Wagons west!

Why go west?

In the 1840s thousands of people moved west to Oregon and California. Why did they go? After reading the accounts of some of their journeys you might find this a difficult question to answer. And remember that most people thought that the Plains, the first barrier on such a journey, were uninhabitable. Maps of the Plains at this time were labelled 'The Great American Desert'.

People went partly because there were factors 'pushing' them away from the places where they lived, and partly because there were things about Oregon or California which 'pulled' them west. After reading through this section you should be able to work out what the 'push' and 'pull' factors were.

To many people in the United States in 1840 there were two places that sounded as if they might be paradise on earth. The first was California. The trappers described it as a place where the sun always shone and fruit grew everywhere. The second place was Oregon where, the trappers reported, there was a never-ending supply of furs, rivers that were full of fish and land that was perfect for farming.

Of course, these stories might not be true. Why take the risk in going west if you were comfortable where you were? But suddenly, in 1837, the lives of people in the East became less comfortable than they had been.

In 1837 the United States was hit by an economic depression. In the East banks collapsed and people lost their savings, wages were cut by 40 per cent and unemployment grew. In 1839 20,000 unemployed people demonstrated in Philadelphia.

The situation was no better in the Midwest. Farmers in the Mississippi valley faced ruin because the price of the wheat and corn they grew had collapsed. They began to wonder – why not go west? Things could not be any worse there, and they might be a lot better.

There was another factor, one which you might find hard to understand. Some of the farmers in the Mississippi valley were beginning to feel 'crowded'. One complained that people were settling right under his nose (his nearest neighbour was 19 km away). But remember that these farmers' grandparents had moved to states like Missouri to get away from it all. The population of Missouri grew from 14,000 in 1830 to 353,000 in 1840!

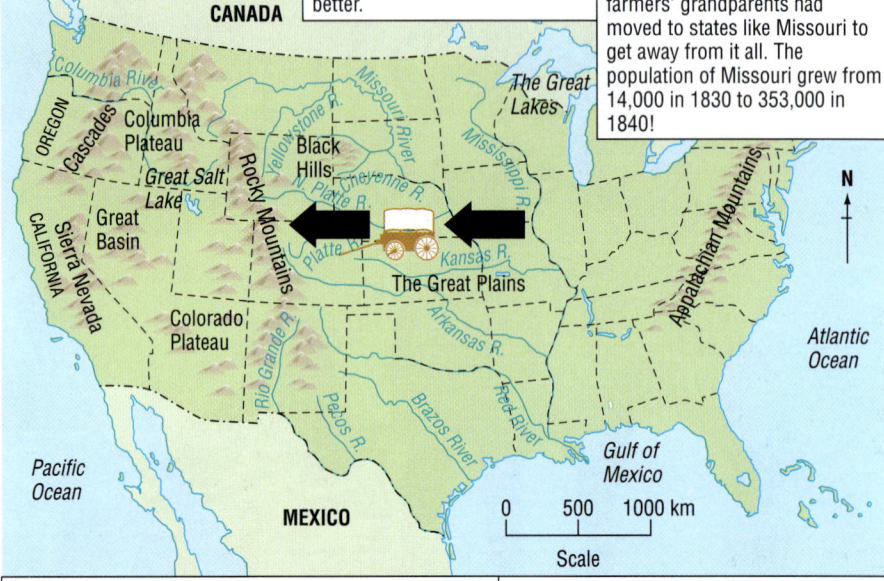

The West offered land in enormous quantities. In California it was there for the taking! And in 1842 the government passed a Pre-emption Bill which applied to the land in Oregon. This said that a farmer who squatted on a piece of land, built a house and cleared the trees could buy the land at a minimum price without being outbid by speculators. This meant that if you did move west and worked hard on the land you would not be wasting your efforts.

In the early 1840s reports began to make their way back East about how wonderful the far West was. Some of these reports were from missionaries who wanted more people to come and help them convert the Indians to Christianity; others came from people who were hoping to make money from the new settlers.

SOURCE 2 'Push' and 'pull' factors which encouraged people to move west. The year 1843 was called the year of the 'Great Emigration', when 1000 people emigrated. In 1845 it was 5000, in 1849 30,000, and in 1850 it went up to 55,000

SOURCE 3 A settler remembers what persuaded her father to take the risk and move to Oregon in 1843

One Saturday morning father said that he was going to hear Mr Burnett talk about Oregon. Mr Burnett hauled a box out on to the sidewalk, took his stand upon it, and began to tell us about the land flowing with milk and honey on the shores of the Pacific. He told of great crops of wheat which it would be possible to raise in Oregon, and pictured in glowing terms the richness of the soil and the attractions of the climate, and then with a little twinkle in his eye, he said, 'and they do say, gentlemen, that out in Oregon the pigs are running about under the great acorn trees, round and fat, and already cooked, with knives and forks sticking in them so that you can cut off a slice whenever you are hungry'.

SOURCE 1 A widely published letter of 1840 from Dr John Marsh, who had settled in California

The whole of California is remarkably adapted to the culture of the vine. Wine and brandy are made in considerable quantities. Olives, figs and almonds grow well. Apples, pears and peaches are abundant and, in the southern part, oranges. Cotton also succeeds well.

WAGONS WEST!

Getting ready

Whether you were going to Oregon or California, you started your journey at one of the many little towns along the Missouri River, such as Independence or St Joseph. Emigrants would spend the winter in these towns, hard at work preparing for the journey. They knew that they would have to leave early in April – as soon as the snows had started to melt. Some families sold all their belongings and their farms or houses to pay for the journey. Others saved for years to raise the $1000 that was needed.

Several guide books were written to help the emigrants to prepare. *The Emigrants' Guide to Oregon and California*, published in 1845, recommended that each family take:

- 200 pounds of flour
- 150 pounds of bacon
- 10 pounds of coffee
- 20 pounds of sugar
- 10 pounds of salt.

They would also need chipped beef, rice, tea, dried beans, dried fruit, baking soda, vinegar, pickles, mustard and tallow. The equipment required included a kettle, frying pan, coffee pot, tin plates, cups, knives and forks.

There would be further expenses during the journey. Stores would need to be replaced, the charges of the ferrymen at river crossings would have to be paid, and enough food would have to be bought to get them through their first winter in their new home.

■ TASK

Make a list of the 'push' factors that made people go west, and a list of the 'pull' factors.

Which do you think were the more important, the push or the pull factors?

SOURCE 4 The 'Prairie Schooner'. The most important and most expensive pieces of equipment were the wagon and the oxen. This is a photograph of a typical wagon, now in a museum in the USA

The emigrants built their own wagons. The wagon bed was made from a hardwood such as maple, which would survive the extremes of temperature, the river crossings and mountain travel. The bed was about 1 m wide and 3 m long. The sides were nearly 1 m high. Either four or six oxen would pull the wagon.

The spokes, axles and wheels were liable to break and spares would be carried under the wagon bed.

A grease bucket would hang under the wagon bed. Water barrels and heavy rope would also have to be carried somewhere.

There were many water crossings ahead so a tar bucket would hang from the side. Tar was used to fill in the gaps between the slats of wood, to make the bed of the wagon waterproof.

The wheels were made of wood, with iron tyres.

The cover was a double thickness of canvas – they often used sailcloth. This was spread over a frame of hickory.

What was it like to travel west?

THE JOURNEY TO California was 3800 km long and took from April to November or even December. Emigrants to Oregon and California started in groups. The best way of understanding what it must have been like to travel west is to study in detail particular groups that went west. We are going to have a look at three such groups. As you read through these accounts, make some notes about the difficulties they faced.

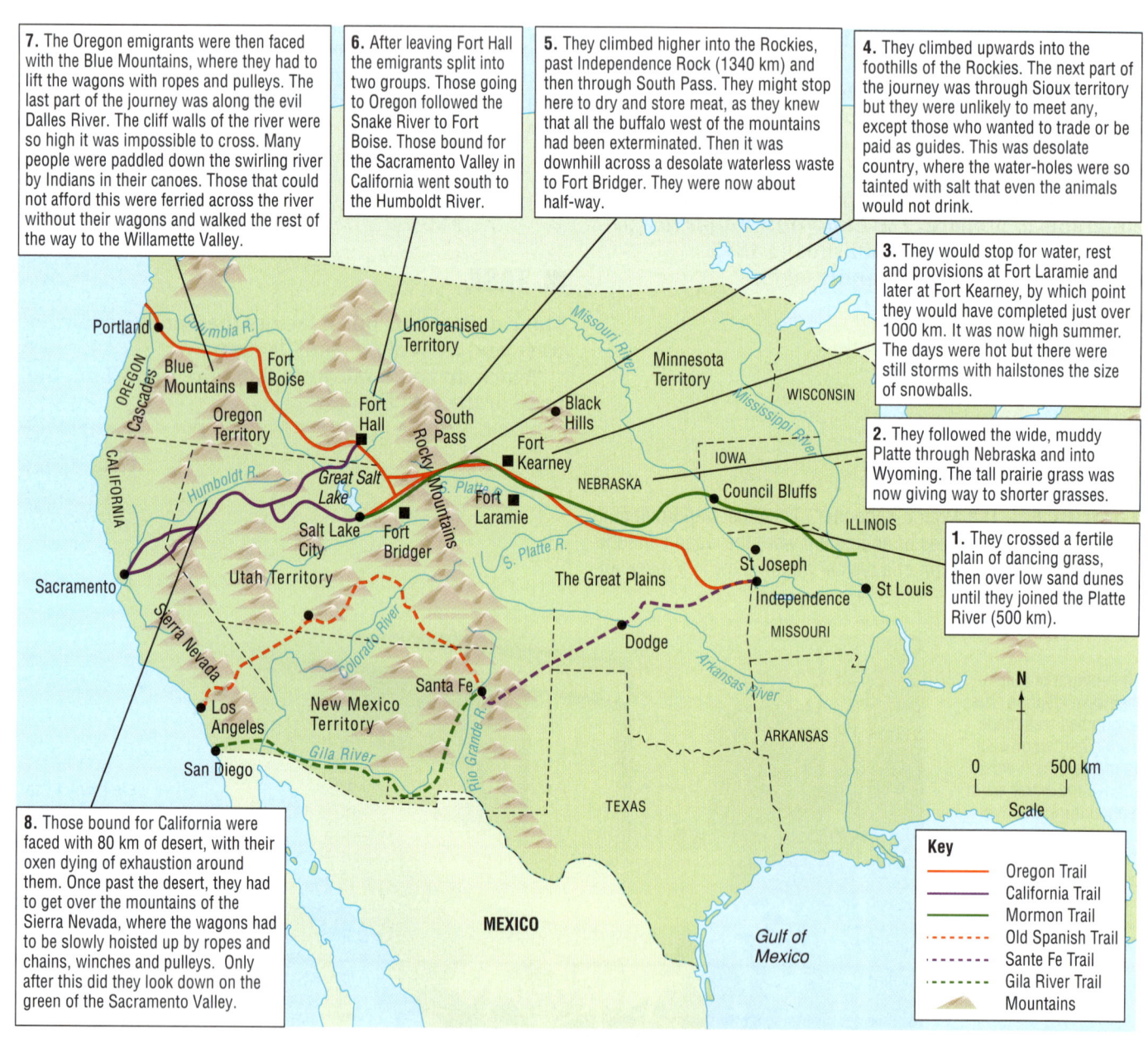

7. The Oregon emigrants were then faced with the Blue Mountains, where they had to lift the wagons with ropes and pulleys. The last part of the journey was along the evil Dalles River. The cliff walls of the river were so high it was impossible to cross. Many people were paddled down the swirling river by Indians in their canoes. Those that could not afford this were ferried across the river without their wagons and walked the rest of the way to the Willamette Valley.

6. After leaving Fort Hall the emigrants split into two groups. Those going to Oregon followed the Snake River to Fort Boise. Those bound for the Sacramento Valley in California went south to the Humboldt River.

5. They climbed higher into the Rockies, past Independence Rock (1340 km) and then through South Pass. They might stop here to dry and store meat, as they knew that all the buffalo west of the mountains had been exterminated. Then it was downhill across a desolate waterless waste to Fort Bridger. They were now about half-way.

4. They climbed upwards into the foothills of the Rockies. The next part of the journey was through Sioux territory but they were unlikely to meet any, except those who wanted to trade or be paid as guides. This was desolate country, where the water-holes were so tainted with salt that even the animals would not drink.

3. They would stop for water, rest and provisions at Fort Laramie and later at Fort Kearney, by which point they would have completed just over 1000 km. It was now high summer. The days were hot but there were still storms with hailstones the size of snowballs.

2. They followed the wide, muddy Platte through Nebraska and into Wyoming. The tall prairie grass was now giving way to shorter grasses.

1. They crossed a fertile plain of dancing grass, then over low sand dunes until they joined the Platte River (500 km).

8. Those bound for California were faced with 80 km of desert, with their oxen dying of exhaustion around them. Once past the desert, they had to get over the mountains of the Sierra Nevada, where the wagons had to be slowly hoisted up by ropes and chains, winches and pulleys. Only after this did they look down on the green of the Sacramento Valley.

Key
— Oregon Trail
— California Trail
— Mormon Trail
---- Old Spanish Trail
---- Sante Fe Trail
---- Gila River Trail
Mountains

SOURCE 1 The journey to the West

SOURCE 2 Catherine Sagar, aged nine, describes leaving St Joseph on 14 April 1844

Some wept at the thoughts of leaving all they held dear for a long and uncertain journey, and the children wept for fear of the mighty waters that came rushing down and seemed as though they would swallow us up; so that it was a sad company that crossed over the Missouri River that bright spring morning.

WHAT WAS IT LIKE TO TRAVEL WEST?

SOURCE 3 An emigrant family by their wagons. They are (left to right at the back): Sarah (aged 11), Elizabeth (aged 6), Nancy (aged 37), Nancy (aged 17) and Hannah (aged 30). Left to right at front: Hyrum (aged 8), Janette (aged 2) and Joseph Henry (aged 39).

1. Look at Sources 3 and 4. Do they give a similar or different impression of the journey west to that given by Sources 1–4 on pages 50–51?

SOURCE 4 Wagons heading west to Oregon, painted by N.C. Wyeth

WHAT WAS IT LIKE TRAVEL WEST?

SOURCE 5 *The Attack on an Emigrant Train*, painted by Charles Wimar, 1856

Case study 1: the Sagars

Henry Sagar had moved his family four times in as many years. By 1844 the Sagars and their six children were in St Joseph, Missouri. He then decided to take his family to Oregon, and joined up with other PIONEERS. Altogether there were 323 people and 72 wagons in the Sagars' group.

The Sagars' journey was difficult from the start. The rain turned the prairies to mud. The swollen rivers were difficult to cross. Five weeks into the journey, Naomi Sagar gave birth to her seventh child, and she had to care for the infant with water running through the wagon's cover and saturating the bedclothes.

On 4 July they rested near the Platte River. Here, they saw their first herd of buffalo and stopped for two days, shooting far more than they could use. Arguments broke out about this and the captain resigned his post, leaving them without a leader for the rest of the journey.

Henry was finding it difficult to control his ox team. The wagon overturned several times, once nearly killing Naomi. On 1 August there was another accident as they passed Scotts Bluff. Catherine, one of the Sagars' daughters, tried to hop off the wagon as it was moving.

SOURCE 6 Catherine describes the accident

" The hem of my dress caught on an axle-handle, precipitating me under the wheels, both of which passed over me, badly crushing the left leg before Father could stop the oxen. "

Catherine had broken her leg. It was put in a splint and she spent the rest of the journey either riding in the jolting wagon or walking with crutches.

A sickness they called 'camp fever' then struck the wagon train. Henry and three of his children went down with the disease. Near Fort Laramie they suffered from a buffalo stampede and Henry, still weak from sickness, died trying to turn the buffalo from his wagon. Worse was to follow. As they followed the Snake River, Naomi went down with 'camp fever'.

SOURCE 7 Catherine's description of her mother's death

" She soon became delirious. Her babe was cared for by the women of the train. The kind-hearted women were also in the habit of coming in when the train stopped at night to wash the dust from her face and make her comfortable. The day she died we travelled over a very rough road, and mother moaned pitifully all day. When we camped for the night her pulse was nearly gone. She lived but a few moments more. "

WHAT WAS IT LIKE TO TRAVEL WEST?

The seven Sagar children were now orphans. The wagon train moved slowly on, and by October it had reached a PRESBYTERIAN MISSION run by the Whitmans in south-eastern Oregon. The Whitmans had lost their own daughter when she was two and they agreed to look after the Sagar children. For the next three years they lived peacefully. Then, in 1847, disaster struck.

Measles, carried west by the emigrant trains, swept through the villages of the local Indians, the Cayuse. The Indians noticed that none of their own children survived, while many of the white children did. The Whitmans worked tirelessly caring for the Indians who went down with the disease but rumours began to spread that they were secretly spreading the disease rather than trying to cure it. In November 1847 three Cayuse shot and hacked Marcus Whitman to death. They then killed the two Sagar boys. Hannah Sagar, who was ill with measles, died shortly afterwards. The remaining four Sagar girls were taken captive by the Cayuse. They were later released after payment of a ransom.

SOURCE 8 Nancy Osborne, who survived the Whitman Massacre by hiding under the floorboards, drew this sketch of the Whitman compound. The Whitmans lived in building 1, emigrants were housed in 3, and their wagons were repaired in 2

WHAT WAS IT LIKE TO TRAVEL WEST?

Case study 2: the Goulds

The extracts on this page were written by Jane Gould. She, her husband Albert, and their two sons travelled to California from Iowa in 1862. They travelled with Albert's father, his brother, Charlie, and Charlie's wife, Lou. Their family group was part of a larger wagon train.

SOURCE 9 An engraving showing settlers camping on the Plains

> **April 27** Left home this morning. We came sixteen miles.

> **May 1** Took an hour to build a fire this morning, the ground was very wet and the wind blew cold from the Northwest.

> **May 16** Most of the women of our company are washing. I am baking. I made some yeast bread for the first time in three weeks.

> **May 17** Raining hard as it could pour down. The men went out of the wagon, made some coffee and warmed some beans. It had grown very cold through the day, most of the men are wet through.

> **June 3** In the afternoon we passed a lonely nameless grave on the prairie.

> **June 4** A beautiful morning. Clear, bright and warm. We travelled nearly ten miles along the banks of the Platte. The boys waded across to an island and brought some chips [dried dung] in a sack which were sufficient to cook our supper with.

> **June 24** Bought some antelope meat which was delicious from the Indians. We passed through a small Indian village. We saw they had over a hundred ponies. There were sixteen wigwams.

> **June 25** The Indians came around. They were anxious to swap moccasins and LARIATS for money, powder and whiskey. Charlie traded a little iron kettle for a lariat.

> **June 28** Did not travel today. Stayed to let the cattle have a rest. Albert set the tyre of his wagon wheels and set some shoes on the horses. I did a large washing and Lucy did a large quantity of cooking.

> **July 22** Our men went to work this morning to build a raft. Had to take the wagons apart and float the box and cover behind.

WHAT WAS IT LIKE TO TRAVEL WEST?

SOURCE 10 A wagon train at Independence Rock

SOURCE 11 Pioneer wagon train crossing the Platte River in Nebraska, painted by Dorenceau in the 1850s

August 3 We passed a camp of six wagons. They had just buried the babe of a woman who died days ago, and were just digging a grave for another woman that was run over by the cattle and wagons when they stampeded yesterday.

August 10 We came to the Snake River. We learned that a train of eleven wagons had been attacked by Indians. The wagons had been plundered and all that was in them, and the teams taken and the men killed.

August 13 We came to a wagon that had been stopped. We saw the bodies of three dead men. They had been dead two or three weeks. One had his head and face cut out, another his legs, a third his hands and arms. Oh! It is a horrid thing. I wish all of the Indians in Christendom were exterminated.

August 15 Most of the train slept under the wagons, dug a trench and blockaded the outside of the wagon. Set up flour sacks and all manner of stuff.

August 21 We saw some Indians today. They were Snakes. Three of our men burned their wigwams. They were very indignant about it and wanted us to pay for it. They got a good deal of bread and bacon from different ones in our camp. After being in trouble with them for so long, we are glad to let them be friendly.

August 29 We camped on the Humboldt River for which we were very thankful.

September 7 They say there is no grass between here and Carson River.

September 14 We are nearly out of provisions. We have to pay five cts. per lb for hay. Lou and I walked a great deal. The roads are lined with wagon irons and piles of bones.

September 15 We saw the trees on Carson River and thought we were almost there but we kept going and going and it seemed as if I never could get there.

October 3 Arrived at the first house in the settlement in the San Joaquin Valley. Pitched our tent. In this part of the country all of the water is pumped by power of windmills. The orchards are small and the trees so near together. Every garden and orchard has its windmill to irrigate it. "

WHAT WAS IT LIKE TO TRAVEL WEST?

Case study 3: the Donner party

Lansford W. Hastings first visited California in 1843. From then on, he had only one ambition – to take California from Mexico and establish an independent country with himself as President. For this, he needed thousands of settlers. The problem was that Oregon was the more popular destination – partly because it involved a shorter journey. There was only one answer – to find a short cut to California. By examining maps and explorers' reports, he found one.

Although he had not actually used the short cut himself, he advised wagon trains to leave the normal route at Fort Bridger, go south-west to the Great Salt Lake, and then rejoin the usual route. It saved hundreds of kilometres but was to cause disaster for the Donner party in 1846. This group was organised by two well-to-do brothers, Jacob and George Donner. It consisted of 60 wagons and 300 emigrants.

At first everything went well. The party left Independence in May and made good progress. By July they had reached the Little Sandy River. The Donners were keen to travel with Hastings along his short cut but most of the party wanted to follow the usual route. As a result, the company split into two, with 88 people going with the Donners.

Hastings had agreed to meet them at Fort Bridger. But when they arrived there at the beginning of August Hastings had already left with another party. However, he promised to mark the trail for the Donners.

They started off, but soon came across a note from Hastings stuck into a forked stick. It told them to wait until he could find a way through the Wasatch Mountains. For eight days they camped. At last, instructions came telling them to follow another trail. This turned out to be almost impossible. For days they pushed aside boulders and guided their cattle along twisting paths. Eventually they emerged on to the blinding-white alkali flats of the Great Salt Lake Desert.

According to Hastings, it should have taken two days to cross the desert. It actually took nearly a week. Behind them in the sand the emigrants left four wagons and 300 head of oxen and cattle. Paiute Indians began to raid the stock. They were now in desperate trouble. Quarrels broke out, fights started. One member of the party, James Reed, killed another in self-defence and was banished to the desert. Their food supplies were almost gone and it was already well into September; their chances of crossing the Sierras before snow began to fall were disappearing.

They sent two men ahead to Fort Sutter to bring back supplies. On 19 October one of them returned with a mule-train of food and two Indian guides. They rested and fed at Truckee Meadows. Not until 23 October did they leave the grassy meadows and start into the Sierras. But they thought they had plenty of time. It usually did not start to snow until mid-November. They began the 600-metre climb. On the night of 28 October they made camp fairly happy. When they awoke the next morning there was 15 cm of snow on the ground. The snows had come a month early!

The passes ahead of them were covered by drifts. Sleet coated the rocks with slippery ice. Further storms buried the mountains under a metre of snow. Their animals died of the cold and of suffocation in the drifts. They were snowbound in the High Sierras with blizzards howling down the mountain.

SOURCE 12 *On the Way to the Summit,* an engraving showing the Donner party struggling over the Sierra Nevada mountains

WHAT WAS IT LIKE TO TRAVEL WEST?

They built crude shelters and huddled together. The snow deepened and the numbing cold grew. Their food supplies were dwindling fast. The first emigrant died of starvation on 15 December. By this time they were eating anything they could chew, including bones, twigs and the bark of trees.

It was clear that someone had to go for help. Fifteen people (eight men, including two Indian guides, and five women volunteered to try to reach Sutter's Fort. This small group – the 'Forlorn Hope' – started on 16 December. They had starvation rations for six days. It would be 32 days before they saw the first signs of civilisation.

By Christmas Day they had been without food for four days. They agreed that one of them must die to allow the others to live. They drew lots. But no one had the heart to kill the loser. The storms got worse. After two days huddled under their blankets, four of them were dead. The survivors stripped the flesh from their bones, roasted it and ate it. When they moved on they packed the last of the flesh – carefully labelling each piece so that no one would eat their husband or wife. When this food ran out, the Indians, who had refused to eat human flesh, were shot and butchered. At last, on 10 January, the seven survivors (two men and five women) stumbled into Johnson's Ranch.

Rescue parties were sent out, and the first reached the camp on 19 February. It found half the emigrants dead, and the others half-mad. Twenty-three of them were strong enough to be led out of the Sierras but the rest had to wait for the main rescue party. This was delayed, and the emigrants had to resort to cannibalism. The main rescue party arrived at the end of February. It was led by James Reed, who had found his way to California alone after being banished to the desert. He found his wife and four children all alive.

SOURCE 13 An illustration of the Donner party emigrants who were trapped in the Sierras for almost four months

SOURCE 14 A description of what he found at the camp by Captain Fellun, who led one of the rescue parties

"A horrible scene presented itself. Human bodies terribly mutilated, legs, arms and skulls scattered in every direction. At the mouth of a tent stood a large kettle, filled with human flesh cut up, it was the body of George Donner. His head had been split open and the brains extracted."

1. Why did the Donner journey end in disaster?

■ TASK

1. Trace the three journeys described on pages 62–67 on your own copy of the map on page 60.
2. From these three journeys, what impression do you get of:
   a) the Indians?
   b) the role of women?
3. Which group would you rather have belonged to? Why?
4. Make a list of all the dangers and difficulties each group faced. Did the different groups face different dangers and difficulties or the same ones?
5. Design and write a small booklet entitled *The Emigrants' Guide to Travelling to Oregon and California*. In it, you are going to advise people:

- how to prepare for the journey and when to leave
- which routes to take
- how to survive the journey and what dangers to look out for
- what they can look forward to when they arrive.

You might want to include examples from the Donner story about how not to do things.

67

The California Gold Rush

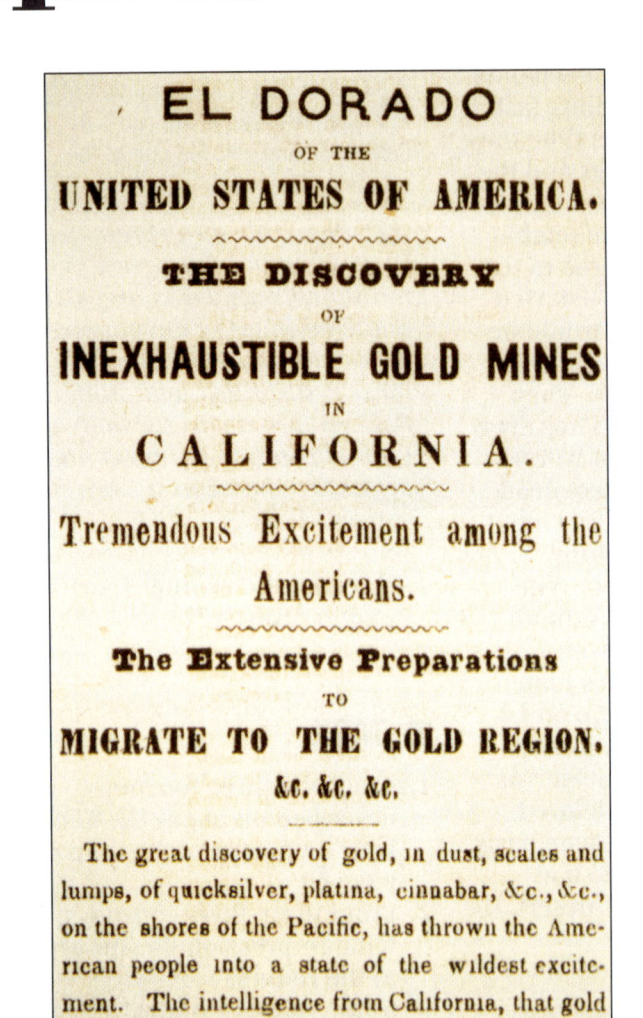

THE TRICKLE OF emigrants moving westwards was suddenly turned into a flood by an accidental event – the discovery of gold in one of the rivers that cascaded westward from the Sierras.

In January 1848 a group of men were building a sawmill in the Sierra foothills when one of them, James Marshall, noticed the glint of yellow at the bottom of the ditch. He collected some samples, which responded to every test for gold he knew. Marshall and his fellow workers, some of whom were Mormons, finished the sawmill and then began to mine what became known as the Mormon Diggings.

In May they were visited by Sam Brannan, a Mormon who owned businesses in San Francisco. He quickly opened a store right next to the sawmill and returned to San Francisco to tell everyone about the gold. Suddenly, everyone in San Francisco was caught up in 'gold fever', as Source 2 explains.

SOURCE 1 A newspaper headline about the discovery of gold in 1849

SOURCE 2 Extract from *The Far Western Frontier* by Ray Allen Billington, 1956

> *Overnight carpenters dropped their hammers, masons their trowels, bakers their loaves, clerks their pens, to rush to the diggings. Schools were closed as both teachers and pupils deserted; shopkeepers hung signs on their doors – 'Gone to the Diggings' – and disappeared. By June 15 San Francisco was a ghost town with houses and shops empty, and all who could walk, ride, or crawl rushing toward the Sierras.*

SOURCE 3 An American cartoon published in 1849. The cartoonist is proposing that an India-Rubber Air Line be set up, to hurl eager gold-seekers across America

1. What point is the cartoonist in Source 3 making about the 1849 Gold Rush?
2. Which of Sources 1–4 tells you the most about the Gold Rush?

Soon two thirds of the able bodied men in Oregon had joined the search for gold. Little notice was taken back east until December 1848. Then the newspapers took up the story, making the most extravagant claims. Guidebooks appeared, telling of people who were making $1000 a day. By mid-December the docks at New York and Boston were jammed with men and women hoping to travel west to make their fortune. About 25,000 people reached California by boat, either round Cape Horn or via Panama. Most experienced storms, seasickness, and stale water and food for ten or twelve weeks.

This was a mere handful compared to the thousands who followed the cheaper overland route in their wagons. They packed the frontier towns such as Independence and St Joseph. So many wagon trains were leaving that there was often only a few hundred metres between groups. Five thousand people died on the journey, many from cholera.

When they arrived in California in the summer of 1849 most people were in for a terrible disappointment. All the good mining sites had been taken. They toiled away at back-breaking work, earning no more than $3 a day. During 1849 the mines yielded $10 million of gold but most of this went to a lucky few. The rest carried on searching, their hopes being kept alive by rumours about men who had struck it rich.

Few had any knowledge of mining but this was hardly a problem, since all they had to do was scrape the gold out of the dry beds of former streams with spoons and knives. Then they moved on to 'wet diggings' where they used 'washing pans'. The washing pan was submerged in a stream, the water carried away the light gravel and the gold was left behind. Later, the 'cradle' was developed. This was an oblong box mounted on rockers. Dirt was shovelled in at one end and water was poured in. The cradle was rocked until the dirt was washed away, leaving the heavier gold.

SOURCE 4 A drawing of miners using washing pans and cradles in a Californian gold mine

THE CALIFORNIA GOLD RUSH

SOURCE 5 Miners working a sluice (a trough for washing gold from sand) in California, 1849

SOURCE 6 A map of the mining areas

Life in the mining towns

Mining towns sprang up, often consisting of one street, ankle-deep in dust or mud depending on the season. The miners lived in shacks made from old blankets spread over wooden frames. They laboured all day, returning to their shacks to eat bread, beans or greasy pork and coffee. Scurvy, diarrhoea, dysentery and even malaria were common.

Living in such conditions, it is hardly surprising that the miners went to the SALOONS for their pleasures. On the days when they were not working they drank all day. In 1853 San Francisco had 537 saloons! Gambling was so common that tables were even set up in the streets. A great deal of what the miners earned was handed over either to shopkeepers who charged fantastically high prices, or to prostitutes who charged $16 for soothing words and $400 for a night.

THE CALIFORNIA GOLD RUSH

SOURCE 7 Mark Twain in his book *Roughing It*, first published in 1872. He visited the mining areas

" They fairly revelled in gold, whisky, fights and fandangoes, and were unspeakably happy. The honest miner raked from a hundred to a thousand dollars out of his claim a day, and what with the gambling dens and the other entertainments, he hadn't a cent left the next morning. "

3. How far do Sources 7 and 8 agree about the miners?
4. Bearing in mind all the other information you have about the miners, which of these two descriptions of miners do you think is the more accurate?

SOURCE 8 A description of the miner's lot

" The miseries of a miner might fill a chapter of woes. Digging and delving with eager anxiety day after day, up to the waist in water, exposed now to the rays of the burning sun and now to cold. With liberal doses of whisky during the day and mad carousels at night, flush with great buckskin bags of gold dust and laid low with regular disappointments, it was more than a man could endure. When disease made him its prey, there was no gentle hand to minister to his wants. Lying on the hard earth, or rolling in feverish agony on the shelf-bed of his cabin, often alone and unattended throughout the long day, while the night was made hideous by the shouts and curses of rioters. "

By 1852 the surface gold in California had gone. The gold that was left had to be reached by deep shafts or blasted out of hillsides. Big machinery was needed for this. The days of the 'forty-niners' were over. Many headed home. On their way home, some did strike it lucky in the Colorado Rockies. There were later discoveries of gold in Nevada, Montana, Oregon, Arizona and Dakota. The discovery in the Black Hills of Dakota would lead to PROSPECTORS swarming all over the Sioux's most hallowed ground. Later in this book you will find out what the result of this was.

In the Californian mining towns big business moved in. Miners brought their families out west and permanent towns began to develop. In the other areas where gold was discovered a few miners always stayed once the initial rush was over, and with them stayed merchants, farmers, businessmen, doctors and lawyers. Where these communities survived, the railroad, the telegraph and the stage-coach followed. In this way the discovery of gold made an important contribution to the settling of the West.

Law and order

Problems of law and order were common, because of CLAIM-JUMPING and the fact that the gold attracted the 'dregs of society'. With no US government law officers to protect them, people had to make their own arrangements. Each town held a mass meeting where a chairman and officers were chosen. They drew up a 'mining code'. Claims to mines had to be recorded with the district recorder. Disputes over claims were dealt with by a committee of miners. A sheriff would be appointed to arrest lawbreakers, and a court of all the miners would decide on punishments. The trials did not take long and the most common punishments were flogging, banishment or hanging.

Many other nationalities came to the mining towns to make their fortunes. Most camps banned Mexicans, Chinese and Indians from mining in the area. Mobs would drive Mexicans from their claims. The Chinese were left to rework old exhausted claims but even then were often harassed and murdered. The Indians were just slaughtered. Most miners refused to work alongside black people. Despite this, some 2000 free blacks did prospect, and when in 1850 Texas slave-owners arrived with their slaves the white miners made them leave.

■ **ACTIVITY**

Imagine you are a 'forty-niner'. Write a letter back home about your experiences in the gold mines. Mention your hopes, your life and work in the camp, and whether or not it has all been worth it.

Why were the Mormons so unpopular in the East?

SALT LAKE CITY is one of the largest and richest cities in the USA today. Behind this city there is an extraordinary story – the story of the Mormons.

Joseph Smith and the start of the Mormon movement (1820–31)

Most of the emigrants who went west were God-fearing people. We have already seen that some went as missionaries to convert the 'heathen' Indians. The most important religious group to go west was the 'Church of Jesus Christ of the Latter-Day Saints' – the Mormons.

For the beginning of this story we have to go back to 1820 and to Palmyra in New York State. Here, a great religious revival was taking place. There were dozens of preachers making claims and counter-claims about their own teachings. One fourteen-year-old boy, Joseph Smith, found all this confusing, and in a grove behind his father's house he prayed for guidance. According to Smith, a pillar of light appeared before him. He was told not to join any religious sect but to prepare himself for a great work.

As Smith grew up on his father's farm he experienced further visitations. In one, an angel appeared to him, as he explains in Source 1.

> **SOURCE 1** Joseph Smith
>
> *He called me by name and said unto me that his name was Moroni, that God had work for me to do. He said that there was a book deposited, written upon gold plates, giving an account of the former inhabitants of this continent and the source from which they sprang.*

In 1827 the angel told Smith where the book was to be found. Smith claimed he dug it up on a hillside near Manchester, New York. Source 2 is his description of what he found.

> **SOURCE 2** Joseph Smith in a letter to *Times and Seasons Magazine*, Nauvoo, 1 March 1842
>
> *These records were engraven on plates which had the appearance of gold. Each plate was six inches wide and eight inches long and not quite so thick as common tin. They were filled with engravings, in Egyptian characters and bound together in a volume, as the leaves of a book, with three rings running through the whole. The volume was [something near 15 cm] in thickness.*

The plates told a rather different story from the one you will find in the Bible. According to the plates, the lost tribes of Israel migrated to America long before Christ was born. They had fought each other until Christ appeared in America to establish his Church there. Later, the fighting started again. One of the few survivors was a man called Mormon who spent the rest of his life recording the story of his people on the plates. The person who found the plates was to restore the true Church of Christ in America, before Christ reappeared to begin his thousand-year reign.

You would think that an easy way to check Smith's story would be to examine the plates, or at least check whether or not other people had seen them. However, Smith claimed that no one else was allowed to see the plates. He said he returned the plates to the hillside. When he was translating the plates he dictated to his wife and some friends who sat on the other side of a blanket which was hung up across the middle of the room! However, when Smith's translation was published in 1830 as *The Book of Mormon*, it contained statements by eight people, including his father and two of his brothers, claiming that they had seen the plates.

Smith started with only five followers but by the end of 1830 his energy and his charismatic public speaking had turned this number into several hundred. But they were very unpopular in New York State. People claimed he was a fraud just out to make money for himself, and clergymen denounced *The Book of Mormon* as blasphemous. His house was attacked by mobs and he and his followers were shot at in the streets. After praying for guidance he took his followers to the village of Kirtland, in Ohio, where he planned to set up a City of God.

1. Do you think it matters whether or not Smith's story (Source 1) was true?

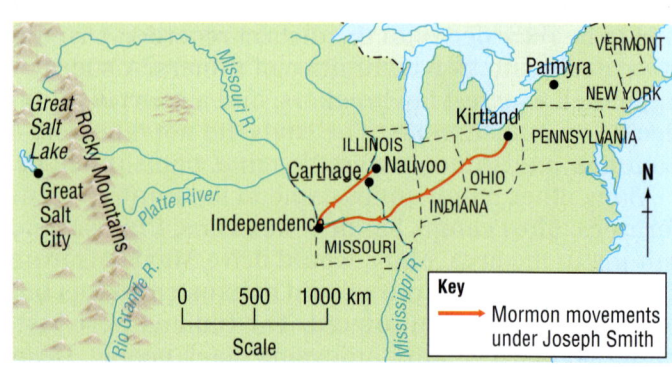

SOURCE 3 A map showing the various places where the Mormons settled

The Mormons in Kirtland (1831–37)

At Kirtland the Mormon movement went from strength to strength. By 1831 it had 1000 members and new colonies were founded in Missouri. In Kirtland their success was their undoing. They worked hard and soon owned a mill, a store, a bank and a printing press. They even started work on a temple. The Mormons soon outnumbered non-Mormons (or gentiles as the Mormons called them), and envy and hatred of the Mormons grew. It looked as if they would take over everything.

Then, in 1837, there was an economic crisis (see page 58) and many banks collapsed. Many non-Mormons had put their savings into the Mormon bank, and when it collapsed all their money was lost. Of course, many other banks collapsed as well. It was clearly not the Mormons' fault but as far as non-Mormons were concerned it was the last straw. The Mormons were chased out of Kirtland.

The Mormons in Missouri (1837–38)

Smith and his followers fled to the colonies which the Mormons had set up in Missouri. But they were no more popular there. Read Sources 4 and 5, which are accounts of what happened in Missouri. They tell us a lot about the attitudes of Mormons and non-Mormons towards one another.

■ TASK

1. What does Source 4 tell you about the Mormons' attitude towards the other settlers?
2. Which words best describe the feelings of the other settlers towards the Mormons: envy, fear, hatred, superiority?
3. What do you think worried the settlers most, the Mormon religion and beliefs, or their growing power and wealth? Explain your answer, referring to Source 5.
4. These two sources seem to show that there was a complete lack of understanding between the Mormons and the non-Mormons. Do you agree?

> **SOURCE 4** A Mormon account of events in Missouri
>
> *Numbers joined the church and we were increasing rapidly. We made large purchases of land, our farms teemed with plenty. Our neighbours were the basest of men and had fled from the face of civilised society to the frontier country to escape the hand of justice. Because we could not join them in their midnight revels, their sabbath breaking, horse racing and gambling, they commenced to persecute us. Finally an organised mob assembled and burned our houses, tarred and feathered and whipped many of our brethren, and finally drove them from their farms.*
>
> *[We moved to other parts of Missouri] where we made large settlements, thinking to free ourselves by settling in places with few inhabitants. But in 1838 we were again attacked by mobs. An exterminating order was issued by Governor Boggs, and organised banditti robbed us of our cattle, sheep, horses and hogs. Many of our people were murdered in cold blood, and we were forced to sign away property at the point of a sword.*

> **SOURCE 5** Extracts from a local newspaper, the *Missouri Intelligencer and Boon's Lick Advertiser*, 10 August 1833
>
> *Little more than two years ago, some two or three of these people appeared on the Upper Missouri and now they number some 1200 souls. Each autumn and spring pours forth its swarm among us, flooding us with the very dregs. Elevated as they mostly are but little above the condition of our blacks, they have become a subject of much anxiety. Well grounded complaints have been already made of their corrupting influence on our slaves.*
>
> *We are told that we are to have our lands taken over by them. The day is not far distant when the government of the county will be in their hands. What would be the fate of our lives and property in the hands of jurors and witnesses who do not blush to swear that they have wrought miracles and supernatural cures and converse with God and his Angels.*
>
> *One of the means they use to drive us to emigrate, is an invitation to freed slaves in Illinois to come here and to claim the rights of citizenship.*

As soon as the Mormons arrived in Missouri attempts were made to stop them from voting in elections. The local settlers rioted and destroyed property (not just property belonging to the Mormons). The governor of Missouri had to send in troops to restore order. The Mormons were held responsible for all the trouble and their leaders, including Smith, were imprisoned and condemned to death. As rumours spread that the Mormons were stirring up the Indians and freeing slaves, the governor declared that they were 'public enemies' who must be 'exterminated or driven from the State if necessary for the public good'.

WHY WERE THE MORMONS SO UNPOPULAR IN THE EAST?

The Mormons in Nauvoo (1839–46)

In the winter of 1838 the Mormons left Missouri. Smith was released from prison on the undertaking that he left with them. Where could they go next? Smith was unwilling to go further west as this would take them into the 'Great American Desert'. Instead, they went to the tiny town of Commerce in Illinois. Smith renamed it Nauvoo and the Mormons were allowed to develop it as an independent city state. They could even make their own laws. This close-knit, co-operative community of hard-working Mormons prospered, and by 1844 Nauvoo was the largest city in Illinois. It was described as the best-built city in the West 'with none of the unfinished temporary appearance of most settlements in the West'. Dominating the city was the giant temple.

The Mormons tried to create an ideal society in which no one was poor or homeless and where the evils of drink and smoking did not exist. There were now 35,000 Mormons, with more on their way from Europe, where Mormon missionaries had been hard at work. Most of these converts came from the poor and downtrodden. They were promised salvation and a chance to begin a new life. It seemed that the Mormons had found peace at last. They governed themselves and they had the well-armed Nauvoo Legion of 4000 men to defend them. Then Joseph Smith made some fatal mistakes.

The success of the Mormons and the fact that they kept themselves to themselves was already making them unpopular with other people in Illinois. But Smith's real troubles came from his own people.

In 1844 he received a revelation from God which, he said, allowed certain Mormons to practise polygamy – that is, have more than one wife. By this time Smith already had more than one wife and his bodyguard, John Scott, had five. (There was a surplus of women in Nauvoo as most of the converts from Europe were women.) Some of the Mormons thought this was wrong and denounced Smith as a false prophet. They criticised him in a newspaper which they had set up. Smith replied by destroying the presses of the newspaper. This led to claims that Smith had turned into a dictator. His critics demanded his arrest, and he was taken to a jail in nearby Carthage.

SOURCE 6 The Mormon settlement of Nauvoo

2. What messages about the Mormons do you think the artist of Source 7 intended to give?

SOURCE 7 A cartoon from the 1840s commenting on polygamy

WHY WERE THE MORMONS SO UNPOPULAR IN THE EAST?

Of course, once news about polygamy reached the non-Mormons they were outraged. They thought it was immoral and they were worried that it would lead to a rapid increase in the Mormon population. They were also upset by the news that Smith was planning to run for President of the the USA. On 27 June 1845 a mob of 200 non-Mormons attacked the jail and shot Smith dead. Mobs now roamed the countryside hunting down Mormons. There was even talk of an attack on Nauvoo.

The Mormons might have been able to defend Nauvoo – they did have their own army – but their new leader had other ideas.

■ TASK

Questions 1 and 2 below are frequently asked in examination papers. For the first question a grid has been provided to help you plan your answer. Copy it out, then read through the story of the Mormons so far and write down as many examples as you can in each column.

1. Why did the Mormons find it impossible to live in the East?

	Examples
Their religious beliefs	
Their attitude towards non-Mormons	
Their success	
Prejudice against them	
Their attitude towards Indians and slaves	
Polygamy	

2. How far were the Mormons to blame for their troubles?

SOURCE 8 The banner of the Nauvoo Legion

■ TASK

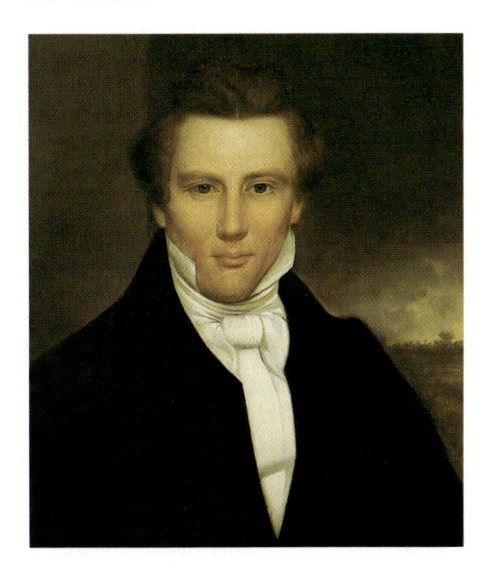

Role of the individual – Joseph Smith

It will be useful for later work if you complete these notes on Joseph Smith now. Write a few sentences under the following headings and try to give examples to support your notes:

- character and personality
- main strengths and main achievements
- main weaknesses and main failures.

SOURCE 9 A portrait of Joseph Smith by Adrian Lamb

Why did the Mormons succeed in the West?

Brigham Young and the decision to go west

After the death of Joseph Smith, the decision on what to do next rested with Brigham Young, the new leader of the Mormons. He was convinced that the Mormons would never be left in peace in the East. What the Mormons needed was somewhere that was isolated and unwanted. He knew from the guidebooks about the Oregon Trail that the most isolated area in all the West was by the Great Salt Lake. And yet these books also talked about the streams fed by snow from the mountains and the good soil and grass. An added attraction was that this part of the Rockies still belonged to Mexico, so if the Mormons moved there they would be outside the control of the US government. So, in September 1845, Brigham Young decided. He agreed with the Illinois authorities that the Mormons would leave Nauvoo in the spring of 1846, in return for freedom from persecution until they left.

SOURCE 1 Brigham Young, with Margaret Pierce Young, one of his many wives

The journey west

The decision to go to the Great Salt Lake created two problems:

- How was Young going to get 16,000 Mormons across the Plains and up the Rockies?
- How would they turn the salt flats into a rich thriving community?

Young was a brilliant organiser (he had organised the move to Nauvoo). He was practical and more down-to-earth than Smith. He was also a very determined man – once he had decided to do something it was as good as done! He was also very considerate – he married eight of Smith's former wives, and in all had 27 wives!

Preparations went on all winter. Wagons had to be built, oxen bought, and equipment and food collected. In February a pioneer band crossed the frozen Mississippi to establish the first way-station, called Camp of Israel, in Iowa. The rest of the Mormons had to follow before they were properly prepared because mobs began looting their homes.

At Camp of Israel Young explained how the journey would be organised. They would be split into a number of separate wagon trains, each made up of a hundred wagons. A captain would be in charge of each wagon train and the wagon train would in turn be subdivided into 'tens', each supervised by a lieutenant.

SOURCE 2 A map showing the journey to Salt Lake

1. What impression of Young does Source 1 give you?

SOURCE 3 An extract from Brigham Young's orders for the journey

" At 5.00 in the morning the bugle is to be sounded as a signal for every man to arise and attend prayers. Then cooking, eating, feeding teams till seven o'clock, at which time the camp is to move at the sound of the bugle. Each teamster to stay beside his team, with his loaded gun in his hands. No man to be permitted to leave his wagon unless he obtains permission from his officer. In case of an attack from Indians, the wagons to travel in double file. The order of encampment to be in a circle with the mouth of the wagon to the outside, and the horses and stock tied inside the circle. At 8.30 the bugle to be sounded again at which time all to have prayers in their wagons and to retire to rest by nine o'clock. "

WHY DID THE MORMONS SUCCEED IN THE WEST?

SOURCE 4 A painting of the Mormons' Winter Quarters by C.C.A. Christensen

SOURCE 5 A description of conditions in the Winter Quarters by Colonel Thomas L. Kane, a US army officer who gave medical help to the Mormons

“The fever prevailed to such an extent that hardly any escaped from it. They let their cows go unmilked. The few who were able to keep their feet, went about among the tents and wagons with food and water. The digging got behind time, and you might see women sit in the open tents keeping the flies off their dead children some time after decomposition had set in.”

Young left with the first wagon train. Every now and then they built a rest camp for those following. At each camp some Mormons stayed behind to plant crops and set up workshops for carpenters and blacksmiths. Soon, a steady procession stretching nearly 500 km was strung out across the flat landscape.

By June 1846 Young and his wagon train had reached the Missouri River. Here they built Winter Quarters. This was where the Mormons would spend the winter. A thousand cabins were built to accommodate everyone. So good was Young's planning that the later wagon trains had little difficulty in reaching Winter Quarters by autumn.

But no matter how well prepared the Mormons were, nothing could control the prairie weather. That winter they huddled in draughty cabins or tents. Fuel and food were short. By spring a plague and the bitter cold had killed 700 people.

In April 1847 Young led forth a 'Pioneer Band' of 143 men, three women and two children. All were carefully chosen for their endurance, and to ensure a balance of farmers and craftsmen. Their job was to lead the way to the Great Salt Lake, to select the site for the new Mormon settlement and to begin work there.

As they entered South Pass they met up with the former mountain man Jim Bridger, who warned them that the valley of the Great Salt Lake was too cold at night for growing corn. Young ignored him.

Later they met Sam Brannan, a Mormon, who urged them to go to California. Young replied, 'If there is a place on this earth that nobody wants, that's the place I'm looking for. God has made the choice – not Brigham Young.' They pressed on. Following the route of the Donner party (see page 66) they laboured with picks and shovels to clear a way for their wagons as they climbed steadily upwards. Finally, in July, they looked down on the salt flats of the Great Salt Lake. Sources 6 and 8 (on page 78) give you their first reactions.

2. Make a list of all the problems and dangers the Mormons faced on their journey.
3. Explain why the Mormons were more successful in their journey than the Donner party (see page 66).

WHY DID THE MORMONS SUCCEED IN THE WEST?

Making a success of Salt Lake

Sources 7 and 8 describe the first reactions to the Great Salt Lake. To carry out his aims of building a Mormon City here, Brigham Young still had many problems to overcome. But he had one enormous advantage: he had total control over the community. The Mormons believed that he was inspired by God and accepted his decisions without question. This total control was necessary to stop people quarrelling over land and water.

Brigham Young decided that there would be no private ownership of land or water. The Church would assign farm land to people according to their needs. The farming land was organised into tiers laid out around Salt Lake City (see Source 9).

SOURCE 6 Brigham Young, 27 July 1847

We do not intend to have any trade or commerce with the gentile world. The Kingdom of God cannot rise independent of the gentile nations until we produce, manufacture and make every article of use, convenience, or necessity among our own people.

SOURCE 7 Description by a member of the 'Pioneer Band'

A broad and barren plain hemmed in by mountains, blistering in the burning rays of the midsummer sun. No waving fields, no swaying forests, no green meadows. But on all sides a seemingly interminable waste of sagebrush – the paradise of the lizard, the cricket and the rattlesnake.

SOURCE 8 From the journal of William Clayton, who kept a daily record of the journey

There is a extensive, beautiful, level-looking valley from here to the lake. There is little timber in sight. There is no prospect for building log houses, but we can make Spanish bricks and dry them in the sun. For my own part I am happily disappointed in the appearance of the valley of the Salt Lake. But if the land be as rich as it has the appearance of being, I have no fear but the Saints can live here and well.

The city
The Temple and the Temple Square were in the centre of the city.
Around the square, wide streets marked off blocks of land all the same size. These were each divided into eight plots for houses and gardens. Each family was given a plot.

Farms between ten and 80 acres for larger families.

Ten-acre plots for those with small families or elderly couples whose children had left home.

Five-acre plots for the young ARTISANS and mechanics who had little time to work on the land.

Water was essential. The Mormons worked together to build a main irrigation ditch through the farming land. Side ditches were then dug so that all the land could be irrigated. Each person was given an exact time when they were allowed to draw water from the main ditch.

SOURCE 9 A plan of Salt Lake City and the surrounding area

SOURCE 10 A description of Salt Lake City by a US government surveyor who surveyed Salt Lake Valley in 1850

A city has been laid out upon a magnificent scale. Through the city itself flows an unfailing stream of pure, sweet water, which, by an ingenious mode of irrigation, is made to travel along each side of every street whence it is led into every garden-spot, spreading life, and beauty over what was a barren waste.

The houses are built, principally, of sun-dried brick, which make a warm comfortable dwelling, presenting a very neat appearance.

WHY DID THE MORMONS SUCCEED IN THE WEST?

SOURCE 13 This well-known photograph, taken around 1875, was long thought to show a Mormon and his several wives. In one school textbook it is entitled *A first view of polygamy*. We now know that it shows Samuel Ashton and his one wife (standing at his right). All the other women are her relatives

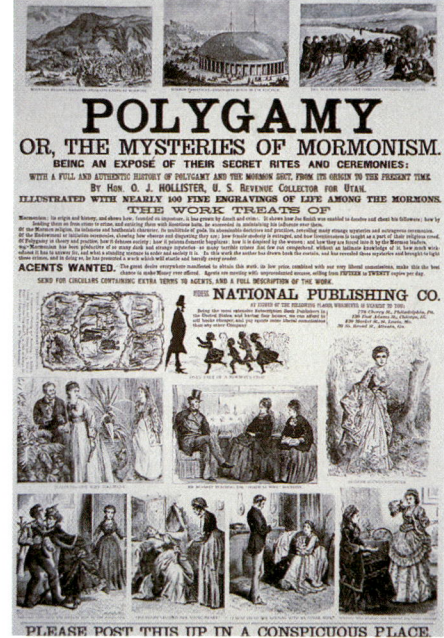

5. Why do you think Source 13 was said to show a Mormon and his several wives?

SOURCE 14 An anti-Mormon poster of 1884 advertising a book that criticised polygamy

Utah becomes a state

The only disagreement left to be settled was that over polygamy. The US government passed an anti-polygamy law in 1862 but it was ignored in Utah. However, in 1890 Utah applied for the fifth time to join the United States of America. The price the US government demanded for admission was a ban on polygamy. This time the Mormons agreed, and in 1896 Utah became a state. Today there are three million Mormons around the world.

■ TASK

Role of the individual – Joseph Smith and Brigham Young
Make some notes under the following headings about the similarities and differences between Joseph Smith and Brigham Young:

- character and personality
- strengths and weaknesses
- the problems they faced
- the solutions they came up with
- main achievements
- main failures.

Then answer the following question: who contributed more to the Mormon movement, Joseph Smith or Brigham Young?

■ REVIEW TASK

1. 'The early pioneers all went west for the same reasons.' Do you agree with this statement?
2. Why were some more successful than others?
3. Look back at the chart for the Task on page 52. If you have not already done so, complete it for the first four groups of pioneers. Which group do you think had the greatest impact on the way of life of the Plains Indians?

81

chapter 5

HOW DID THE HOMESTEADERS AND RANCHERS SETTLE THE PLAINS?

IN CHAPTER 4 YOU investigated different groups who crossed the Plains in order to get to somewhere else. However, in the mid-nineteenth century more and more people moved on to the Plains themselves – on to land occupied by the Plains Indians.

In the second half of the nineteenth century thousands of people like the Bentleys (see Source 1) sold their homes, left their friends and families and travelled, in some cases, thousands of miles to settle on the Great Plains. Why did these people go to the Great Plains? How did they survive when they got there? What happened to the Plains Indians who used to live there? These are three of the important questions we are going to consider in this chapter.

SOURCE 1 The Bentley family, homesteaders, proudly photographed outside their sod house in Custer County, Nebraska, in 1887. Remember that when people had their photographs taken at this time they had to keep perfectly still in the same pose for much longer than we do today. So they couldn't smile for the camera, in case they couldn't hold the smile for long enough! Look at the bushes in the photo. They are blurred. This is because they moved in the breeze that must have been blowing at the time

■ TASK

Study Source 1 carefully.

- What clothes are they wearing?
- What sort of house do they live in?
- What tools do they use?
- What work might they do?
- They are all members of the same family. Can you work out what their relationships might be?
- Look at their faces. What sort of life do you think the Bentleys live?

The homesteaders: why did so many people want to settle on the Plains?

Reason 1: the actions of the US government

The US government recognised the need to populate the West and to help achieve this the Homestead Act was passed in 1862. It was intended to encourage people to settle in the West by allowing each family 160 acres of land. This land was given to them free, provided they lived on it and farmed it for five years. Two later Acts also encouraged settlers. These were:

- **The Timber Culture Act, 1873**
  This gave settlers a further 160 acres of free land, provided they planted 40 acres with trees.
- **The Desert Land Act, 1877**
  This gave settlers the right to buy 640 acres cheaply in areas where lack of rainfall was a particular problem.

The effect of these three Acts was to make millions of acres of land available for homesteaders to settle. Thousands of men and women seized this opportunity and became homesteaders.

Reason 2: the end of the American Civil War

The American Civil War lasted from 1861 to 1865. It was fought between the slave-owning southern states, known as the Confederacy, and the anti-slavery northern states, known as the Union. It was partly triggered by events in the West. A major argument in the years up to 1861 was whether slavery should be allowed in the new western states.

The end of the war marked a turning point in American history. Thousands of DEMOBILISED soldiers and their families were looking to rebuild their lives. Thousands of newly freed black slaves were looking for a new life. The eastern states where they had grown up did not seem to be the best place to do this. One obvious place to look was the West, and that is what thousands of them did. They became the homesteaders, cowboys, miners, soldiers and railroad-builders who transformed the West.

Reason 3: The building of the transcontinental railroads

The US government had long wanted to build a transcontinental railroad to link East and West. In the 1860s two companies started building, one from the East, the other from the West. Eventually they met in Utah.

This had two main effects. Now it was easy for homesteaders to get to the Plains; it was also cheap to buy land, as the railroad companies sold off the land on either side of the line at low prices.

So land was cheap, travel was easy and there were plenty of people looking for a new life. Result: a flood of homesteaders on to the Plains.

SOURCE 1 A map showing the routes of the railroads across the West

SOURCE 2 A railroad land sale poster, 1875

Did all the homesteaders go west for the same motives?

AS WELL AS the general reasons on page 83, each group of homesteaders had their own special reasons for moving west.

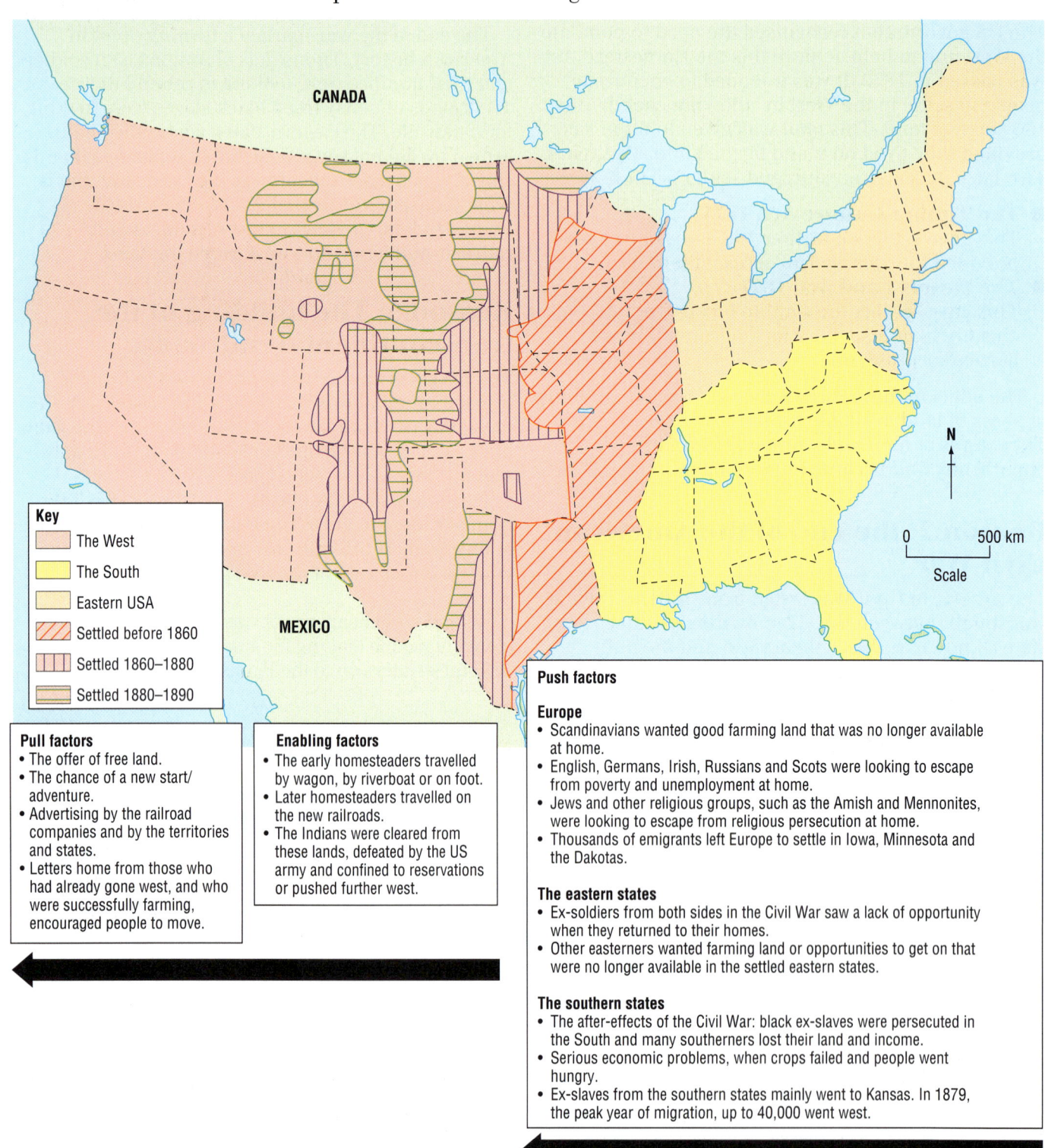

Key
- The West
- The South
- Eastern USA
- Settled before 1860
- Settled 1860–1880
- Settled 1880–1890

Pull factors
- The offer of free land.
- The chance of a new start/adventure.
- Advertising by the railroad companies and by the territories and states.
- Letters home from those who had already gone west, and who were successfully farming, encouraged people to move.

Enabling factors
- The early homesteaders travelled by wagon, by riverboat or on foot.
- Later homesteaders travelled on the new railroads.
- The Indians were cleared from these lands, defeated by the US army and confined to reservations or pushed further west.

Push factors

Europe
- Scandinavians wanted good farming land that was no longer available at home.
- English, Germans, Irish, Russians and Scots were looking to escape from poverty and unemployment at home.
- Jews and other religious groups, such as the Amish and Mennonites, were looking to escape from religious persecution at home.
- Thousands of emigrants left Europe to settle in Iowa, Minnesota and the Dakotas.

The eastern states
- Ex-soldiers from both sides in the Civil War saw a lack of opportunity when they returned to their homes.
- Other easterners wanted farming land or opportunities to get on that were no longer available in the settled eastern states.

The southern states
- The after-effects of the Civil War: black ex-slaves were persecuted in the South and many southerners lost their land and income.
- Serious economic problems, when crops failed and people went hungry.
- Ex-slaves from the southern states mainly went to Kansas. In 1879, the peak year of migration, up to 40,000 went west.

SOURCE 1 The 'push' and 'pull' factors that encouraged people to move west

DID ALL THE HOMESTEADERS GO WEST FOR THE SAME MOTIVES?

SOURCE 2 A flatcar filled with European immigrants being shown potential farming sites in Kansas. This was one way in which railroad companies encouraged settlers to move west

SOURCE 3 Swedish homesteaders in Greeley County, Kansas

SOURCE 4 Extract from an editorial in the *Kansas Farmer*, 1867

" I saw vast areas of unimproved land, rich as the land on the banks of the famous Nile. We saw land before us, land behind us, land at the right hand, land at the left hand. Everywhere there were oceans of land all ready for the plough, as good as the best in America, and unoccupied. "

SOURCE 5 An extract from a letter written home by Paul Hjelm Hansen and published in a Norwegian newspaper

*" Minnesota, July 1869
It is not only my opinion but that of all who have seen it that this land presents so many advantages for Scandinavian farmers that immigrants are likely to stream in here within the next year. The soil is fertile and there is not as much as a stone or a tree stump in the way of the plough. Railroads are to run through the middle of the valley. In the summer months, May, June, July and August, the heat may at times be great, but the atmosphere is always fresh. In the wintertime, the snow is usually two or three feet deep and lies in a solid mass over the whole prairie. "*

SOURCE 6 The Shores family, who settled in Custer County, Nebraska, in 1887

■ TASK

1. Consider Sources 2–6. For each one, explain what might have motivated these people to move to the Great Plains. Consider both the 'push' and the 'pull' factors in Source 1.
2. What do you think were the most important motives of these homesteaders for settling on the Great Plains? You should consider all their motives before reaching your conclusion.

How did homesteaders survive on the Plains?

IN SECTION 1 YOU saw how harsh the conditions on the Plains could be. Thousands of settlers were trying to make a living farming this land, yet just 30 years earlier it was considered impossible to settle the Plains. How did the homesteaders survive?

ACTIVITY

1. Imagine you are a woman or man living on a homestead in Kansas in 1878. You are writing a letter home to your family in England. You know that some of your younger relatives are thinking about emigrating to Kansas to become homesteaders. What advice and information will you give them? You should use the all the material on the homesteaders (pages 86–93) to help you. You might want to comment on:
   - the opportunities
   - the problems of life and farming
   - how tough it is for men and women.

2. Write again in 1890. What do you have to add?

The problems of living on the Plains

Water shortages
In many places out on the Great Plains water was scarce. In such places it was difficult for people to keep either themselves or their clothing clean.

Extremes of weather
The extreme weather, hot in summer and cold in winter, with a low rainfall, made life on the Great Plains very uncomfortable. The Indians had moved with the seasons but the homesteaders remained rooted on one spot. Many grew to hate the fierce winds that howled around their houses for days on end.

Fuel
On the Plains there was no wood to burn for heating and cooking. Instead homesteaders used buffalo or cow 'chips' – dried dung.

Dirt and disease
Sod houses with earth floors, walls and roofs were very difficult to keep clean. They harboured all sorts of pests, such as bed bugs, fleas, mice and snakes. Living in such conditions it was difficult for people to keep clean, especially where a shortage of water was also a problem. It was all too easy for disease to develop and illness was common among homesteaders, particularly their children.

Building materials
Homesteaders who settled in river valleys might be able to use wood for building homes, and wood was also transported from the East to the small number who could afford it. But for the vast majority the only material available for house-building was earth. Blocks of earth (sods) were cut out by hand or with a special plough. These were then used as building bricks to construct the house walls. Windows and doors were fitted. Then the house was roofed with boards, grass and more sods. Finally, the outside walls were plastered with clay-like mud. Such houses were very cheap to build. They could be warm in winter and cool in summer if well built but it was very difficult to stop water leaking in when it rained.

SOURCE 1 A family outside their sod house in Nebraska, c.1890

The problems of farming on the Plains

Water shortages
For farming the shortage of water was a major problem. It could lead to the total failure of crops. This would lead in turn to bankruptcy or starvation. For the Mormons of Salt Lake City irrigation was a solution but out on the Great Plains there were no rivers or lakes from which to draw water. Wells were a possible solution but digging a well was expensive and gave no guarantee of finding water.

Extremes of weather
For farming the extremes of weather were a major problem. Drought in summer and cold in winter could damage or destroy crops. In Kansas, for example, no rain fell between January 1859 and November 1860.

Ploughing
The Great Plains had never been farmed before. So the first task for the homesteader was to plough the land. The grasses had dense, tangled roots and the early cast-iron ploughs needed constant repairs. Ploughing was a slow, back-breaking task.

SOURCE 2 A modern illustration of a farm on the Great Plains

Protecting crops
There was no wood for fencing so there was nothing to protect growing crops from buffalo or straying cattle. Nor was it possible to mark land boundaries clearly, and this could lead to disputes.

Growing crops
The homesteaders planted the crops they had always grown, such as maize and soft winter and spring wheats. These were not well suited to the weather conditions on the Great Plains.

Natural hazards
In the summer, when the grass was so dry, it was easy for prairie fires to start. If they were too big for the people to fight then their crops would be destroyed. The plagues of grasshoppers which swept across the Plains in 1871, 1874 and 1875 were another natural hazard. The insects descended on the land in columns 240 km wide and 160 km long. Hundred-acre cornfields vanished in a few hours.

■ CONNECTIONS
Both the Plains Indians and the homesteaders had to solve the problem of building a home on the Great Plains. Compare the *tipi* to the sod house. Explain how and why their solutions to the problems were different.

HOW DID HOMESTEADERS SURVIVE ON THE PLAINS?

Living and farming on the Great Plains: solutions to problems

Despite the many problems of living and farming on the Great Plains, the majority of homesteaders stayed on after their first year. Not all of them were successful.

One crucial factor was the exact location of their land. Some parts of the Great Plains were less fertile than others.

A second factor was the adaptability of homesteaders. The Great Plains required them to adapt their farming to the conditions. Those who failed to adapt did not succeed.

A third factor, outside their control, was the weather. The severe droughts of the 1870s and 1880s forced thousands into bankruptcy. For example, approximately 11,000 homesteads were repossessed in Kansas between 1889 and 1893.

Those who survived and prospered were helped by a number of inventions and developments.

Windmills

As you have already seen a lack of water was a major problem on the Great Plains. There were two solutions to this. The first was developed in 1874, when Daniel Halliday invented a self-governing windmill: it always kept in line with the wind so that it did not get damaged by the strong winds. This windmill could be used to pump water from underground. First, a high-powered drill was used to get down to the water. Then the wind pump was fitted. It would pump water night and day for people to use in their homes and to irrigate their crops.

Dry farming

The second solution was dry farming. Farmers ploughed their land when there had been heavy rain or snow. This left a thin layer of dust over the surface, which trapped and preserved the moisture in the soil. The land was then left fallow ready for the following year's crop.

Growing a surplus

In their early years on the Great Plains homesteaders would plough enough land to grow food to feed their family. In later years they could plough more land and grow more crops. This would produce a surplus that they could sell. With this money they could buy better equipment and increase their surplus.

Hard winter wheat

Homesteaders recognised that wheat was a more suitable crop than corn. Those who settled on the high Plains realised that it was better to keep animals – sheep and cattle – rather than just to grow crops.

Russian Mennonite immigrants introduced hard winter wheat (Turkey Red wheat). The climatic conditions on the Great Plains were similar to those on the Russian steppes, so these crops flourished and homesteaders who grew it were successful. The Russians accidentally brought Russian weeds mixed in with the wheat seed. These also flourished, notably the tumbleweed (Russian thistle) seen in so many Westerns.

Barbed wire

In 1874 Joseph Glidden invented barbed wire. This provided a cheap and effective solution to the problem of fencing and protecting crops.

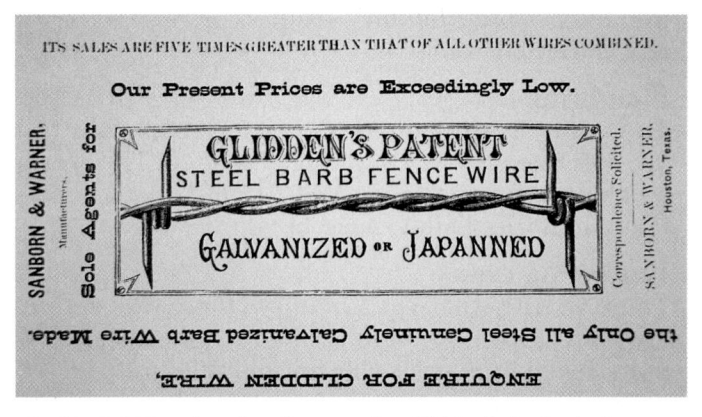

SOURCE 3 An advertisement for Glidden's barbed wire, 1881

1. Some adverts claimed that barbed wire was the greatest invention of the age. Do you agree?

Sod-buster

John Deere invented a particularly strong plough which could deal with the tough grass roots. This was known as a 'sod-buster', the nickname sometimes given to homesteaders by the cowboys.

HOW DID HOMESTEADERS SURVIVE ON THE PLAINS?

Other machinery
From the 1880s other new farming machinery was developed. This included reapers, binders and threshers. These could be easily transported by railroad to the Great Plains and were affordable. The machines increased the area that a homesteader could manage to farm and were well suited to the wide open spaces of the Great Plains.

Hard work
By the 1890s a combination of all these inventions and developments had helped the homesteaders to solve the problems of farming on the Great Plains. The Great Plains became a fertile area for wheat production and the majority of homesteaders prospered. Their success can be explained by their determination, hard work and adaptability. They were supported by the railroads which took them there, brought them equipment and carried their crops to market.

SOURCE 4 The Gillette family, 1886

2. Look at Source 4. The family are 'posed' in their Sunday best for the photograph. Does this mean the photo is of no use for finding out about the lives of homesteaders?
3. Do the Gillette family look like successful homesteaders? How do you know?

■ TASK

Copy the following table. In column 2 describe the problems of living and farming on the Plains. In column 3 record what solutions were found. Remember, not all the problems had a solution.

	Problem	Solutions
Water shortages		
Weather extremes		
Fuel		
Dirt and disease		
Building materials		
Natural hazards		
Ploughing		
Protecting crops		
Growing crops		

How important was the role of women in homesteading?

LIFE WAS HARD for the homesteaders while they were learning to live on the Plains. The main bulk of the work for men was the building of a home and farming the land. So what was the contribution of women? How important was their role?

■ SOURCE INVESTIGATION

Study Sources 1–10 on pages 90–93.

1. List the jobs that women did.
2. Were there any jobs that they shared with their men?
3. What were the hazards that the homesteaders faced in the early years?
4. Could the men have got on with their work without the women?
5. How important was the role of women in homesteading?

SOURCE 1 Extracts from the diary of Luna E. Warner, aged 15, in Kansas in 1871. The Warner family (father, mother and two daughters, plus other related families) had just arrived in Kansas. They had a CLAIM by the Solomon River so water was never a problem. On arrival they lived in a wooden cabin whilst they built a house

March 22 The men went to look at some claims. They found six just the other side of the river about five miles from here. They went over to the land office and filed on their claims.

March 25 We all went up the river to see the claims. I like ours best. Papa bought some potatoes – the first we had for a long time.

March 28 Mamma and I went over to our claim and set out some gooseberry bushes.

March 29 Our family went out on to our land and commenced to dig a cellar. All the men have been at work on Uncle Eli's dugout.

April 6 Temperature 98. We planted peas, turnips and squash on our claim.

April 9 This morning we saw six buffaloes coming down the river. Louie took the rifle and I took the revolver. We lay down and waited until they got near, then Louie fired. How they did run!

April 10 The snow sifted into our faces all night. Our fireplace smokes very badly. It keeps our eyes crying all the time. The cabin is full of mice.

April 14 Rainy. I dug fish worms and went fishing. There have been Indians seen in a good many places. We have to be very careful.

April 18 The wind blew very hard. Everything out of doors blew away, even two pails of water.

April 27 I killed three snakes today. Helped Papa plant onions and peas, sweet corn and melons.

May 5 There was a white frost this morning. The water froze in the water pail. Mamma and I planted 81 hills of melons. At night I drove Mr Ray's cattle away from our garden with buffalo bones.

May 6 Uncle Howard and Henry worked on our house. They raised the frame.

May 10 We planted potatoes. Saw two beavers and a turkey gobbler.

May 17 I am sixteen years old today. I do not feel so old.

HOW IMPORTANT WAS THE ROLE OF WOMEN IN HOMESTEADING?

SOURCE 2 Extracts from the diary of Miriam Davis Colt in Kansas, 1856. The Colt family had just arrived in Kansas to stake their claim. Their farm was not successful and they gave up and left before the end of the year

*"**May 15** Have a fire out of doors to cook by; two forked poles driven into the ground, with a round pole laid thereon, on which to hang our kettles and camp pails, stones laid up at the ends and back to make it as much as it can be in the form of a fireplace, so as to keep our fire, ashes and all, from blowing high and dry, when these fierce prairie winds blow. It is not very agreeable work, cooking out of doors in this windy, rainy weather, or when the scorching sun shines.*

***May 26** Have been washing to-day, and dried our clothes right out in the burning hot sun. We dare not leave them out in the dewy nights for fear of the Indians, who come thieving round, slying about, taking everything they can lay hands on . . . They are soon going two or three hundred miles west on the buffalo hunt, where they go twice a year, staying three months at a time.*

***June 10** I hear that Mrs Clubb felt greatly annoyed while her husband was away, by an intruder at her feet in the night time; in the morning found that a large rattlesnake had been occupying the bed with herself. They are fond of a comfortable place to coil up.*

***June 16** What are we to look for, and what fear next? The mosquitoes have come upon us all of a sudden."*

SOURCE 3 Extracts from the diary of Keturah Penton Belknap, Iowa, 1839–42. The Belknaps kept animals and grew crops on their farm

"All this winter I have been spinning flax and tow to make summer clothes. I have not spent an idle minute and now the wool must be taken from the sheep's back, washed and picked and sent to the carding machine and made into rolls, then spun, coloured and wove ready for next winter. I can't weave so I spin for my mother-in-law and she does my weaving.

. . . Now it is harvest time. I am tending the chickens and pigs and make a little butter (we have two cows).

. . . I have got my work for the winter pretty well in hand. Have made me a new flannel dress coloured blue and red. I am going to try and make me one dress every year then I can have one for nice and with a clean check apron I would be alright. I made some jeans enough for two pair of pants for George."

SOURCE 4 An extract from the autobiography of Thomas Allen Banning

"I have often wondered how my mother stood it with such a family of children and no one to help her except my oldest sister. We used candles, which my mother made by pouring melted tallow into moulds. We used soft soap that my mother made by leaching water slowly through a barrel of wood ash to get the alkali and potash, and then boiling this in a kettle with the scraps of fats she saved. Often she would sit up late at night darning our socks and mending our ragged trousers."

SOURCE 5 Medical remedies reportedly used by homesteader women

Snakebite – apply warm manure to the bite
Ear ache – pour warm urine into the ear
Measles – eat a roasted mouse

91

HOW IMPORTANT WAS THE ROLE OF WOMEN IN HOMESTEADING?

SOURCE 6 A woman collecting cattle chips (dung) for fuel, Kansas, 1880s

SOURCE 8 An incident recorded in *The Pioneers* by H. Horn, 1974

" The two women saw the Cheyenne warriors approaching across the prairie. Mrs Kine plunged into the stream at a point where she was hidden by some overhanging branches and held her baby high to keep it from drowning. But Mrs Alardice, paralyzed with fear, collapsed in a faint surrounded by her four frightened children. The Cheyennes shot the three oldest boys, killing two of them. They then galloped off with Mrs Alardice and her baby. The baby cried so loudly that the Indians choked it to death and left the body beside the trail. "

1. How many pupils were there in the school in Source 7?
2. What ages would you say these pupils were?
3. What problems might the teacher face in teaching such a class?

SOURCE 7 A schoolteacher with pupils outside their school, Oklahoma, 1895

HOW IMPORTANT WAS THE ROLE OF WOMEN IN HOMESTEADING?

SOURCE 9 A family on their porch, 1880s

4. Does Source 9 show a well-off family? How can you tell?
5. Can you suggest reasons why homesteaders might try to have large families?

SOURCE 10 A woman driving a grain binder

■ CONNECTIONS

Now that you have studied the lives of the homesteaders, look back at your notes on the lives of the Plains Indians. How were the lives of women in the two groups similar and different? Which lifestyle would you have preferred to live?

How did the cattle industry develop?

YOU ARE NOW going to leave the homesteaders for a while and look at a second group of settlers who came west: the ranchers.

Beginnings in Texas

Cattle, just like horses, were first brought to America by the European invaders. By the 1850s, southern Texas was the major centre of cattle ranching. The Texas longhorns were a breed that had developed from the original Spanish imports. They were very hardy and could survive on the OPEN RANGE in Texas. Their one drawback was the relatively poor quality of their meat. In the 1850s beef became a popular food, and the Texan cattle ranchers became prosperous. Then came the American Civil War. Texas fought on the losing Confederate side. At the end of the war the Texans returned to their ranches to find their cattle herds had grown dramatically. It is estimated that in 1865 there were roughly five million cattle in Texas.

The need for cattle drives

Cattle were not worth much unless they could be sold. The only way to do this was to drive them to the markets in the eastern states. Here the Texans faced a major problem. Their Texas longhorns carried a disease called Texas fever, which was spread by the ticks that lived on cattle. Whenever they came into contact with other cattle, those cattle sickened and died. So if the Texans tried to drive their cattle north, they would be turned back by homesteaders afraid of the disease spreading to their animals.

■ TASK

The following pages describe how the cattle industry developed in the West. Your task is to make notes on how each of the following factors and individuals contributed to that development:

- the railroads
- the Indians
- the US army
- the demand for beef in the populous eastern states
- Charles Goodnight
- John Iliff
- Joseph McCoy
- the cowboys
- other factors.

Then decide who or what you think was most important.

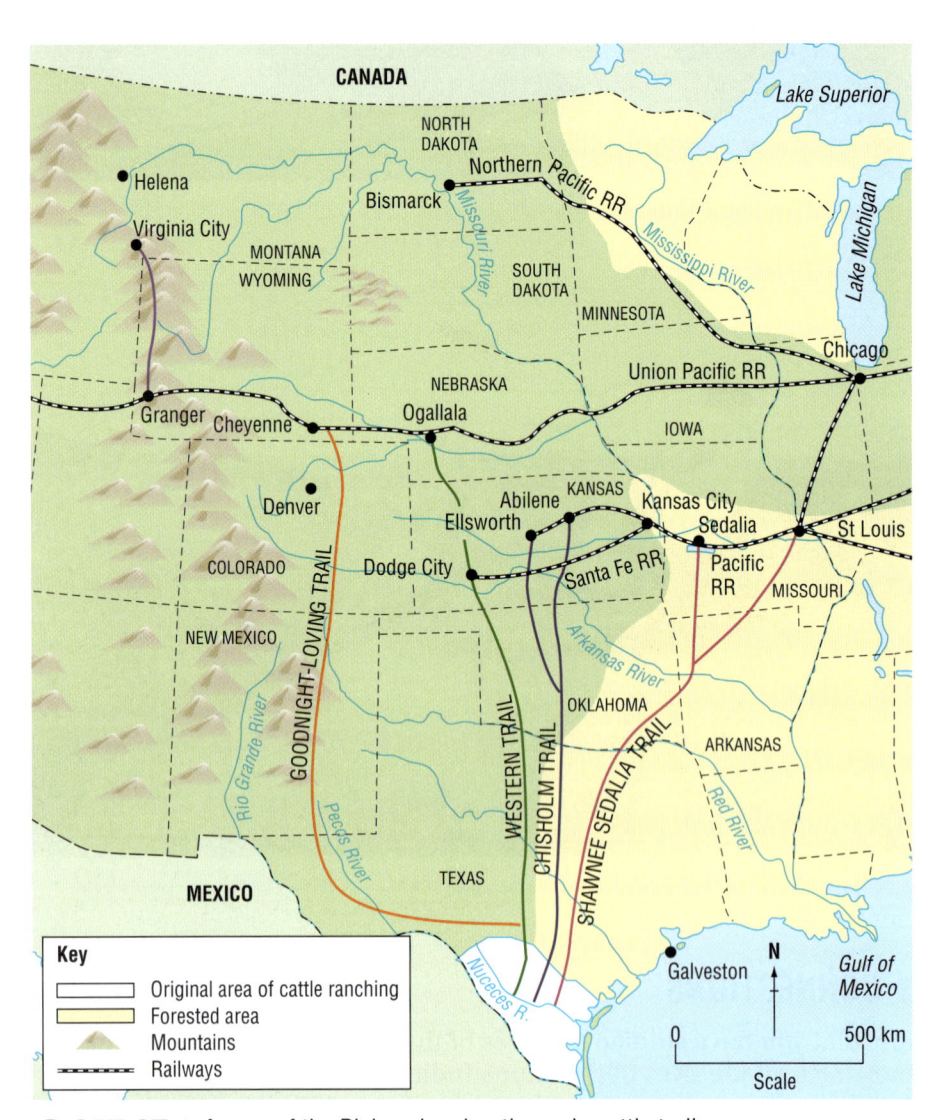

SOURCE 1 A map of the Plains showing the main cattle trails

HOW DID THE CATTLE INDUSTRY DEVELOP?

One solution to this problem was pioneered by Charles Goodnight. In 1860 he had a herd of 180 cattle. In 1865, when he returned from the Civil War, his herd had grown to 5000 cattle. In 1866 he and his partner, Oliver Loving, drove a herd to Fort Sumner, New Mexico. There the cattle were sold to feed the army in their forts and the Indians on their reservations. This began Goodnight's profitable career in the cattle industry.

In the West the US army, the Indians on the reservations, and groups like the miners and railroad builders provided a good market for cattle. By 1870 the US government was buying 50–60,000 head of cattle a year to distribute as rations on the various Indian reservations. The major market, however, was the millions of people who lived in the populous eastern states. So the problem remained: how could the Texans reach this market? The solution was provided by the railroads. In 1866 cattle from Texas were driven to Sedalia, a town on the railroad. This was far enough west to avoid crossing the land of homesteaders.

Cow towns

One man who saw how to exploit this development was a Chicago cattle dealer, Joseph McCoy. He was the man who created the cow town of Abilene in 1867. He bought land, built stock pens and advertised the town as a shipping point. The cattle were driven from Texas to Abilene and then shipped east on the railroad for slaughter and sale (see page 120 for further details). There were great profits to be made from this. An animal worth $5 in Texas could be sold for ten times that amount in Abilene. As the railroad moved further west across the Great Plains new cow towns, such as Dodge City and Newton, developed, and new trails were followed. In the peak years of cattle drives, 1867–85, nearly four million cattle passed through the cow towns.

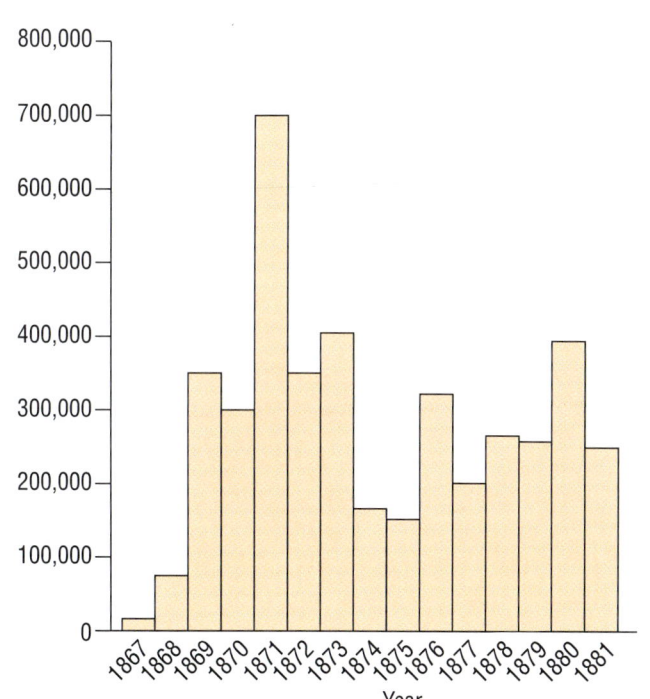

SOURCE 2 Cattle driven north from Texas to the cow towns, 1867–81

SOURCE 3 Joseph McCoy (born 1837 in Illinois, died 1915), the enterprising cattle dealer who developed Abilene. He was also the author of *Historic Sketches of the Cattle Trade of the West and South West* (1874), which is an important source for historians today

1. When was the peak of the cattle drives?
2. Why did the numbers of cattle driven north decline after that?

HOW DID THE CATTLE INDUSTRY DEVELOP?

Cattle drives

The cattle drives took place in the summer. The cattle would be driven from Texas, at an average speed of 24 km a day, to the cow towns for sale. While there were great profits to be made from the cattle drives there were many dangers to overcome. As well as natural hazards, there was an element of danger from Indians. Oliver Loving, Charles Goodnight's partner, died in 1867 as a result of wounds inflicted by a Comanche raiding party.

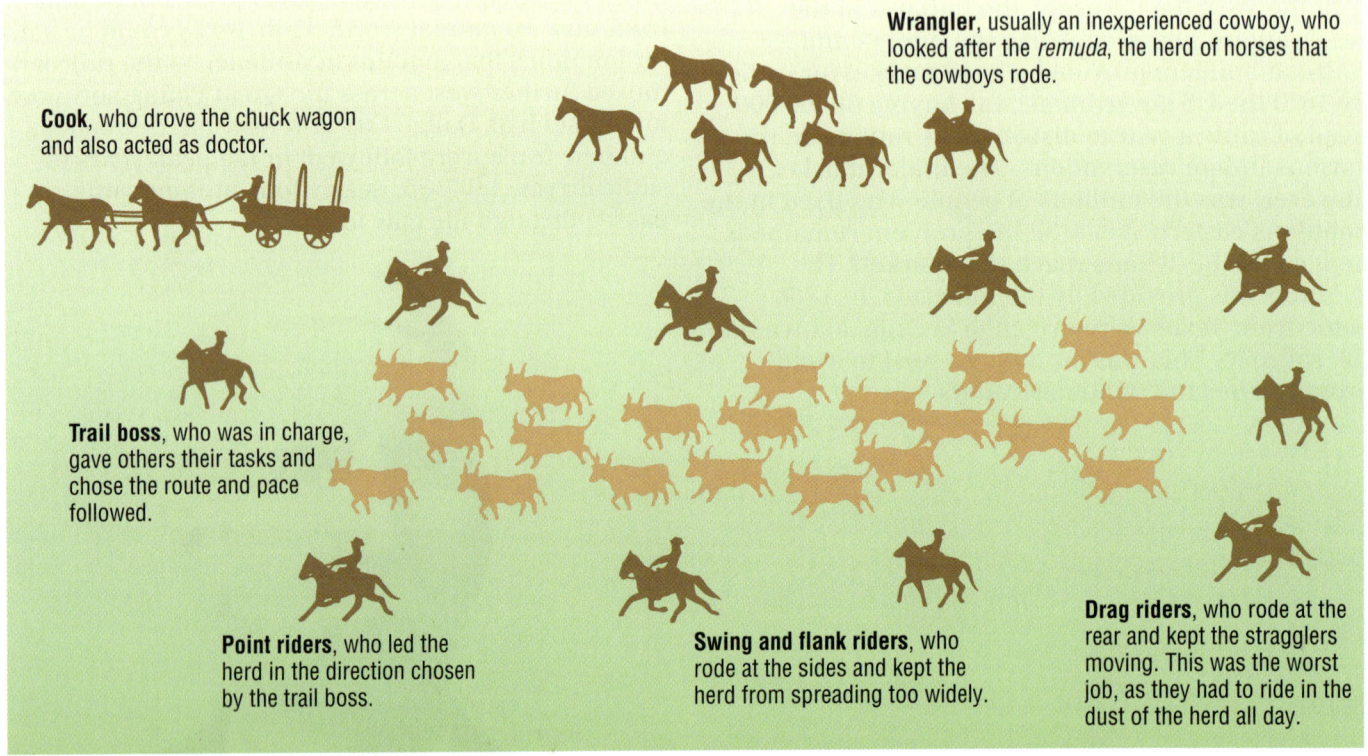

Cook, who drove the chuck wagon and also acted as doctor.

Wrangler, usually an inexperienced cowboy, who looked after the *remuda*, the herd of horses that the cowboys rode.

Trail boss, who was in charge, gave others their tasks and chose the route and pace followed.

Point riders, who led the herd in the direction chosen by the trail boss.

Swing and flank riders, who rode at the sides and kept the herd from spreading too widely.

Drag riders, who rode at the rear and kept the stragglers moving. This was the worst job, as they had to ride in the dust of the herd all day.

SOURCE 4 The jobs carried out by cowboys on the drive. At night everyone took turns to guard the herd

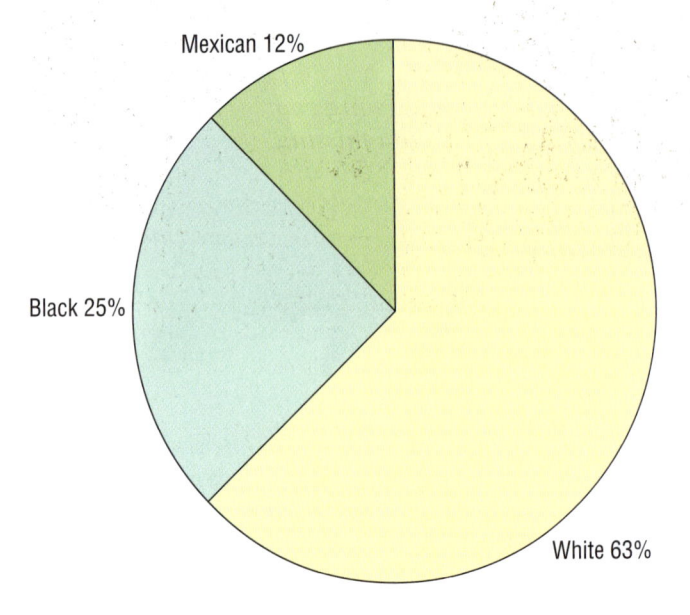

Mexican 12%
Black 25%
White 63%

SOURCE 5 The ethnic origins of cowboys employed on trail drives, 1866–85

3. Do Western films show most cowboys as being white?
4. Can you think of any possible explanations for this?

96

HOW DID THE CATTLE INDUSTRY DEVELOP?

SOURCE 6 Extracts from the diary of George Duffield, who drove a herd of about 1000 cattle from southern Texas to Iowa in 1866. The drive eventually ended on 31 October. Duffield sold 500 cattle, all that was left of the 1000 cattle he set out with

May 1 Big stampede. Lost 200 head of Cattle.

May 2 Spent the day hunting and found but 25 Head. It has been Raining for three days. These are dark days for me.

May 3 Day spent in hunting Cattle. Found 23. Hard rain and wind. Lots of trouble.

May 8 Rain pouring down in torrents. Ran my horse into a ditch and got my knee badly sprained – fifteen miles.

May 9 Still dark and gloomy. River [Brazos] up. Everything looks Blue to me.

May 14 Swam our cattle and Horses and built Raft and Rafted our provisions and blankets over. Swam river with rope and then hauled wagon over. Lost most of our kitchen furniture such as camp Kittles, Coffee Pots, Cups, Plates, Canteens, etc.

May 15 It does nothing but rain. Got all our traps together that was not lost and thought we were ready for off. Dark rainy night. Cattle all left us and in morning not one Beef to be seen.

May 16 Hunt Beeves is the word – all hands discouraged and are determined to go. 200 beeves out and nothing to eat.

May 17 No breakfast. Pack and off is the order. All hands gave the Brazos one good harty damn and started for Buchanan.

May 31 Swimming Cattle is the order. We worked all day in the River [Red] and at dusk got the last Beefe over – I am now out of Texas – This day will long be remembered by me – There was one of our party Drowned today.

June 1 Stampede last night among six droves and a general mix up and loss of Beeves. Hunt Cattle again. Men all tired and want to leave.

June 2 Hard rain and wind Storm. Beeves ran and I had to be on Horse back all Night. Awful night. Men still lost. Quit the Beeves and go to Hunting men is the word – 4pm. Found our men with Indian guide and 195 Beeves fourteen Miles from camp. Almost starved not having had a bite to eat for 60 hours. Got to camp about 12 midnight. Tired.

June 19 Fifteen Indians came to Herd and tried to take some Beeves. Would not let them. Had a big Muss. One drew his knife and I my Revolver. Made them leave but fear they have gone for others.

June 27 My Back is Blistered badly from exposure while in the River [Arkansas] and I with two others are suffering very much. I was attacked by a Beefe in the River and had a very narrow escape from being hurt by Diving.

SOURCE 7 The chuck wagon exhibit in the American Museum, Bath, England. This reconstruction has been carefully researched and some of the artefacts in it are authentic

SOURCE 8 Teddy 'Blue' Abbott, cowboy, describing a stampede

And that night it come up an awful storm. It took all four of us to hold the cattle and we didn't hold them, and when morning come there was one man missing. We went back to look for him, and we found him among the prairie dog holes, beside his horse. The horse's ribs was scraped bare of hide, and all the rest of horse and man was mashed into the ground as flat as a pancake. The only thing you could recognise was the handle of his six-shooter. We tried to think that the lightning hit him, and that was what we wrote to his folks down in Texas.

5. Look at Sources 6 and 8. What were the main hazards and dangers facing cowboys on the cattle drives?

The development of ranching on the Plains

IN THE 1860s A conflict began to develop over the Great Plains themselves. Who would get the Plains: the ranchers or the homesteaders?

Early ranchers

The major problem for the cattlemen in driving their herds northwards was the spread of homesteaders. As they settled across the Plains the routes of the cattle drives were blocked. The eventual solution to this was the development of ranching on the plains.

One of the earliest ranchers on the plains was John W. Iliff. Having failed to strike it rich as a gold miner at Pikes Peak in 1859, he set up a store near Cheyenne. He discovered that cattle could survive the winter on the plains. He went on to build up his herd by buying lame and footsore cattle from settlers travelling to Oregon. In 1866 he bought cows and bulls from Goodnight and Loving. Eventually he had a herd of 35,000 cattle on his ranch. He sold beef to the railroad builders and in 1868 secured a US government contract to supply beef to the Sioux reservations.

In 1870 Charles Goodnight bought land in Colorado, stocked it with Texas longhorns and began ranching. Other Texans followed his example. Whilst his Colorado ranch was unsuccessful, the ranch he set up later, the JA ranch in Texas, was very successful. By 1877 it covered one million acres and had 100,000 cattle. In 1878 a large band of starving Comanches and Kiowas left their reservation to hunt for buffalo. Finding none, they took some of Goodnight's cattle. Hearing of this, Goodnight arranged a meeting. The Indians agreed to allow Goodnight to keep his cattle on their land if he paid them two beef cattle a day. He agreed, knowing that the US army would soon arrive and force them back on to their reservation. That is exactly what happened.

Why was unfenced ranching on the Great Plains successful?

The ranches on the Great Plains were successful for a number of reasons.

- The Plains Indians were defeated and confined to reservations.
- The buffalo that had previously grazed on the Great Plains were gone, slaughtered by the hunters.
- It was discovered that if Texas longhorns were held on the northern plains during the winter then the cold would kill the disease-carrying ticks.
- The railroads that were crossing the Plains were able to take the cattle to market. The cattle were shipped live to Chicago where they were slaughtered in huge slaughterhouses. Then they were refrigerated and sent east for sale. This was made possible by the work of Gustavus Swift, who developed refrigerated rail cars.

SOURCE 1 A modern illustration of a ranch

THE DEVELOPMENT OF RANCHING ON THE PLAINS

Experiments in cattle breeding from the 1870s onwards solved another problem. By interbreeding the Longhorns with better-quality animals from the East, ranchers were able to improve their animals. These cattle put on weight more easily and provided better meat.

The 'open range'
The ranches themselves were typically 'open ranges', unfenced land which was claimed by the rancher. Every open range needed a water supply. Often the boundaries between ranches were watersheds. At the centre of the ranch were the buildings where the ranch-hands – cowboys – lived and worked. You can find out more about cowboys on pages 100–103.

As the land was not fenced there was a problem of how to establish ownership of the cattle that wandered and mixed on the open range. For that reason the cattle were branded. This also acted as a defence against rustlers who might steal and drive off cattle.

1. If you were a cattle rustler, which of the brands in Source 2 would you find easiest to alter?

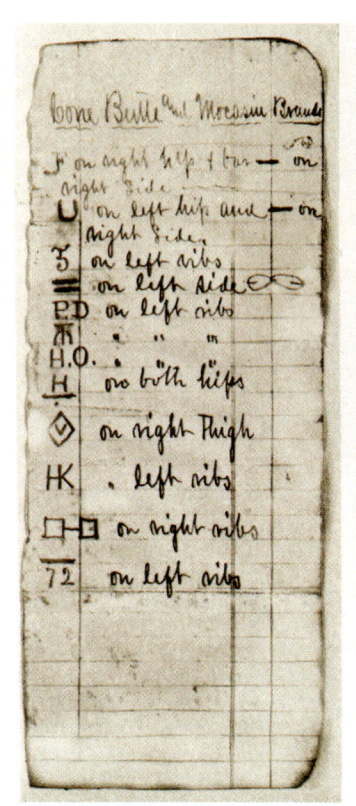

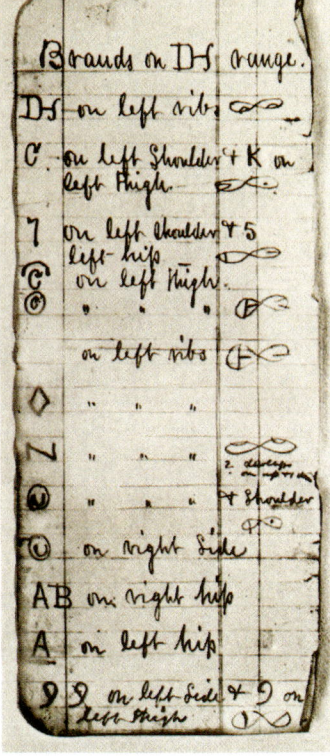

SOURCE 2 A handwritten list of brands, 1886. These lists were produced in every state and brands had to be registered

The end of the 'open range'
The period 1880–85 was the peak period of ranching on the plains. Ranching was seen as a sure way to make money. As cattle prices rose, cattle ranchers put more and more animals on to the open range. This put pressure on the stock of grass. The drought of 1883 added to this problem, as the grass withered.

At the same time, the demand for beef in the East began to fall and so, therefore, did the prices paid for cattle. Since prices were falling, the ranchers kept their cattle on the range instead of sending them for slaughter, which increased the pressure on the grass stocks even more. Then came the final blow. The winter of 1886–87 was especially severe. Thousands of cattle died in the icy blizzards and freezing cold. Something like fifteen per cent of herds died in the worst-hit areas – it was impossible to be sure since ranchers never knew exactly how many cattle they had. So the 'open range' was already under pressure. The Johnson County War (see page 106) made the problems of the open range still worse.

The cattle-ranching boom was over and many cattle men had gone bankrupt. The character of cattle ranching changed. The open range was replaced by smaller ranches which were fenced off using barbed wire. The use of barbed wire kept out competition, and cut labour costs by preventing animals from straying. Wind pumps were put up to supply water, and ranchers concentrated on breeding fewer but better animals. The life of the cowboy on such a ranch changed completely.

SOURCE 3 Numbers of cattle on the Great Plains, taken from the US Census, 1880

State or territory	1860	1880
Colorado	none	791,492
Kansas	93,455	1,533,133
Montana	none	428,279
Nebraska	37,197	1,113,247
Wyoming	none	521,213

■ TASK

Draw your own spider diagram to summarise the reasons for the end of the open range.

Who were the cowboys and what was their life like?

THE ORIGINAL COWBOYS were the Spanish *vacqueros* in what was later to become Texas. The word 'cowboy' came into general use in the 1870s. It was used to describe the men who worked with cattle on the cattle drives and ranches. Many of these men were from the southern states and they included large numbers of blacks and Mexicans. Their work consisted of looking after the cattle, line riding in winter (see below), and the peak-time work of rounding up and driving the cattle in spring and summer. This work was not well paid. Average wages were $25–40 per month, plus room and board. In 1883 a strike for higher wages in Texas was broken by the cattle companies.

Line riding

The job of line riding was a lonely one. Line riders stayed alone at line shacks on the ranch boundaries. From these, they patrolled the boundary, herding stray cattle back on to the ranch and driving off strays from neighbouring ranches, so that they did not eat the precious grass. They also tried to discourage rustling, pulled animals from bogs and the deep winter snows, treated sick animals and shot predators, particularly wolves.

With the introduction of barbed wire they became 'fence riders', who also had to repair damaged fences. This made the job even more boring, since they could no longer follow their own routes but had to follow the wire.

Round-up and branding

In spring the cattle would be rounded up and identified by their brands. Young animals would be branded for the first time. These jobs required skilled horsemanship and hard physical effort.

■ SOURCE INVESTIGATION

1. On page 101 is a series of sources describing aspects of the life and work of cowboys. Use them to help you to decide what sort of men they were. Were they ordinary, hard-working men? Were they the lowest of the low? Or were they romantic heroes? How would you portray them?
   You should also look back at the information on the cattle drives on pages 96–97 to help you with this work.
2. Now use this information and your judgement to help you to devise a simple game based upon cowboy life. You could look back at the 'Living on the Plains' game on page 40 for ideas. This game should have historical authenticity. It should also be simple and enjoyable for players. To test it, give it to some other members of your class to play. You may wish to base it on an example your teacher gives you.

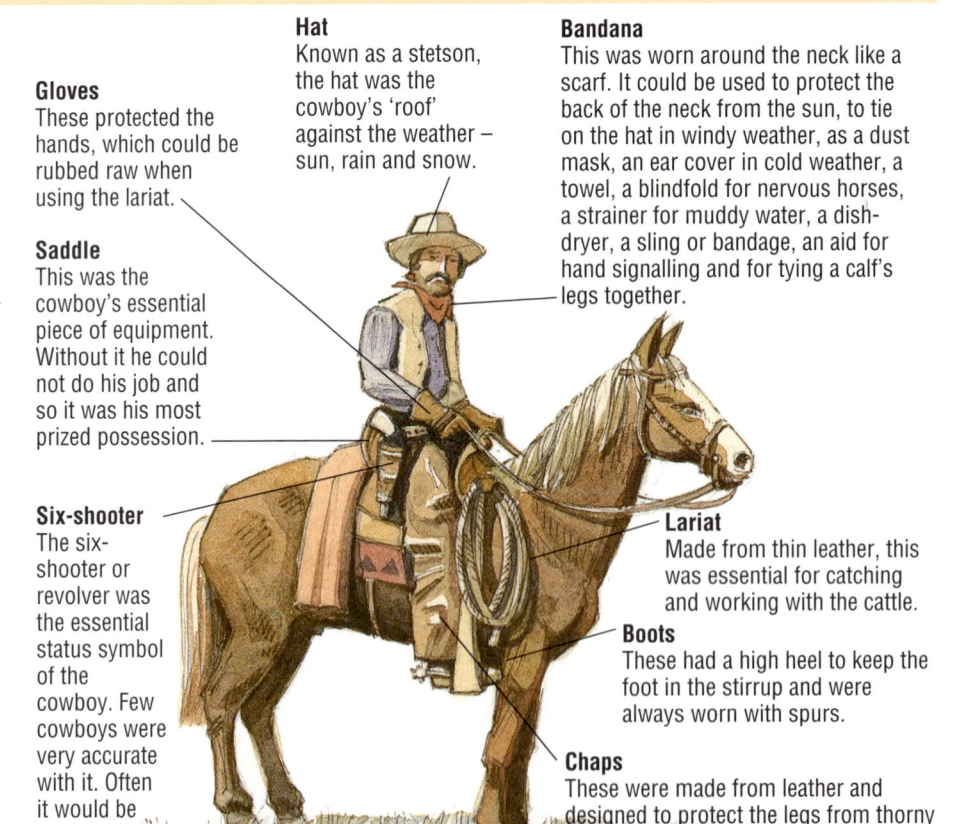

Gloves
These protected the hands, which could be rubbed raw when using the lariat.

Saddle
This was the cowboy's essential piece of equipment. Without it he could not do his job and so it was his most prized possession.

Six-shooter
The six-shooter or revolver was the essential status symbol of the cowboy. Few cowboys were very accurate with it. Often it would be left in the chuck wagon.

Hat
Known as a stetson, the hat was the cowboy's 'roof' against the weather – sun, rain and snow.

Bandana
This was worn around the neck like a scarf. It could be used to protect the back of the neck from the sun, to tie on the hat in windy weather, as a dust mask, an ear cover in cold weather, a towel, a blindfold for nervous horses, a strainer for muddy water, a dish-dryer, a sling or bandage, an aid for hand signalling and for tying a calf's legs together.

Lariat
Made from thin leather, this was essential for catching and working with the cattle.

Boots
These had a high heel to keep the foot in the stirrup and were always worn with spurs.

Chaps
These were made from leather and designed to protect the legs from thorny vegetation, from chafing on a long ride, and to give some protection in a fall.

SOURCE 1 A modern illustration of a cowboy and his equipment

WHO WERE THE COWBOYS AND WHAT WAS THEIR LIFE LIKE?

Opinions of the cowboys

At the time, views of the cowboys varied. Sources 2–4 are all from Western newspapers. The writers would have seen cowboys in town after cattle drives.

SOURCE 2 Extract from the *Topeka Commonwealth* (Kansas), 15 August 1871

"The Texas cowboy is a character, the like of which can be found nowhere else on earth. He is unlearned and illiterate, with few wants and little ambition. His diet is mainly navy plug [chewing tobacco] and whiskey and the occupation dearest to his heart is gambling.

He generally wears a revolver on each side, which he will use with as little hesitation on a man as on a wild animal. Such a character is dangerous and desperate and each one has generally killed his man."

SOURCE 3 Extract from the *Las Vegas Optic* (New Mexico), 28 June 1881

"It is possible that there is not a wilder or more lawless set of men in any country than these cowboys."

SOURCE 4 Extract from the *Rio Grande Republican* (New Mexico), 18 December 1884

"Those cowboys who are not professional thieves, murderers and various blacklegs who fled to the frontier for reasons that require no explanation are men who totally disregard all of the amenities of Eastern civilization. They fear neither God, nor man nor the devil. He is the best man who can draw the quickest and kill the surest."

Sources 5–7 were all written by men who worked with cowboys on the range and on cattle drives.

SOURCE 5 Extract from the *Texas Live Stock Journal*, 21 October 1882

"The cowboy is a fearless animal . . . he is as chivalrous as the famed Knights of old. Rough he may be, but no set of men have higher respect for women and no set of men would risk more in the defence of their person or honour."

SOURCE 6 Joseph McCoy writing in *Historic Sketches of the Cattle Trade of the West and South West*, 1874

"He lives hard, works hard, has few comforts and fewer needs. He has little taste for reading. He would rather fight with pistols than pray, loves tobacco, whiskey and women better than any other trinity. His life borders upon that of an Indian."

3. What do these writers think is best about the cowboys?
4. In what way do Sources 5–7 agree with Sources 2–4?
5. Which writers would you consider to be more reliable and why?

■ CONNECTIONS

Both the cowboys and the Plains Indians lived on the Great Plains. Joseph McCoy, in Source 6 below, thought that there were similarities between their lives. How were their lives similar? How were their lives different? Which lifestyle would you have preferred to live and why? You should consider the following:

- horsemanship
- code of honour
- family life
- homes, food and clothing
- weapons
- bravery.

1. What are the main faults that cowboys are accused of by these newspapers?
2. Can you think of any reason why they would be so hostile to cowboys?

SOURCE 7 John Baumann writing in the *Fortnightly Review*, 1 April 1887

"He is on the whole a loyal, long enduring, hard working fellow, grit to the backbone, and tough as whipcord; performing his arduous and often dangerous duties, and living his comfortless life, without a word of complaint about the many hardships he has to undergo."

WHO WERE THE COWBOYS AND WHAT WAS THEIR LIFE LIKE?

Charles Russell (1864–1926)

Known as the 'cowboy artist', Charles Russell worked on cattle ranches between 1880 and 1892. He took up painting full time in 1893. While his paintings are mostly action-packed, he was drawing upon his experience to depict the reality of cowboy life. He was attempting to preserve the past. According to the art historian Brian W. Dippe, 'His West was a compound of memory, imagination and research.'

■ SOURCE INVESTIGATION

With the rest of your group study Sources 8–11, which are all paintings by Charles Russell.

1. Try to decide exactly what is going on in each painting. You should consider the setting, the expressions and actions of the main subjects, the clothing and equipment of the cowboys, and the small clues, particularly in Sources 8 and 11.
2. What view of cowboy life is Russell trying to give us? How does he try to do this?
3. Now consider another group of sources, the Western films you have seen. What does the typical cowboy look like in them? Does he look like Russell's cowboys? Is either set of sources entirely accurate?

SOURCE 8 *Just a Little Pleasure*, c.1898

SOURCE 9 *Laugh Kills Lonesome*, c.1925

WHO WERE THE COWBOYS AND WHAT WAS THEIR LIFE LIKE?

SOURCE 10 *The Roundup*, 1913

SOURCE 11 *Gunfight*, 1902

Why was there conflict between cattle ranchers and homesteaders?

THE CATTLE RANCHERS wanted the same land as the homesteaders. It will not surprise you that the success of the cattle ranchers led to conflict between cattle ranchers and homesteaders from the 1850s onwards. Early conflicts were caused when the homesteaders tried to stop the cattle drives. They were afraid of damage to their crops and of Texas fever infecting their animals. This conflict was one of the reasons for the end of cattle drives.

From the 1870s onwards, when cattle ranchers settled on the Plains, conflicts continued. These disputes were about land and access to water. The cattle ranchers were anxious for the range to be 'open range' with access to water for their cattle. The homesteaders wanted to fence off their crops to protect them from straying cattle, as well as wild beasts. This could cut off access to water and bring the two sides into direct conflict.

SOURCE 1 Teddy 'Blue' Abbott describes the conflict from the cowboy's point of view

> *There was no love lost between settlers and cowboys on the trail. Those jayhawkers would take up a claim right where the herds watered and charge us for water. They would plant a crop alongside the trail and plough a furrow around it for a fence, and then when the cattle got into their wheat or garden patch, they would come cussing and waving a shotgun and yelling for damages. And the cattle had been coming through there when they were still raising pumpkins in Illinois.*

Sheep farmers

By the 1880s flocks of sheep were a serious threat to cattle, as they were competing for grazing. Sheep rearing was most common in the south-western states. There were five million sheep in New Mexico, sheep out-numbered cattle ten to one in Arizona, and there were also large numbers of sheep in California and Utah. The advantage of sheep-rearing was that it required a smaller initial investment and offered quicker returns than cattle. So it was an attractive option for men starting out.

There was some violence by cattle ranchers, which took the form of killing shepherds, slaughtering sheep and burning the hay of farmers who sold fodder to sheep farmers. Racial and religious intolerance fed this hostility. The sheep owners were often immigrants who were not of European origin: Mexican-Americans, Navaho Indians, or sometimes Mormons. Many of the shepherds were Scots, Basques or Mexican-Americans.

SOURCE 2 A shepherd and his flock

WHY WAS THERE CONFLICT BETWEEN CATTLE RANCHERS AND HOMESTEADERS?

Barbed wire

In some places the invention of barbed wire led to trouble. Homesteaders used it to fence off their land. This initially aroused the hostility of the cattle ranchers. Later, cattle ranchers realised the value of fencing, and on some large cattle ranches vast areas of range were fenced off. Smaller ranchers fought back to avoid being cut off from water or squeezed out. They did this by fence cutting, as happened in Texas in the mid-1880s (see Source 3).

SOURCE 3 A staged photograph showing ranchers cutting a barbed-wire fence

1. This photograph was staged. Does this mean it is of no use to us as historians studying the West?
2. Look back at your answer to the question about barbed wire on page 88. Does what you have just read change your answer?

105

Case study: the Johnson County War

Causes

Johnson County in Wyoming had been settled by cattle ranchers in the 1870s. These men ran large-scale ranches and were known as cattle barons. They became very powerful in the state and joined together in the Wyoming Stock Growers Association. This association met in Cheyenne and among its members were the governor of Wyoming and other state senators. Its purpose was to protect the interests of its powerful members. By the 1880s three threats had developed to those interests.

First were the problems in cattle ranching itself. Beef prices were falling. Droughts in 1883 and the harsh winter of 1886–87 also severely damaged income from ranching.

The second threat was the growing number of homesteaders and small ranchers settling in Wyoming. This led to disputes over land ownership. These people were settling on land which the cattle barons claimed was their land. Not surprisingly, the cattle barons resented these newcomers.

Finally, the most annoying threat was from rustling. This had always been a problem on the open range. In Texas a tradition had developed that a maverick (a motherless calf) could be branded and claimed by anyone. To some men this was not a crime but a way of starting a herd. To others it was rustling. The cattle barons in Wyoming lost cattle to rustlers and blamed the homesteaders and small ranchers. It was hard to get juries of local men to convict men accused of rustling. So the cattle barons took the law into their own hands. They hired Frank Canton, a gunfighter, as their chief detective to hunt down rustlers.

The chain of events

The first killings took place in 1889. Jim Averill, who ran a small store and saloon, and his partner, a prostitute called Ella Watson, were living on land claimed by one of the cattle barons. In April Averill wrote in the local paper that the cattle barons were land-grabbers. In July he and Ella were LYNCHED outside their cabin. No one was prosecuted for this crime, although the cattle barons were known to be responsible. The cattle barons claimed that the two were rustlers. Ella was said to accept cattle as payment for her services. Other killings and murder attempts followed, leaving another three of the small ranchers dead.

In 1892 the cattle barons went a stage further. They planned a full-scale invasion of Johnson County, led by Major Frank Wolcott. The acting governor of Wyoming knew about it and even supplied a case of guns. A death-list of 70 names was drawn up, and 24 gunfighters were recruited. Their pay was $5 a day plus expenses and a $50 bonus for every 'rustler' they killed. They were brought to Wyoming on a special train provided by the Union Pacific Railroad Company. With them were two newspaper reporters. The gunfighters and cattlemen made up an invasion force of roughly 50. The plan was to capture the town of Buffalo, kill the sheriff and then kill the rest of the men on the list.

1. The invaders brought two newspaper men with them and readily posed for photographs. Is that the action of men who think they are in the wrong?

SOURCE 1 'The Invaders', Johnson County Cattle War, 4 May 1892

CASE STUDY: THE JOHNSON COUNTY WAR

The invaders began by cutting the telegraph wires to cut off Johnson County from the outside world. But then the plan began to go wrong. The invaders stopped to attack the KC ranch. There they were held up by the heroic resistance of Nate Champion. Single-handed, after the death of his friend Nick Ray, he held off the invaders all day until they finally burnt him out of his cabin. While this was going on the invaders were spotted by some passing riders. By the time Nate Champion was dead the alarm had been raised in Buffalo. Next day, as the invaders approached Buffalo, they heard that the local people were armed and ready. They then retreated to the TA Ranch. Here, they were besieged by nearly 300 men, until the US cavalry arrived to save them. The invaders were taken into protective custody at Fort D.A. Russell. The war had ended with two dead, Nate Champion and his friend Nick Ray, and several wounded.

Results

The defeated cattle barons were brought to trial but never convicted for their actions. However, they were widely condemned. They never had the same power in Wyoming again and the homesteaders and small ranchers were able to continue their lives in peace.

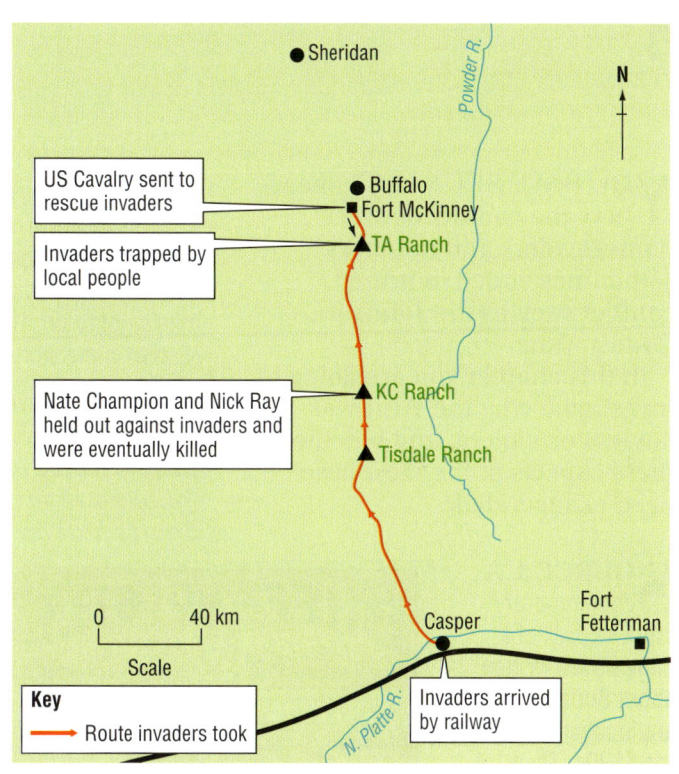

SOURCE 2 A map showing the route taken by the invaders during the Johnson County War

■ ACTIVITY

A TV company is making a programme about the American West. As a researcher on the programme you have been asked to prepare the script for a five-minute section. This should describe cattle ranching on the Plains and why it declined.

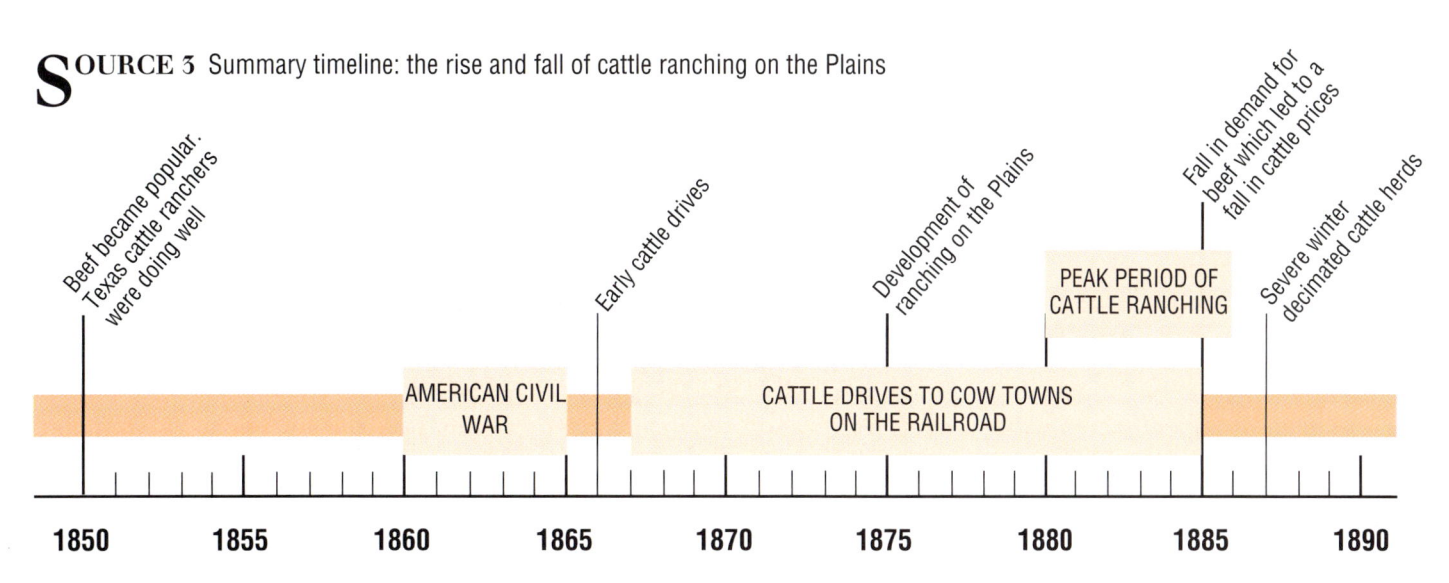

SOURCE 3 Summary timeline: the rise and fall of cattle ranching on the Plains

- 1850: Beef became popular. Texas cattle ranchers were doing well
- 1860–1865: AMERICAN CIVIL WAR
- 1866: Early cattle drives
- 1867–1885: CATTLE DRIVES TO COW TOWNS ON THE RAILROAD
- 1875: Development of ranching on the Plains
- 1880–1885: PEAK PERIOD OF CATTLE RANCHING
- 1885: Fall in demand for beef which led to a fall in cattle prices
- 1887: Severe winter decimated cattle herds

chapter 6
HOW WILD WAS THE WEST?

YOU HAVE SEEN in Chapter 5 how the conflict between homesteaders and ranchers sometimes ended in armed conflict such as the Johnson County War.

In this chapter you are going to investigate why the West was lawless or violent, and whether these aspects of the West have been exaggerated.

SOURCE 1 A contemporary artist's cover of a dime novel, written about Buffalo Bill and published in the 1890s. The term 'dime novel' was kept, even when, as here, the price had increased

Dime novels
Dime novels appeared in the 1860s and were amazingly successful. After just four years the publishers, Beadle and Adams, had five million of their dime novels in circulation. Although they were often based upon real people, the plots were entirely fictional and often wildly exaggerated. There were, for example, over 120 'Buffalo Bill' novels. These novels created the myth of the noble frontier hero instinctively doing the right thing. Since they were so popular they helped to create the myth of the West and of the cowboys who appeared in their pages from the 1870s onwards.

SOURCE 2 'The walkdown', an extract from *The Virginian* by Owen Wister, 1902. The Virginian, the cowboy hero of the story, has a dilemma. Trampas the villain has given him until sunset to get out of town. If he leaves town people will think him a coward. If he stays his bride-to-be will not marry him. But a man's got to do what a man's got to do. The Virginian has stayed and is now about to walk out into the street. (Earlier in the story a man called Shorty has been shot dead by Trampas)

The Virginian walked out into the open, watching. He saw men here and there, and they let him pass, without speaking. He saw his three friends, and they said no word to him. But they turned and followed in his rear at a little distance, because it was known that Shorty had been shot from behind. The Virginian gained a position soon where no one could come at him except in front.

'It is quite a while after sunset,' he heard himself say.

A wind seemed to blow his sleeve off his arm, and he replied to it, and saw Trampas pitch forward. He saw Trampas raise his arm from the ground and fall again, and lie there this time, still. A little smoke was rising from the pistol on the ground, and he looked at his own, and saw the smoke flowing upward out of it.

'I expect that's all,' he said aloud.

But as he came nearer Trampas, he covered him with his weapon. He stopped a moment, seeing the hand on the ground move. Two fingers twitched, and then ceased; for it was all. The Virginian stood looking down at Trampas.

'Both of mine hit,' he said, once more aloud. 'His must have gone mighty close to my arm. I told her it would not be me.

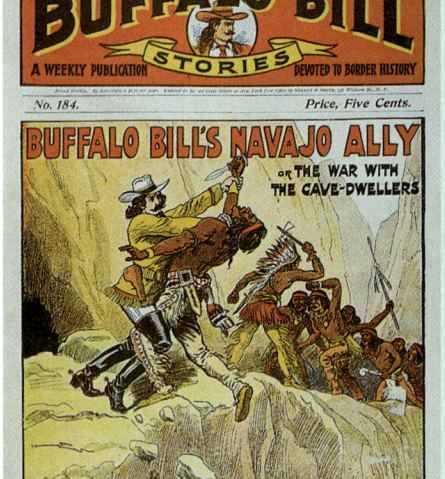

The Virginian
The Virginian is a work of historical fiction which sold 50,000 copies in just two months. The author, Owen Wister, had travelled in the West and was attempting to 'faithfully report' the West. Source 2 is believed to be based upon a real-life incident that happened in Springfield, Missouri, on 21 July 1865. Davis Tutt, an ex-Confederate soldier and skilled shot, had a dispute with Wild Bill Hickok. They confronted each other in the town square and walked towards each other. When they were roughly 50 metres apart, Tutt drew his pistol, fired and missed. Hickok drew his pistol and, before Tutt could recock his pistol, shot him through the heart. Hickok was arrested, tried and acquitted. The verdict was self-defence, and Hickok had gained a national reputation as a gunfighter. In reality, pistols were very inaccurate weapons and most cowboys were not good shots. The 'walkdown' has since become part of the myth of the West.

HOW WILD WAS THE WEST?

■ **SOURCE INVESTIGATION**

Much of what we think we know about the West comes from three types of source:

■ Western fiction, such as Source 2
■ Western art, such as Source 3
■ Western films, such as Source 4.

1. Study Sources 2–4 on pages 108–109.
   a) What is happening in each source?
   b) Do they make you think that the West was wild?
2. Now read the notes on each source. Essentially, each source is an interpretation of the West. Each author, artist or director is giving his own interpretation of what the West was like. What interpretation is this in each case? Why are they doing this? Do you still think the West was wild?

SOURCE 4 Two stills from the film *Butch Cassidy and the Sundance Kid*, made in 1969

SOURCE 3 *What an Unbranded Cow Has Cost*, painted by Frederic Remington for *Harper's Weekly* in 1895 to illustrate a story by Owen Wister

Butch Cassidy and the Sundance Kid
This film still of the outlaws, played by actors Paul Newman and Robert Redford, shows them blowing open a railroad express car with dynamite. Some parts of the film were well researched. These two outlaws did exist and they did blow up railroad express cars to rob them. However, where there was no surviving evidence of what actually happened the film 'filled in the gaps' and deliberately gave a romanticised version of these two outlaws' lives.

What an Unbranded Cow Has Cost
No Western gun battle over unbranded cattle (rustling) ever claimed as many lives as Remington's painting suggests.

109

Why was there lawlessness or violence in the West?

■ TASK

The diagram below shows some of the main factors which led to lawlessness and violence in the West. Your task is to consider how these factors help to explain the crimes described on pages 111–13. Are there any factors you want to add yourself?

1. Copy and complete the table below.
2. In column 3 add other factors if you wish. Do not limit yourself to the ones we have listed.

Type of crime	Example	Factors that help to explain this crime

Political factors
The new mining and cow towns which sprang up so quickly were particularly lawless in their early years. There was a shortage of reliable law-enforcement officers and politicians did not think the issue was important enough to spend money on employing and training more, or better, officers.

Geographical factors
The West was a vast area and transport was very slow. This made it very difficult to enforce law and order.

Social factors
There were many potential sources of conflict between the different ethnic groups: blacks, Chinese, Europeans, Indians, Mexicans and settlers from the eastern USA.
After the Civil War thousands of soldiers, Confederates and Unionists, were demobilised. For many, readjusting to civilian life was difficult. Also, many people on both sides were unable or unwilling to forgive or forget what had happened.

Why was there lawlessness or violence?

Economic factors
There were many potential sources of conflict between the different economic groups: between cowboys and townspeople; homesteaders and ranchers; miners and hunters; sheep herders and ranchers; cattle barons and small ranchers.

Values and attitudes
The West was dominated by a primitive code of honour. It was your responsibility to settle things for yourself. You had no duty to retreat in a confrontation. Since most Westerners carried guns this meant that an argument could end in a shooting. If you shot a man in self-defence, then you had not broken the law, as long as the other man was armed. This attitude lay behind the willingness of big businessmen, cattle barons and railroad owners to resort to violence.

WHY WAS THERE LAWLESSNESS OR VIOLENCE IN THE WEST?

Types of crime

Bank robbery
Immediately after the Civil War some of the ex-Confederate guerrilla fighters turned to bank robbery. The most famous were the James–Younger Gang, who carried out a series of robberies between 1866 and 1882. Their raid on the bank in Northfield, Minnesota, in 1876 went badly wrong. The townspeople armed themselves and fought back. Two gang members were killed and the others were wounded.

SOURCE 1 An artist's impression of the James–Younger Gang's raid on Northfield in 1876

Cattle rustling
The herds of cattle roaming freely on the range were an easy target for rustlers. The use of brands, as described on page 99 in Chapter 5, helped to identify cattle, but brand marks could be altered and young cattle stolen before they had been branded. It was a way in which cowboys could get started as small ranchers. As you have seen, this was one of the factors that led to the Johnson County War.

Claim jumping
In the gold- and silver-mining areas claim jumping was a particular problem, as late arrivals tried to steal the land others had already claimed. When mining first began in these areas, the nearest forces of law and order were a long way away (see page 71).

Fence cutting
Fence cutting occurred in the 1880s and 1890s, when homesteaders and small ranchers cut the barbed-wire fences being put up by cattle barons. The cattle barons were trying to enclose vast areas, whilst the smaller ranchers were trying to avoid being cut off from water or forced out altogether.

Horse stealing
Horse stealing was regarded as a serious crime. Not only was a horse extremely valuable, it was also essential for survival on the Great Plains. Horse thieves were frequently hanged. Of course, for the Plains Indians horse stealing was an essential part of their way of life. It was one way in which warriors gained honour.

WHY WAS THERE LAWLESSNESS OR VIOLENCE IN THE WEST?

Racial attacks
Thousands of Chinese were encouraged to emigrate to the United States, where they made a major contribution to the building of the railroads. However, they were often the victims of racial attack in the mining and cow towns. These attacks were motivated by fears about job competition. The worst incident took place at a coal-mining centre, Rock Springs, Wyoming, in 1885, when 51 Chinese were killed and over 400 others expelled from the town. Other groups who suffered racial attack were blacks, Indians and Mexicans. According to one historian, in one Texas town a Texan killed a black soldier. When two more black soldiers came to arrest him he shot them too. A white jury found him not guilty.

Shootings
Some historians have estimated that between 1866 and 1900 20,000 people died of 'lead poisoning' (shooting) in the West. That works out at approximately 600 a year. Other historians have argued that such figures are exaggerated. Much has been made of the violence in cow towns but one historian, Robert Dykstra, claimed in his book *The Cattle Towns* (1968) that only 45 killings took place between 1867 and 1885 in these towns. Whatever the final numbers, some men became famous as gunfighters. The later part of this chapter deals with three such men: Billy the Kid, John Wesley Hardin and Wild Bill Hickok.

SOURCE 2 An illustration of an anti-Chinese riot in Denver, Colorado, 1880

SOURCE 3 The Chinese Exclusion Act, 6 May 1882

" Whereas in the opinion of the Government of the United States the coming of Chinese labourers to this country endangers the good order of certain localities ... Be it enacted, That ... the coming of Chinese labourers to the United States be suspended ... "

1. Which source, 2 or 3, is more reliable as evidence of the racial tensions in the West?

WHY WAS THERE LAWLESSNESS OR VIOLENCE IN THE WEST?

Robbery (road agents)

In the vast open spaces of the West robbery was a common crime. Individual travellers and stage-coaches could be held up well away from the towns and the forces of law and order. Stage-coach companies responded by hiring armed guards to 'ride shotgun'. In some cases the US army was called in to help.

SOURCE 4 A photograph of Butch Cassidy and the Wild Bunch, train robbers. From left to right: Harry Longbaugh (The Sundance Kid), William Carver, Ben (The Tall Texan) Kilpatrick, Harvey Logan (Kid Curry), Robert Parker (Butch Cassidy)

Train robbery

In 1866 the first train robbery took place outside Seymour, Indiana. The Reno brothers stole $13,000 from the Ohio & Mississippi Railroad. Between 1870 and 1880 gangs of outlaws regularly robbed the express cars on trains. The most famous gang was Butch Cassidy and the Wild Bunch. The robberies forced the railroad companies to take counter-measures. These included strengthening the doors of express cars, employing tougher guards and giving guards better weapons. Yet by the 1890s robberies were common on all the major railways. The basic problem was the distances involved out in the West. Robberies could take place far from the nearest town. The solutions eventually taken up by the railroad companies included the use of express cars made entirely of steel, several armed guards, and 'posse vans' full of armed lawmen ready for immediate pursuit. Train robberies reached a peak by 1900 and then began to tail off.

2. Compare Source 4 to the view of the gang you get from the film still on page 109. Do they differ?

SOURCE 5 The posse that trailed Butch Cassidy and the Wild Bunch, preparing to board their train

WHY WAS THERE LAWLESSNESS OR VIOLENCE IN THE WEST?

The forces of law and order

- **US marshals** were appointed by the President to oversee a state or territory. As this was such a large area the marshals appointed deputies who worked on a more local basis.
- **Town marshals** were appointed by the people of a town, often on a yearly basis.
- **Sheriffs** were elected by the people of a county for a two-year period of office. Often they had to cover too wide an area to be effective.
- **The Texas Rangers** (established in 1820) were a small army of lawmen employed to enforce the law in the state of Texas. There were also Arizona Rangers.
- **The Pinkerton Detective Agency** was a private company that was hired by banks and railroad and stage-coach companies to provide protection. Sometimes the Agency was hired to catch particular outlaws, such as the James–Younger Gang.
- **Judges** were appointed by the President to try cases. There were three to supervise each state or territory. Obviously this was too few. Prisoners had to be held for a long time before trial; sometimes they were lynched before a trial could take place.

Few men made a career out of being a lawman, since it was both badly paid and dangerous. The quality of lawmen ranged from admirable to bad. At one extreme was Bill Tilghman, deputy marshal of Oklahoma, who had a distinguished career. At the other extreme was Henry Plummer, sheriff of Bannack, Montana, who combined this job with leading a band of outlaws. His double life ended when he was hanged by vigilantes.

Were vigilantes a force for good or evil?

Vigilantes were people who took the law into their own hands. When they identified someone whom they believed to be a criminal they punished them. They might run them out of town or lynch them. There were over 200 vigilante groups west of the Mississippi. Often, they were led by local elites, the well-to-do members of frontier communities.

One example of a vigilante group at work was in Bannack, Montana. In 1864 the area was being terrorised by a gang who robbed travellers and miners. The gang was believed to be over 100 strong and was well informed about valuable stage-coaches to rob. The local law officers seemed unable to stop the robberies. Eventually a vigilante committee was established. It turned out that the sheriff, Henry Plummer, was also the leader of the robbers. In 1865 he was captured, tried and lynched by the vigilantes.

A second example was in Downieville, California. In 1851, vigilantes lynched a Mexican woman, Josefa, who had killed a drunken miner who had molested her. A newspaper at the time commented, 'Had this woman been an American instead of a Mexican, instead of being hung for the deed, she would have been praised for it. It was not her guilt that condemned this unfortunate woman, but her Mexican blood.'

WHY WAS THERE LAWLESSNESS OR VIOLENCE IN THE WEST?

■ **SOURCE INVESTIGATION**

Study the sources below. They show that opinions on vigilantes varied at the time. Do Sources 6–10 see vigilantes as a force for good or evil?

SOURCE 6 Professor T.J. Dimsdale, writing in *The Vigilantes of Montana*, 1866

" Such was the lawless state of affairs that five men in Virginia City and four in Bannack started the Montana Vigilantes. In a few weeks it was known that the voice of justice had spoken. The vigilantes struck from his hand the weapon of the murderer, warned the thief to steal no more and forced the ruffians, who had so long maintained a reign of terror in Montana, to flee the territory. Justice and protection from wrong to person and property are the birthright of every American citizen. When justice is powerless as well as blind, self preservation is the first law of nature. "

SOURCE 7 A description of a lynching by Edward Buffum, a journalist working as a miner. He describes how five men were caught robbing a gambler and were given 39 lashes each. Three of them were then accused of murder and an attempted robbery that had happened three months earlier. Two hundred jurors then sentenced them to death. The three could not speak English – two were French and one Chilean

" Vainly they called for an interpreter, for their cries were drowned by the now infuriated mob. The wagon was drawn from under them, and they were launched into eternity. "

SOURCE 8 A Denver newspaper report on a vigilante hanging in 1879

" The hanging was not only well deserved but a positive gain to the country, saving it at least five or six thousand dollars. "

SOURCE 9 The victims of a vigilante hanging

SOURCE 10 The editor of the *Idaho World*, 2 September 1865

" A general lawlessness prevails through all these territories of Montana, Idaho, Colorado and Utah resolving itself in the form of these vigilante committees. Everywhere they have brought trouble upon the community. The remedy for the existing evils is greater than the evils. "

Billy the Kid: hero or killer?

HENRY MCCARTY, ALIAS William H. Bonney, alias Billy the Kid, was born in New York in 1859. As a child he moved with his mother and brother to New Mexico, where his mother remarried. Little is known of his early life. In his teens he was imprisoned for stealing, only to escape from jail, a feat he repeated more than once. His most serious brush with the law was apparently in 1877, when he killed a man who had been bullying him. After this he became a cattle rustler but inevitably there is little hard evidence of this.

He then worked as a cowboy for an English rancher, John Tunstall. This led to his involvement in the Lincoln County War of 1878. This war was similar to the Johnson County War but with one important difference. In Lincoln County the struggle was not between cattle barons and small ranchers. Instead it was between two rival groups of businessmen and cattle barons.

On 18 February 1878 John Tunstall was murdered, triggering a range war. This war involved cowboys and gunfighters on both sides. It continued until July, ending in a three-day battle in the main street of Lincoln. Billy was drawn into the conflict and by its end had gained a reputation as a top gunfighter. Afterwards his efforts to live within the law failed and he became an outlaw. The sources that follow trace his later career. He was shot dead by Sheriff Pat Garrett on 14 July 1881 at Fort Sumner, New Mexico.

These are generally agreed to be accurate details of Billy's life. But around him have developed a number of myths – that he killed 21 men, one for each year of his life, and that he was more a hero than a murderer, particularly to the Mexicans. Why have such myths developed?

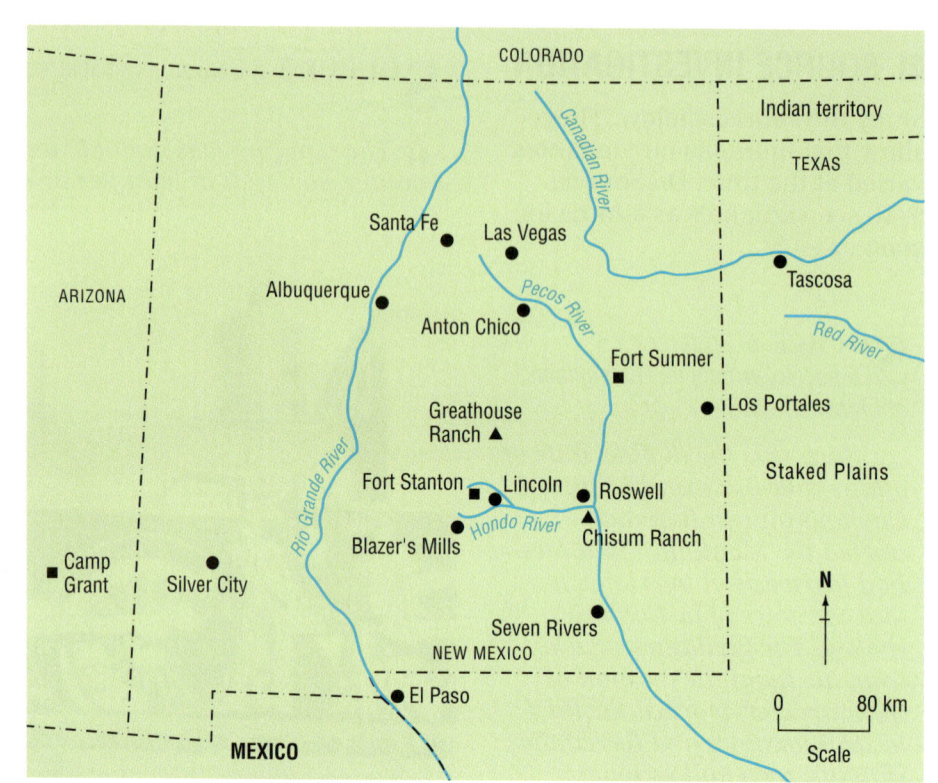

SOURCE 1 A map of New Mexico

■ TASK

Your task is to decide on the following questions.

1. Do you think it is likely that Billy the Kid killed 21 men?
2. Is the myth that he was a gunfighting hero believable?
3. How has that myth developed?

The sources on the next three pages will help you to decide. As you study each source, record your ideas on a table like the one below.

Source	
What was the purpose of its author?	
Is it reliable?	
Is it sympathetic to Billy?	
Was Billy a gunfighter?	
Was Billy an outlaw?	
Was Billy a killer? (of how many?)	

You should now be able to reach answers to questions 1–3. Are your answers the same as those of other people in your group, or different?

BILLY THE KID: HERO OR KILLER?

SOURCE 3 The cover of a dime novel, August 1881. Wildly inaccurate dime novels about Western characters appeared both during their lives and after their deaths

SOURCE 2 A tintype (a type of photograph) of Billy taken at Fort Sumner in 1880. As tintypes are reversed images this image has sometimes been printed back to front. This has confused people into thinking that Billy was left-handed. One Hollywood film of his life, made in 1957, was actually called *The Left Handed Gun*

1. How does the cover (Source 3) try to 'sell' the book?

SOURCE 4 The Cover of Pat Garrett's biography of Billy, 1882. The biography was on sale shortly after Billy's death. Although it sold relatively few copies it is important since so many later writers used it as a reference source

2. How does the cover (Source 4) try to 'sell' this book?
3. Why would Pat Garrett want to write such a book?
4. Which of the two books, Source 3 and Source 4, would you expect to be more accurate? Why?

117

BILLY THE KID: HERO OR KILLER?

SOURCE 5 Billy's killing of Deputy Robert Olinger, taken from Pat Garrett's biography of Billy, 1882. This incident took place when Billy was escaping from arrest. He shot Olinger from the balcony of the building in which he was being held prisoner. Billy used a shotgun

SOURCE 7 An illustration of Billy killing a man, taken from a dime novel. It shows Billy with two right hands

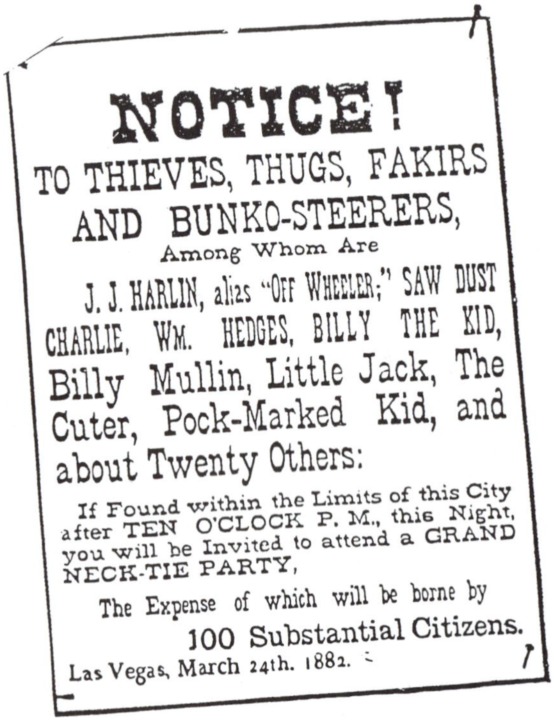

NOTICE!
TO THIEVES, THUGS, FAKIRS AND BUNKO-STEERERS,
Among Whom Are
J. J. HARLIN, alias "OFF WHEELER;" SAW DUST CHARLIE, WM. HEDGES, BILLY THE KID, Billy Mullin, Little Jack, The Cuter, Pock-Marked Kid, and about Twenty Others:
If Found within the Limits of this City after TEN O'CLOCK P. M., this Night, you will be Invited to attend a GRAND NECK-TIE PARTY,
The Expense of which will be borne by
100 Substantial Citizens.
Las Vegas, March 24th. 1882.

SOURCE 6 A vigilante poster from Las Vegas

5. Does the fact that the artist (Source 7) has drawn Billy with two right hands make you discount this as a source?
6. Do you think it is possible that the artist never witnessed this event but made it up?

BILLY THE KID: HERO OR KILLER?

SOURCE 8 The cover of a biography of Billy by the historian Robert M. Utley, 1989

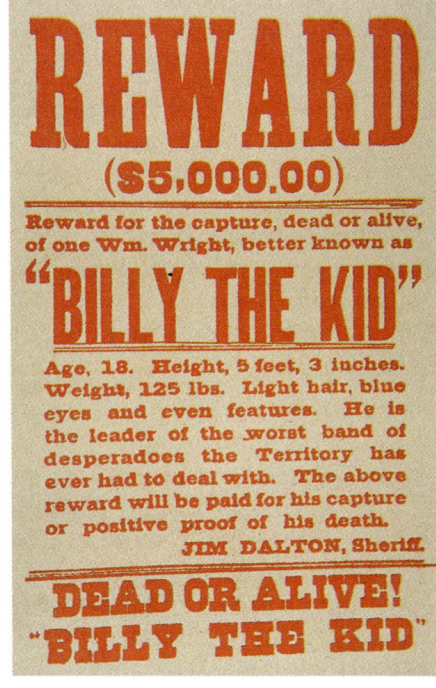

ROBERT M. UTLEY
Billy the Kid
A Short and Violent Life

REWARD
($5,000.00)
Reward for the capture, dead or alive, of one Wm. Wright, better known as
"BILLY THE KID"
Age, 18. Height, 5 feet, 3 inches. Weight, 125 lbs. Light hair, blue eyes and even features. He is the leader of the worst band of desperadoes the Territory has ever had to deal with. The above reward will be paid for his capture or positive proof of his death.
JIM DALTON, Sheriff.

DEAD OR ALIVE!
"BILLY THE KID"

SOURCE 9 Wanted poster produced by the governor of New Mexico, 13 December 1880

7. Compare this poster with Source 6, the vigilante poster. Which is more likely to give accurate information? Why?

8. How does the film director attempt to glamorise Billy and his companions in this scene?

SOURCE 10 A still from the film *Young Guns*, the most recent film version of the Billy the Kid story, 1988. There have been more than 40 Hollywood films based upon his life

Abilene: law and order in a cow town

IN 1867 ABILENE WAS just a collection of huts but it had the four essentials needed to become a shipping point for cattle.

- It was on the Kansas Pacific Railroad, linking it to the markets in the East.
- It had a river to provide water for cattle herds and good grazing to feed them while they were being held before shipment.
- It was at the northern end of the Chisholm cattle trail from Texas.
- It had military protection from nearby Fort Riley.

Its potential was recognised by Joseph McCoy, who built shipping pens and advertised it to Texas cattlemen and to the Chicago cattle buyers. The first herd was shipped east in 1867. For the next five years Abilene was a booming cow town, thanks to McCoy's enterprise.

The cattle drives brought prosperity to Abilene and its citizens but also brought problems of law and order. With the cattle came the cowboys. At the end of the 1600-km drive they were paid their wages. After hard months on the townless trail and with money in their pockets they expected to celebrate, as you have already seen on pages 100–103. They spent their money in the saloons, at the gambling tables and at the brothels. The town population in winter was approximately 500 but by June this had jumped to something like 7000. This was due to the arrival of the cowboys and those who came to make money out of them, the gamblers, HURDY-GURDY GIRLS and prostitutes.

Their wild behaviour was made worse by the ill-feeling that remained at the end of the Civil War. Most of the cowboys were Texans, southerners and supporters of the Confederacy, whilst the people of Abilene were supporters of the Union.

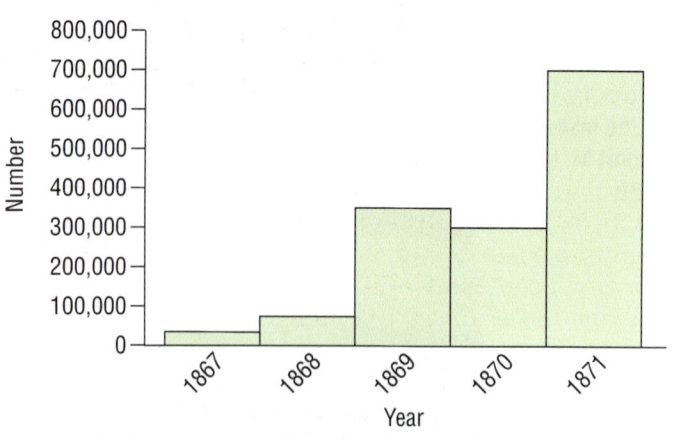

SOURCE 1 Numbers of cattle shipped east from Abilene by the Kansas Pacific Railroad

1. The average-sized herd of 1500 to 3000 cattle was driven by a crew of between twelve and twenty cowboys. In 1871 roughly how many cowboys may have passed through Abilene?

Wild Bill Hickok (1837–76)

In 1871 the citizens of Abilene hired James Butler (Wild Bill) Hickok as town marshal. During the Civil War Hickok had fought for the Union. He had made his name as a gunfighter in 1865 when he killed Davis Tutt. Since then he had killed at least three men. While he was marshal of Hays City he had arrested Tom Custer, brother of George (see page 140). In fighting off a revenge attack Hickok shot and killed a soldier. He was forced to escape on the Kansas Pacific Railroad from the angry men of the Seventh Cavalry.

SOURCE 2 Wild Bill Hickok, with his trademark ivory-hilted pistols worn reversed for a quick draw. He claimed to have killed more than 100 men but the evidence suggests he killed fewer than ten

As town marshal of Abilene he was paid $150 per month and he added to his income by gambling. Some of the town's citizens disapproved of him as he drank too much and lived with a succession of prostitutes. But he did keep the cowboys under control and enforced a ban on carrying weapons in the town. Eventually, in a gunfight, over either gambling or a woman, he killed a man called Phil Coe and, accidentally, his own deputy, Mike Williams. After that his contract was not renewed. One citizen commented, 'He acted only too ready to shoot down, to kill outright.' Others valued his success in maintaining law and order.

In 1872 the citizens of Abilene made it known that the cattle and cowboys were no longer welcome. The cattle drives moved on to other towns and Abilene no longer needed a highly paid gunfighter to keep the peace.

In 1873 Hickok toured with Buffalo Bill in the melodrama *Scouts of the Plains*. He then went back to drifting from one Western town to the next, drinking and gambling. In 1876, while he was playing poker at the Number Ten Saloon in Deadwood, he was shot in the back of the head by Jack McCall. McCall blamed Hickok for the murder of his brother. Hickok died holding a hand of a pair of aces and a pair of eights. This became known as a 'dead man's hand'.

John Wesley Hardin (1853–95)

Hardin was the son of a Methodist minister, but became the most feared gunfighter in Texas. In 1871 he arrived in Abilene at the end of a cattle drive. Wild Bill Hickok had received a handbill offering a reward for the arrest of Hardin. Hickok told Hardin that he would not arrest him for any crimes he had committed in Texas. Instead Hickok warned that if Hardin killed anyone in Abilene he would not get out of town alive.

One night Hardin did kill a man. There are two versions of the story. In one, the man unlocked and entered Hardin's room while he was in bed. In the other, Hardin shot the man through the bedroom wall because the man's snoring was disturbing him. Whatever the truth, Hardin escaped. Another story concerns two incidents while he was working as a cowboy on a cattle drive. In the first, he shot an Indian who was demanding a toll. In the second, he got into a row with five Mexican cowboys and shot them all. He was eventually captured and imprisoned for his crimes in 1874. After his release he was finally shot from behind, and killed, by a policeman whom he was threatening.

SOURCE 3 The Texas outlaw, John Wesley Hardin. In his autobiography he claimed to have killed 42 men but the evidence suggests he killed 20, and that many of these killings were racially motivated. This still makes him the West's deadliest gunfighter

ABILENE: LAW AND ORDER IN A COW TOWN

■ **ACTIVITY**

You are going to write a Western short story set in Abilene in 1871. You already know a lot about ranchers and homesteaders from your work in Chapter 5. You also know about outlaws and lawmen from your work in Chapter 6. You should use this knowledge to help you.

Study the artist's illustration of Abilene. This will give you an idea of what the town was like. Read the description of how the town developed. Discuss with a partner what sort of people would be living in the town and what they might do. Don't forget that as well as the cowboys from the cattle drives there will be local homesteaders who come into town for supplies.

For your short story you must follow this recipe.

1. The year is 1871. It is the last night of a cattle drive. The cattle are waiting outside the town. Your story can cover a period of no more than one or two days.
2. Your story may have no more than three main characters. These can be real people such as Wild Bill Hickok and John Wesley Hardin, or they can be fictional. They can include some cowboys – a hot-headed drunken cowboy, a young heroic cowboy, a new and inexperienced trail boss. You might also want to include a saloon girl or a homesteader's wife.
3. The events of your story can happen in only two places, Abilene and the camp fire by the chuck wagon.
4. Your story must include a storm.
5. Your story should have a twist in it.

Don't forget that a good Western is one which is exciting but believable. You need characters and a plot that your reader will find believable, and a historical setting that is authentic.

SOURCE 4 A modern illustration of Abilene in 1871

ABILENE: LAW AND ORDER IN A COW TOWN

SOURCE 5 A saloon girl in the 1880s

section 3

WHY DID THE INDIANS LOSE THE STRUGGLE FOR THE PLAINS?

Conflict on the Plains: a chronology

WHEN OUTSIDERS AND Indians first met on the Great Plains their relations were generally good. As you have seen earlier in this book, the Indians and mountain men lived peacefully together, with some of the mountain men marrying Indian women. Even when there were growing numbers of travellers crossing the Plains to California, Oregon and Salt Lake City there was relatively little conflict. It was only when outsiders began to settle on the Plains, on land the Plains Indians regarded as their own, that trouble began.

In this section we are going to examine that conflict, analyse its causes and look at the reasons why it ended as it did, with the defeat of the Indians at Wounded Knee. The timeline below summarises these events.

SOURCE 1 A timeline showing the key phases in the conflict over the Great Plains

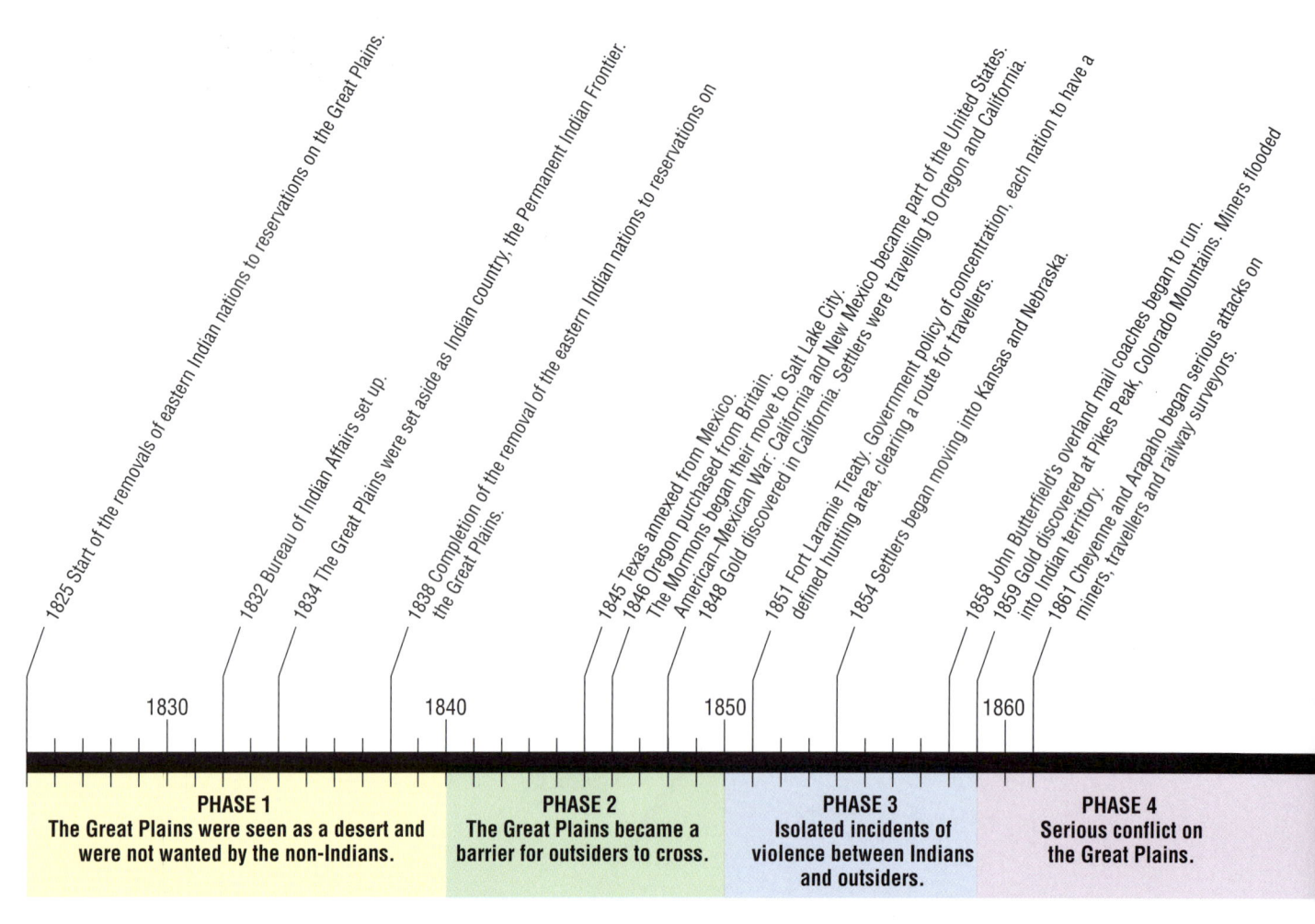

- 1825 Start of the removals of eastern Indian nations to reservations on the Great Plains.
- 1832 Bureau of Indian Affairs set up.
- 1834 The Great Plains were set aside as Indian country, the Permanent Indian Frontier.
- 1838 Completion of the removal of the eastern Indian nations to reservations on the Great Plains.
- 1845 Texas annexed from Mexico.
- 1846 Oregon purchased from Britain. The Mormons began their move to Salt Lake City.
- American–Mexican War. California and New Mexico became part of the United States.
- 1848 Gold discovered in California. Settlers were travelling to Oregon and California.
- 1851 Fort Laramie Treaty. Government policy of concentration, each nation to have a defined hunting area, clearing a route for travellers.
- 1854 Settlers began moving into Kansas and Nebraska.
- 1858 John Butterfield's overland mail coaches began to run.
- 1859 Gold discovered at Pikes Peak, Colorado Mountains. Miners flooded into Indian territory.
- 1861 Cheyenne and Arapaho began serious attacks on miners, travellers and railway surveyors.

PHASE 1 The Great Plains were seen as a desert and were not wanted by the non-Indians.

PHASE 2 The Great Plains became a barrier for outsiders to cross.

PHASE 3 Isolated incidents of violence between Indians and outsiders.

PHASE 4 Serious conflict on the Great Plains.

The defeat of the Indians and the destruction of their way of life is a complex story. Many different factors combined to allow the settlers to win the struggle for the Plains. In this section you will examine three of the most important factors in detail:

- the role of the US army – 'the military solution'
- the destruction of the buffalo herds
- the reservation policy.

On pages 157–158 you will be able to pull these factors together with the others which you have investigated in Chapters 1–6, and reach your own conclusions as to why the settlers won, and the Indians lost, the struggle for the Plains.

So, first, the story of the 'Indian wars' . . .

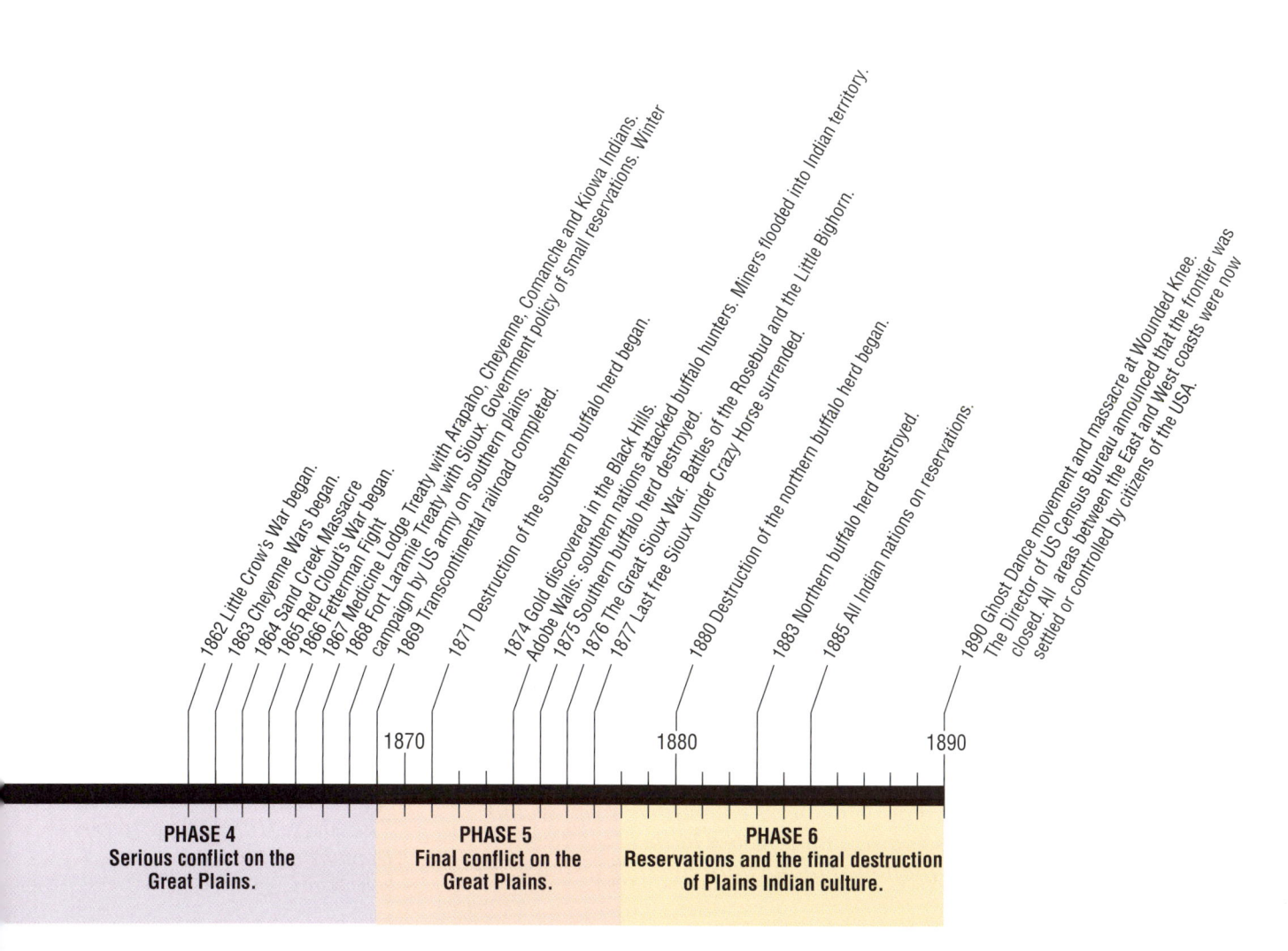

1862 Little Crow's War began.
1863 Cheyenne Wars began.
1864 Sand Creek Massacre
1865 Red Cloud's War began.
1866 Fetterman Fight
1867 Medicine Lodge Treaty with Arapaho, Cheyenne, Comanche and Kiowa Indians. Government policy of small reservations. Winter campaign by US army on southern plains.
1868 Fort Laramie Treaty with Sioux.
1869 Transcontinental railroad completed.
1871 Destruction of the southern buffalo herd began.
1874 Gold discovered in the Black Hills. Adobe Walls: southern nations attacked buffalo hunters. Miners flooded into Indian territory.
1875 Southern buffalo herd destroyed.
1876 The Great Sioux War. Battles of the Rosebud and the Little Bighorn.
1877 Last free Sioux under Crazy Horse surrendered.
1880 Destruction of the northern buffalo herd began.
1883 Northern buffalo herd destroyed.
1885 All Indian nations on reservations.
1890 Ghost Dance movement and massacre at Wounded Knee. The Director of US Census Bureau announced that the frontier was closed. All areas between the East and West coasts were now settled or controlled by citizens of the USA.

PHASE 4 Serious conflict on the Great Plains.

PHASE 5 Final conflict on the Great Plains.

PHASE 6 Reservations and the final destruction of Plains Indian culture.

chapter 7

WHAT ROLE DID THE US ARMY PLAY IN THE DEFEAT OF THE PLAINS INDIANS?

Negotiate or exterminate?

FROM THE 1840s ONWARDS the Plains Indians were seen as a problem, the 'Indian Problem'. They occupied land that was wanted by travellers, settlers, ranchers, miners and the railroad companies. They stood in the way of the United States' 'Manifest Destiny'. Opinions differed as to the best solution to this problem.

The 'negotiators'

On the one hand there were the people who wanted a negotiated solution to the Indian problem. These were mainly people living in the East. They did include some Westerners, government officials such as Indian agents who by working with the Indians had gained some understanding of them and their way of life. These people believed that aggressive tactics would only make matters worse. After the four bloody years of the Civil War they had had enough of fighting. They believed that responsibility for Indian affairs should be kept with the Bureau of Indian Affairs and not given to the US army. Once a negotiated solution had been achieved, they wanted to follow a policy of cultural assimilation. In other words, they hoped through education and missionary work to transform the Plains Indians into good Christian farmers.

The 'exterminators'

On the other hand there were the exterminators. These were mainly people living in the West: settlers, ranchers, miners and the soldiers sent to protect them. They were both the people with most to gain if the Indians were removed, and those most likely to have suffered from Indian hostility. These people believed that the only solution was to destroy the Plains Indians, a solution that we would call genocide today. As far as they were concerned the Indians were savages. They believed that the soldiers had experience of and were firm with the Indians. They believed that the Bureau of Indian Affairs should be under the control of the army. They wanted a military solution to the Indian problem, the destruction of the Indians. This group also included some of those who profited by selling beef and other supplies to the US army.

■ **SOURCE INVESTIGATION**

How should the government deal with the Indians? Study Sources 1–8. With your partner discuss which sources you would use to support your argument in a debate if you were either:

a) a 'negotiator', or
b) an 'exterminator'.

You need to prepare your argument and list the points you wish to make to back it up.

You may wish to use other sources from elsewhere in this book.

SOURCE 1 A description of the Sand Creek Massacre by Major E. W. Wynkoop, taken from his testimony before the military tribunal in November 1864

From the evidence of officers at this post, I understand that on 28 November 1864, Colonel J.M. Chivington, with the third regiment of Colorado cavalry, attacked the camp of friendly Indians, the majority of whom were women and children. Everyone whom I have spoken to agrees that the most fearful atrocities were committed; women and children were killed and scalped; children shot at their mothers' breast, and all the bodies mutilated in the most horrible manner.

SOURCE 2 An extract from a speech by Senator Morrill to Congress in 1867

We have come to the point in the history of the country that there is no place beyond the white population to which you can remove the Indian, and the precise question is will you exterminate him, or will you fix a lasting place for him.

SOURCE 3 From a speech by Sitting Bull

We want no white men here. The Black Hills belong to me. If the whites try to take them, I will fight.

NEGOTIATE OR EXTERMINATE?

SOURCE 4 An engraving showing an Indian attack on homesteaders

SOURCE 5 An editorial from the *New York Times* commenting upon a speech by Red Cloud

"The clear view that this unlettered savage has of what he claims as his rights, and what he resents as the wrongs against him, shows very plainly the need for negotiating with the leaders of the aboriginal 'nations', on some straightforward and intelligible principle.

The attempt to flatter and fool the Indians as if they were stupid, ought to be abandoned, as should the policy of hunting them down like wild beasts."

SOURCE 6 A speech attributed to Red Cloud

"The white man made us many promises, more than I can remember, but they never kept but one; they promised to take our land, and they took it."

SOURCE 7 A comment by General William Tecumseh Sherman

"We must act with vindictive earnestness against the Sioux, even to their extermination, men, women, and children."

SOURCE 8 A print from an engraving by Frederic Remington showing cavalrymen discovering the bodies of their fallen comrades. Their dead bodies have been shot full of arrows

Why did the Sioux go to war?

THE DEBATE ON page 126 was not a balanced one, since those who favoured a military solution were the ones with most influence where it really mattered, in the West. It was events in the West which finally decided government policy towards the Indians.

The diagram on the right shows the pattern of events which we find repeated again and again from the 1840s onwards.

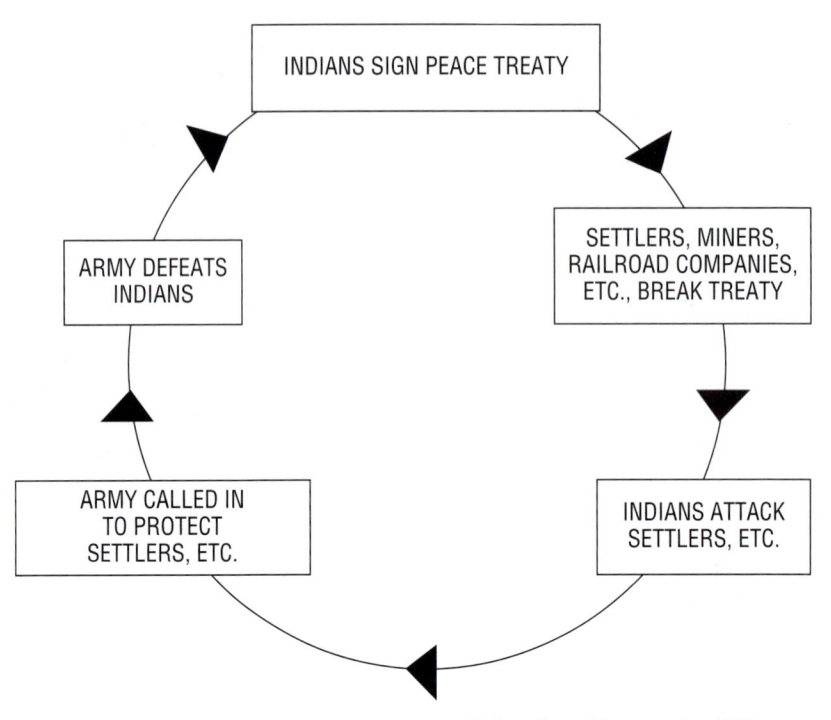

```
           INDIANS SIGN PEACE TREATY
         ↗                           ↘
   ARMY DEFEATS              SETTLERS, MINERS,
     INDIANS                 RAILROAD COMPANIES,
                             ETC., BREAK TREATY
         ↑                           ↓
   ARMY CALLED IN              INDIANS ATTACK
   TO PROTECT                  SETTLERS, ETC.
   SETTLERS, ETC.
         ↖                           ↙
```

■ TASK

In order to understand how and why this happened we are again going to concentrate on one Indian nation, the Sioux. There were three major conflicts between the Sioux and the US army. You are going to construct a summary table of these wars.

	Little Crow's War	Red Cloud's War	The Great Sioux War
When was the war?			
What allies did the Sioux have?			
What caused the war?			
Was the US army called in to protect settlers or miners?			
Who won?			
What did the settlers gain or lose?			
What did the Sioux gain or lose?			

SOURCE 1 Big Eagle (Wamditanka), a Santee Sioux leader

The whites were always trying to make the Indians give up their life and live like white men – go to farming, work hard and do as they did – and the Indians did not know how to do that, and did not want to anyway ... If the Indians had tried to make the whites live like them, the whites would have resisted, and it was the same way with many Indians.

Little Crow's War (1861–62) – an early failure of the reservation system

In 1861 the reservation solution was introduced by the US government. Plains Indians were to be moved to special areas called reservations. There they would receive annual cash payments from the government and would be taught how to become self-sufficient farmers.

Causes of the war

The 12,000 people of the Santee Sioux lived on a reservation in southern Minnesota. Life for them was hard, and in 1861 cutworms devastated their corn crops. They were forced to live on credit but when their annual cash payment did not arrive in June 1862 their credit at the government store was stopped. The Santee Sioux were then unable to buy food, and as their situation got worse the threat of violence grew.

WHY DID THE SIOUX GO TO WAR?

SOURCE 2 Little Crow, a Santee leader, speaking to the Indian agent Thomas Galbraith, August 1862

We have waited a long time ... We have no food, but here are these stores, filled with food. We ask that you, the agent, make some arrangement by which we can get food from the stores, or else we may take our own step to keep ourselves from starving. When men are hungry they help themselves.

SOURCE 3 Andrew Myrick, a trader at the Santee Sioux Agency, June 1862. He was killed in the Agency attack, his body mutilated and his mouth stuffed with grass

If they are hungry let them eat grass or their own dung.

SOURCE 4 A survivor of the attack on New Ulm

They came down upon us like the wind.

SOURCE 5 General John Pope

You have no idea of the uncontrollable panic everywhere in this country. The most horrible massacres have been committed; children nailed alive to trees and houses; women violated and then disembowelled – everything that horrible ingenuity could devise.

The chain of events

Little Crow tried to restrain his starving people but violence erupted on 17 August 1862, when four Santee Sioux men killed five settlers, three men and two women. The next day Little Crow led an attack on the Indian Agency. Of the people at the Agency, twenty men were killed, ten women and children were captured and 47 escaped, many helped by their friends among the Santee Sioux. Later Little Crow ambushed the company of 45 soldiers marching to the aid of the Agency; only 24 escaped alive.

The fighting continued until September. During that time Little Crow attacked, but failed to capture, Fort Ridgely and the town of New Ulm. He was never again able to hold together a large enough force of warriors to defeat the army. Nor was he able to persuade other Indian groups to join him. Instead, numerous smaller settlements were attacked. There was indiscriminate killing of settlers by undisciplined bands of young Santee Sioux while their leaders were fighting the army. Over 700 settlers were killed. Massive army reinforcements were sent in, withdrawn from Civil War battlefields. By September the Santee Sioux realised that they could not win. While Little Crow and some of his followers set off westwards the rest of the Santee Sioux surrendered to General Sibley.

Results

By October, 2000 Santee Sioux had been captured or surrendered. General Sibley tried them by military commission, and by 5 November 303 Santee Sioux warriors had been sentenced to death. The evidence against them was weak and President Abraham Lincoln commuted the sentences of all but 38. These 38, including three who were wholly innocent, being the victims of mistaken identity, were hanged in December 1862.

The remainder of the Santee Sioux, roughly 2000, were transferred to a new reservation, Crow Creek on the Missouri River, in 1863. The land was barren, the water unfit for drinking and food scarce. During the first winter nearly 400 died. Amongst their visitors during this period of hardship was Sitting Bull. The situation he found there would later affect his attitude to the settlers and outside authorities.

SOURCE 6 A photograph of Little Crow taken before the war. He was shot near Hutchinson, Minnesota, by a farmer who caught him picking raspberries in his field, in June 1863. The farmer received a reward of $500 for Little Crow's scalp, which was displayed at the state historical society in St Paul, Minnesota

WHY DID THE SIOUX GO TO WAR?

SOURCE 7 A contemporary engraving of the execution of Santee Sioux warriors in 1862

SOURCE 8 A transcript from a Channel 4 TV programme, *The Wild West*, 1995

"They were hanged on the chilly morning of 26 December in Mankato, while a few whites taunted and jeered."

SOURCE 9 A contemporary engraving of the execution

■ **TASK**

Sources 7 and 9 are engravings that show the execution of the 38 Santee warriors sentenced to death. A single rope was pulled by Captain William J. Duley to spring the traps underneath the warriors simultaneously.

1. List the differences and similarities between these two illustrations of the event. You could comment on the buildings, crowd, scaffold and soldiers.
2. Read Source 8. Which illustration is best supported by Source 8?
3. Can you suggest reasons why these two interpretations of the same event are different?

130

WHY DID THE SIOUX GO TO WAR?

Red Cloud's War (1865–68)

Causes

In 1862 gold was discovered in the Rocky Mountains of Montana. New mining towns such as Virginia City sprang up as miners rushed to the area along a new trail, the Bozeman Trail. This new trail left the Oregon Trail near Fort Laramie and crossed Sioux lands. It broke the existing peace treaty. The government failed to stop these miners from breaking the peace treaty, and the reaction of the Sioux was to attack travellers along the trail.

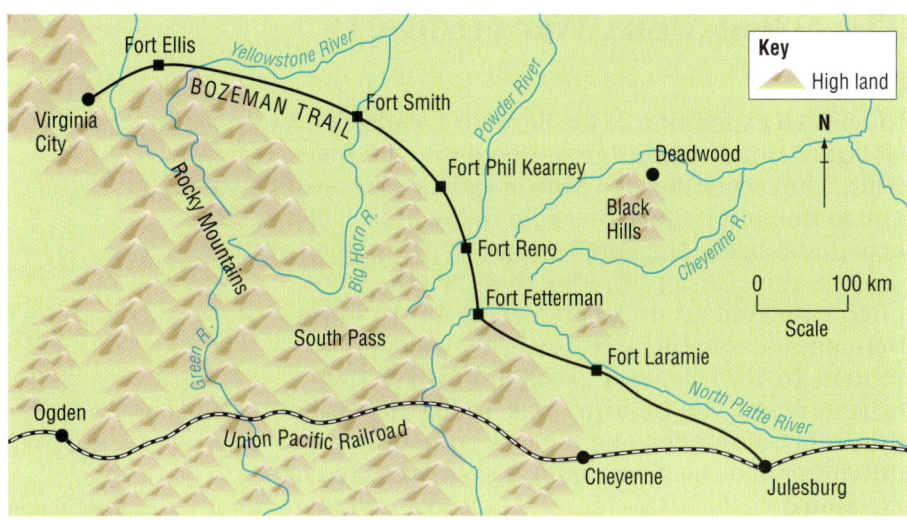

SOURCE 10 A map showing the Bozeman Trail and the chain of forts established along it

The chain of events

Sioux attacks on travellers continued until 1866, when the government tried to solve the problem. Their first step was to open peace talks with the Sioux leader, Red Cloud. However, at the same time the government also ordered the US army to begin work on a chain of forts along the trail. Red Cloud broke off the peace talks in disgust and attacked the army. By the winter of 1866 the soldiers were under siege in their forts. The Sioux were not strong enough to capture the forts, which were equipped with artillery. They did wipe out one detachment of 80 men, led by Captain William Fetterman, who were lured into a trap outside Fort Phil Kearney. In this fight the Indians suffered heavy casualties, one estimate being almost 200 killed and wounded. This reflected the advantage the better-armed soldiers had.

Since the superior firepower of the soldiers prevented the capture of Fort Phil Kearney, Red Cloud made sure that it was ringed by his warriors. The army could not move safely outside the fort and no travellers could use the Bozeman Trail. This was the major achievement of Red Cloud: that he kept together a force of several Sioux bands, plus some of their allies, the Arapaho and the Cheyenne. He managed to keep them fighting through the winter months. He also had the vision to try to persuade the Crow, traditional enemies of the Sioux, to fight with him. Although he was unsuccessful in this he did keep the army on the defensive.

Results

In 1868 the government was forced to admit defeat and change its policy. The government realised that the Sioux and their allies could not be defeated militarily. At the same time an alternative route to the gold-mining areas had been opened. So the government agreed to withdraw from the forts and under the terms of the Fort Laramie Treaty the Great Sioux Reservation was created. No non-Indian settlers were to be allowed ever to enter this land. Red Cloud agreed to this treaty. When the soldiers withdrew the Sioux moved in and burned the forts to the ground. The Sioux had won – or had they?

For Red Cloud it marked the end of his fighting against the US army. From this point on he lived peacefully on the Sioux reservation. However, not all the Sioux agreed with the peace treaty. Red Cloud's power decreased and many of the Sioux went on to follow younger, more militant leaders such as Sitting Bull and Crazy Horse.

SOURCE 11 Red Cloud, photographed by Charles M. Bell in Washington DC, 1880. He was born around 1819 near the forks of the Platte River, and died in 1909. He was the successful war leader of the Sioux up to 1868. Afterwards he remained a respected councillor on the reservation. In 1880 he worked successfully to show the corruption of the Indian agent running the Sioux reservation

WHY DID THE SIOUX GO TO WAR?

The Great Sioux War (1876–77)

Causes
In 1874 an expedition of the Seventh Cavalry led by George Armstrong Custer was sent into the Black Hills. They were there to protect railway surveyors and to find out if there was gold in the area. This expedition broke the Fort Laramie Treaty signed six years earlier. Custer reported that the hills were filled with gold 'from the grassroots down'. From that moment the Black Hills were invaded by miners. In 1875 General Crook found over 1000 miners there. The US army was unable to prevent this influx of miners, and the government was unwilling to do so. Some miners were attacked by the Sioux.

The government then made an offer of $6,000,000 to buy the Black Hills or $400,000 a year for the mineral rights. This was a ridiculous offer to the Sioux: to them the Black Hills were sacred as the place where their nation began. The government offer was rejected. Relations between the Sioux and the government were very poor.

The chain of events
In December 1875 all Sioux were ordered to return to their reservation. In winter it was impossible for them to obey this order even if they wished to. There were approximately 7000 Indians with Sitting Bull and Crazy Horse in the Powder River country, mainly Sioux but also Arapaho and Cheyenne. This number shows two things: the strength of the Indians' anger over the Black Hills, and Sitting Bull's great reputation as a leader. Since his visit to the Santee Sioux back in 1863 he had been consistently hostile to outside authorities. He had refused to live on the reservation and many Sioux had turned to his leadership.

By February 1876 the army was instructed to treat all Indians outside the reservation as hostile. General Philip Sheridan ordered a three-pronged campaign. The campaign that followed led to the Battle of the Little Bighorn, a great victory for the Indians and a serious defeat for the army. You will study this more closely on pages 138–45.

Results
News of the defeat reached the rest of America on 4 July – the hundredth anniversary of the USA's independence. The public reaction was one of great shock. No effort was spared in supporting the army campaign that followed. Two new forts were built on the Yellowstone River and 2500 reinforcements were sent west.

SOURCE 12 A photograph of Sitting Bull. Born at Grand River, South Dakota, in around 1834, he became an important chief of the Sioux after Red Cloud made peace in 1868. He refused to live on the Great Sioux Reservation. After the Battle of the Little Bighorn he led his followers to safety in Canada. By 1881 hunger forced him and his followers to return to live on the reservation. He was still widely respected among the Sioux. On his return from Canada he took part in Buffalo Bill's Wild West Show for a while but returned to the reservation when there was a government attempt to take more Sioux lands

After the Battle of the Little Bighorn, the Indians had split up into their bands. These bands were followed and attacked throughout the autumn and winter. There were too many soldiers for the Indians to fight while also trying to protect their women and children. Also, they were all short of ammunition and their food and supplies were destroyed or exhausted. One by one, the bands gave in and returned to the reservation. By the autumn most were back. On 5 May 1877 Crazy Horse and his followers rode into the reservation and surrendered. The day before, Sitting Bull and his followers had escaped over the border into Canada. The armed resistance of the Sioux was over.

Back on the reservation the Sioux were forced to sell the Black Hills, the Powder River country and the Bighorn Mountains. They were put under military rule. Eventually the reservation itself was split up into smaller reservations, and more land was taken from the Sioux. Finally, their horses and weapons were taken away from them. Never again were the Sioux able to fight in any great numbers against the army.

SOURCE 14 The death of Sitting Bull. When the government learned in 1890 that Sitting Bull was involved with the Ghost Dance Movement (see page 155), Sioux Indian Police were sent to arrest him. In the confrontation that followed he was shot dead on 15 December 1890

MASSACRED

GEN. CUSTER AND 261 MEN THE VICTIMS.

NO OFFICER OR MAN OF 5 COMPANIES LEFT TO TELL THE TALE.

3 Days Desperate Fighting by Maj. Reno and the Remainder of the Seventh.

Full Details of the Battle.

LIST OF KILLED AND WOUNDED.

THE BISMARCK TRIBUNE'S SPECIAL CORRESPONDENT SLAIN.

Squaws Mutilate and Rob the Dead

Victims Captured Alive Tortured in a Most Fiendish Manner.

What Will Congress Do About It?

Shall This Be the Beginning of the End?

SOURCE 13 News of the Battle of the Little Bighorn as it appeared in the *Bismarck Tribune* on 6 July 1876

■ **TASK**

Write an essay comparing the leadership of Little Crow, Red Cloud and Sitting Bull.

a) Write a paragraph on each one, considering their achievements and failures.
b) Write your conclusion as to which of the three achieved most for the Sioux.

Was the US army well equipped for war with the Plains Indians?

IN THE 1840s AND 1850s the Army of the West was relatively weak. By 1856 an expanded army of 15,715 officers and men, in a network of 52 forts, was responsible for keeping the peace between Plains Indians and travellers and settlers over four million square kilometres. Trained to fight an enemy in fixed battles, they spent most of their time garrisoning the forts, patrolling the overland routes or searching in vain for the Indians. The fact that so many of them were infantry made the problem worse. Cavalry units were more expensive to maintain but infantry were little use against the well-mounted Plains Indians. The Indians fought only in small raids, not major battles. Close combat, unless the odds overwhelmingly favoured them, was avoided. So the two sides were fighting completely different kinds of war. One company commander commented, 'In fighting a campaign against Indians the front is all around, and the rear is nowhere.'

SOURCE 1 Everyday problems for enlisted men in the Army of the West

Poor food and living conditions
Poor-quality uniforms
Long periods of boredom
Long separation from family and friends
Low pay
Harsh, and often brutal, discipline
Hard field service
Harsh winters
Few opportunities for promotion
Danger of death from disease or enemy action

SOURCE 2 Six troopers from the Seventh Cavalry, photographed at Fort Lincoln

SOURCE 3 Members of the Tenth US Cavalry, an all-black regiment. Four black regiments served in the West: the Ninth and Tenth Cavalry and the Twenty-Fourth and Twenty-Fifth Infantry. According to legend, the Sioux called these men 'buffalo soldiers' because their tight curly hair and fighting spirit reminded them of the buffalo. They certainly gained a good reputation. Eleven black soldiers received the Medal of Honour for their bravery in fighting the Indians. Cavalrymen were equipped with single-shot or repeating rifles and sabres. The sabre was not very effective for fighting against Indians. The Seventh Cavalry did not carry theirs in the Little Bighorn campaign

WAS THE US ARMY WELL EQUIPPED FOR WAR WITH THE PLAINS INDIANS?

Enlisted men

Recruits to the army included not only Americans, but also many European immigrants. At times up to 50 per cent of recruits were Irish, whilst the number of German recruits was always high. The quality of the recruits was generally poor. New recruit Eugene Bandel wrote home to his parents in Germany, 'The greater part of the army consists of men who either do not care to work, or who, because of being addicted to drink, cannot find employment.' Two major consequences of this were drunkenness and desertion. In his memoirs Sergeant Percival Lowe wrote that ten per cent of his company could usually be found in the guardhouse for offences committed while drunk. In 1853 the Secretary of War declared that in an army of 10,000 nearly 1300 would receive a dishonourable discharge, whilst nearly 1500 would desert. In the year 1856 a total of 3223 men deserted.

Forts

The forts in the West were built to protect the overland routes and to keep watch over reservations. They served as a base from which soldiers could patrol the routes and also attack the Plains Indians. Although the Indians attacked forts on a number of occasions, such as the attack on Fort Ridgely during Little Crow's War and on Fort Phil Kearney during Red Cloud's War, they never managed to capture one. The combination of men and artillery, sometimes protected by walls, was too strong. This ensured that the army always had a defensive base on the Great Plains and helped them to launch the offensives that eventually inflicted military defeat on the Plains Indians.

SOURCE 4 General William Tecumseh Sherman's description of the forts in the West

Some of what are called military posts are mere collections of logs, ADOBES or mere holes in the ground, and are about as much forts as prarie dog villages might be called forts.

SOURCE 5 *Fort Laramie,* Wyoming, in 1837, painted by A.J. Miller

SOURCE 6 A map showing army forts in 1860

SOURCE 7 A typical fort described by a cavalryman in 1852

Some, I suppose, have a vague idea of what a fort is like in this country. The buildings are built of mud brick in a hollow square, leaving in the centre what is called a 'parade ground' where the military parades are held every morning. One side of the square is used as officers' quarters; the opposite side as a guard house, commissary department, offices, etc. The other two sides are soldiers' barracks. There is a flag staff in the centre from which the stars and stripes flash and wave in the breeze. Out of this square are to be found a hospital, dragoon stables, yards, etc.

135

WAS THE US ARMY WELL EQUIPPED FOR WAR WITH THE PLAINS INDIANS?

Indian scouts

In all its major campaigns the army was helped by its own Indian scouts. These were recruited from other Indian nations. For example, the Crow and the Shoshone, traditional enemies of the Sioux, fought for the army in numerous campaigns. They were invaluable for their knowledge of the country and of Sioux battle tactics. At the Battle of the Rosebud they saved General Crook's force from suffering heavier casualties than it actually did. The failure of the different nations to fight together against the US army contributed to their eventual defeat. Some far-sighted leaders, such as Red Cloud, attempted to get traditional enemies to fight together but the pattern of old warfare was too strong to break.

The impact of the Civil War

With the start of the American Civil War in 1861 the regular troops were withdrawn to fight in the East. They were replaced by volunteers. Lacking the discipline of the regular army, and sometimes led by men with political ambitions, the volunteers often made relations with the Plains Indians worse. The most notable example of their excesses was the Sand Creek Massacre. Colonel Chivington and his Colorado Volunteers attacked a Cheyenne village, killing 28 men and 105 women and children. This caused outrage in the East and led to the Cheyenne and their allies fighting a full-scale war against settlers and travellers for the next four years.

SOURCE 8 Curley, the Crow scout who survived the Battle of the Little Bighorn and carried the news back to General Terry. The Crow nation lost the Powder River country to the Sioux in war but now have it back. It is where the US government sited their reservation

At the end of the Civil War in 1865 the regular army replaced the volunteers. These seasoned soldiers, well led by experienced commanders, were able to police the West more effectively. They were also better armed, with modern rifles, revolvers and artillery. In encounter after encounter with the Indians this superior firepower enabled them to win, often against much greater numbers.

WAS THE US ARMY WELL EQUIPPED FOR WAR WITH THE PLAINS INDIANS?

New strategies

Two new strategies also helped to ensure eventual military success.

Total war

The first was the strategy of total war. This strategy had been successfully used by Generals Sherman and Sheridan during the Civil War and they brought it into use against the Plains Indians. 'Total war' meant waging war against a whole enemy population, not just against the fighting troops. However, it did not mean the killing of women and children. Instead it meant destroying all the food, shelter, clothing, possessions and animals of the Plains Indians. This left the victims with a choice between starvation, going to their relatives for help, or else going into the reservation and surrendering. This strategy demoralised the Plains Indians and strengthened the arguments of those in the bands who were in favour of peace.

Winter campaigns

The second strategy was that of winter campaigns. The Plains Indians were vulnerable to attack in winter. With the heavy snow and sub-zero temperatures, it was the time of year when they needed to stay in one place for long periods of time. It was also the time when they needed to conserve food supplies and the strength of their ponies. Defeat at such a time could be devastating.

The combination of all these factors enabled the army to defeat the Plains Indians in battle. However, the army was not the only reason for the final defeat of the Indians. The sections that follow tell you about the other important reasons for this defeat.

SOURCE 9 General Philip Henry Sheridan, born Albany, New York, 1831, and died Nonquitt, Massachusetts, 1888. Sheridan was one of the most successful generals during the American Civil War. Afterwards he was made commander-in-chief of the Army of the West. He was famously quoted as saying, 'The only good Indians I ever saw were dead', but he always denied saying this. He was responsible for the planning of the Little Bighorn campaign of 1876

■ TASK

1. What problems did the US army face in the wars against the Plains Indians?
2. The following were all equally important reasons for the army's success:

   ■ the network of forts
   ■ the use of Indian scouts
   ■ the development of 'total war'
   ■ the end of the American Civil War.

   Do you agree? Explain your answer.

■ CONNECTIONS

The US cavalryman fought the Indian warrior in the Plains Wars.

1. Compare their way of life. How were they similar? How were they different? You should compare where they lived, how they fought and the weapons they used. You should also consider their beliefs, their reasons for fighting and their idea of bravery.
2. What opinion would they have been likely to have of each other? What effect might this have on the conflict in the West?

Was Custer responsible for the defeat of the US army at the Battle of the Little Bighorn?

SOURCE 1 *Custer's Last Battle*, a painting completed by Edgar Paxson in 1893 after years of research. He visited the site and interviewed many of the survivors from both sides

THE BATTLE IN Sources 1 and 2 is generally known as the Battle of the Little Bighorn but is known as the Battle of the Greasy Grass by the Sioux.

At this battle on 25 June 1876 a US army regiment of 600 men was defeated by a combined force of Sioux, Cheyenne and Arapaho numbering approximately 2000 warriors. Out of the 600 US army soldiers, George Armstrong Custer and 263 officers and men were killed. Indian sources report their casualties as roughly 58 killed and over 60 wounded.

It is one of the most studied and painted battles in American history. There are over 950 paintings of this battle. It was the worst defeat of the US army by Indians. But artists and writers turned it into a heroic last stand. For many decades the battle made Custer famous as a great American hero.

WAS CUSTER RESPONSIBLE FOR THE DEFEAT OF THE US ARMY AT THE BATTLE OF THE LITTLE BIGHORN?

Nowadays, however, people see the battle in different ways. Some explain the defeat of the US army as Custer's fault. Others say it was the mistake of other army leaders. Some say it was the inspired leadership of Crazy Horse which was responsible. See what you think. Was Custer totally responsible for the defeat of the US army at the Battle of the Little Bighorn?

Let's start with Custer himself.

1. Compare Sources 1 and 2. Both show the same battle. In what ways are they similar? How are they different?

SOURCE 2 *The defeat of Custer at the Little Bighorn*, painted in about 1890 by Kicking Bear, who was involved in the battle. Kicking Bear was commissioned by Frederic Remington to paint this picture

WAS CUSTER RESPONSIBLE FOR THE DEFEAT OF THE US ARMY AT THE BATTLE OF THE LITTLE BIGHORN?

Viewpoints on Custer

Source 3 is a career chart of Custer. This interpretation of his career shows how different events contributed to his status as a hero. Over the next four pages you will decide whether you think it is an accurate assessment of Custer. Sources 5–9 give you the views of his contemporaries. Which of these people would agree with the interpretation given in the chart?

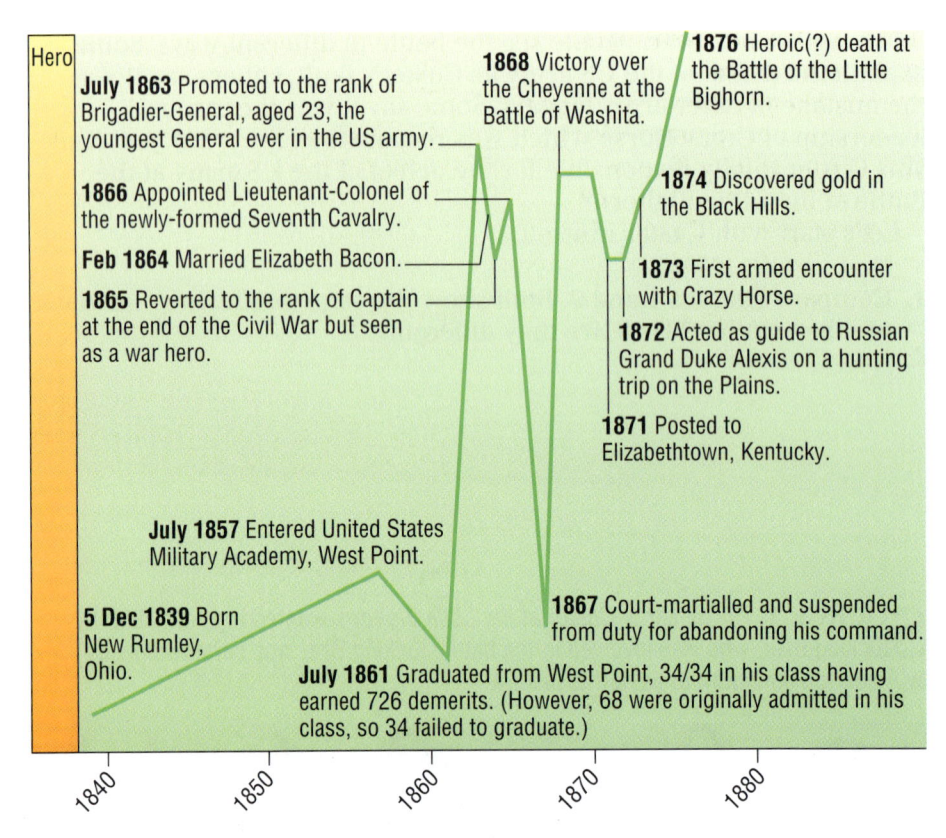

Hero

- **5 Dec 1839** Born New Rumley, Ohio.
- **July 1857** Entered United States Military Academy, West Point.
- **July 1861** Graduated from West Point, 34/34 in his class having earned 726 demerits. (However, 68 were originally admitted in his class, so 34 failed to graduate.)
- **July 1863** Promoted to the rank of Brigadier-General, aged 23, the youngest General ever in the US army.
- **Feb 1864** Married Elizabeth Bacon.
- **1865** Reverted to the rank of Captain at the end of the Civil War but seen as a war hero.
- **1866** Appointed Lieutenant-Colonel of the newly-formed Seventh Cavalry.
- **1867** Court-martialled and suspended from duty for abandoning his command.
- **1868** Victory over the Cheyenne at the Battle of Washita.
- **1871** Posted to Elizabethtown, Kentucky.
- **1872** Acted as guide to Russian Grand Duke Alexis on a hunting trip on the Plains.
- **1873** First armed encounter with Crazy Horse.
- **1874** Discovered gold in the Black Hills.
- **1876** Heroic(?) death at the Battle of the Little Bighorn.

SOURCE 3 The career of General George Armstrong Custer

SOURCE 4 *Portrait of Custer as Major General of Volunteers*, 1864. This is one of many paintings and photos for which Custer posed. He recognised the value of good publicity and at the Little Bighorn was accompanied by a newspaper reporter. This portrait was hung in his study at Fort Abraham Lincoln where he wrote his autobiography at the age of 25, *My Life on the Plains*. He wrote of himself, '... when I was verging upon manhood, my every thought was ambitious – not to be wealthy, not to be learned, but to be great'

2. Why do you think Custer chose to have this particular portrait hanging in his study?

WAS CUSTER RESPONSIBLE FOR THE DEFEAT OF THE US ARMY AT THE BATTLE OF THE LITTLE BIGHORN?

Views on Custer from his contemporaries

Sources 5–7 are the views of some of Custer's men. Source 8 is the view of one of his officers. Between 1 October 1866 and 1 October 1867, 512 men of the Seventh Cavalry deserted, a rate of 52 per cent. Many headed for the gold mines in Colorado and Montana.

SOURCE 5 Private Theodore Ewert, Seventh Cavalry

" The hardships and danger to his men, as well as the probable loss of life were worthy of but little considerations when dim visions of a star [indication of rank] floated before the mind of our Lieutenant Colonel. "

SOURCE 6 Corporal Jacob Horner, Seventh Cavalry

" He was too hard on the men and horses. He changed his mind too often. He was always right. He never conferred enough with his officers. When he got a notion, we had to go. "

SOURCE 7 Sergeant Charles A Windolf, Seventh Cavalry

" Some of the officers were friendly and easygoing with their troopers, but Custer struck me as being aloof and removed. "

SOURCE 8 Extracts from the letters of Captain Albert Barnitz, Seventh Cavalry, to his wife, written at Fort Hayes. Barnitz was wounded at the Battle of Washita in 1868 and this led to his disability retirement in 1870

*" **27 April 1867**
...I dare not tell you how many desertions we are having. They happen nightly. As many as ten non-commissioned officers and men have left in one night, with horses and arms!

17 May 1867
Today General Custer ordered the officer of the day to have the heads of six men shaved close to the head on one side of their head while the other side was left untouched. In this condition the men were transported through all the streets of the camp, to their own humiliation, and the disgust of all right thinking officers and men in the camp.
[Their crime] These men, driven by hunger, had gone to the post, half a mile away, without a pass, in order to buy some canned fruit, they returned in 45 minutes having not missed any roll call or duty.

18 May 1867
...fourteen men of H, E & M troops have just deserted – gone off armed and mounted! – broke through the guards and departed. If General Custer remains long in command, I fear that recruiting will have to go on rapidly to keep the regiment up to strength. "*

SOURCE 9 Elizabeth Custer, speaking about her husband

" He had a very keen sense of his social responsibilities as post commander and believed that our house should be open at all hours to the garrison. "

3. From these sources would you say that Custer was popular with his officers and men?
4. What reasons might his critics have had for trying to discredit Custer?

WAS CUSTER RESPONSIBLE FOR THE DEFEAT OF THE US ARMY AT THE BATTLE OF THE LITTLE BIGHORN?

The campaign

In 1876 the US army was ordered to attack all Sioux who had not returned to their reservation.

Planning the campaign

The plan of campaign was prepared by General Philip Sheridan. It involved three columns co-ordinating their movements. General George Crook would lead a column of 1049 cavalry and infantry northwards from Fort Fetterman. Colonel Gibbon would lead a column of 450 infantry eastwards from Fort Shaw. General Terry, accompanied by Custer, would lead a column of 1000 cavalry, infantry and Gatling guns westwards from Fort Abraham Lincoln. The three would trap the Indians between them.

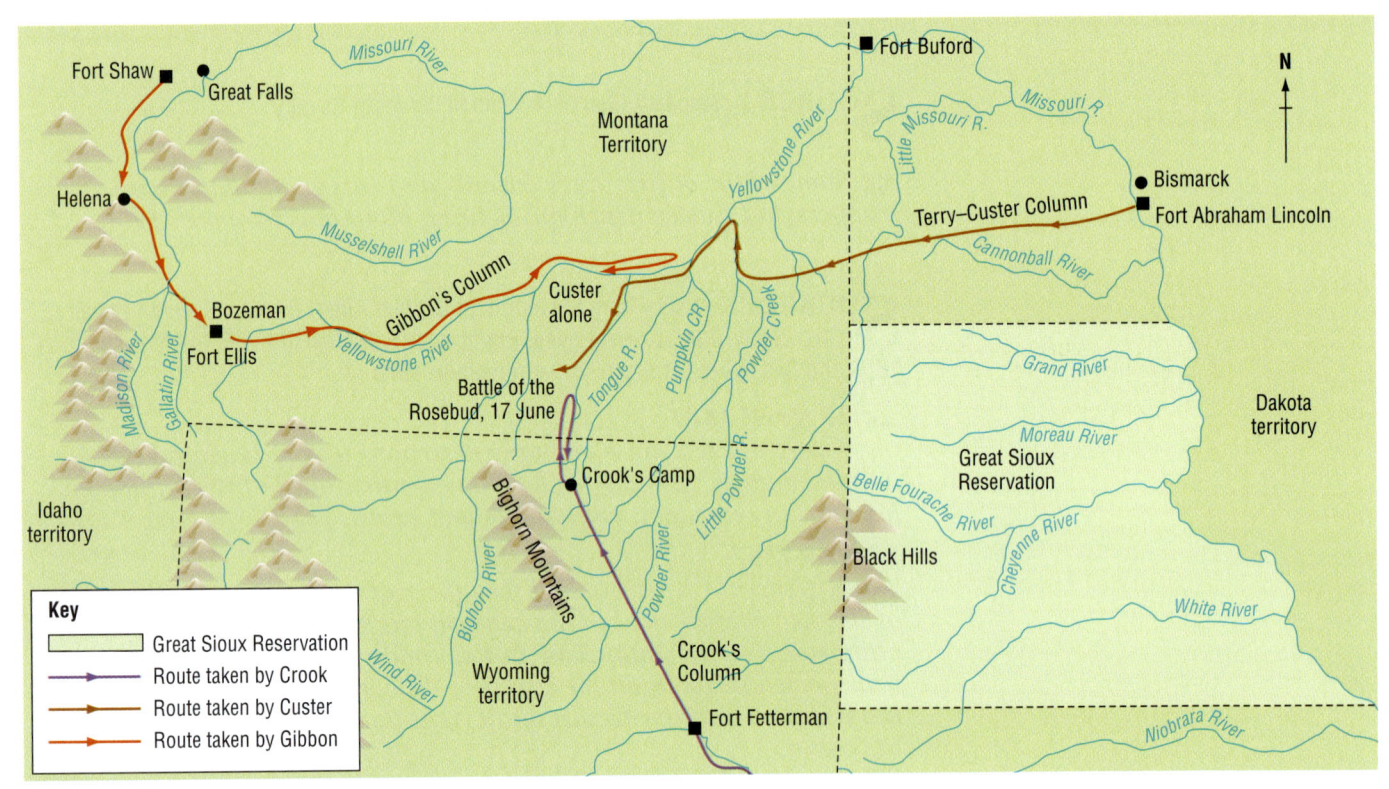

SOURCE 10 A map showing the plan of campaign

5. Who do you think was responsible for the weaknesses in the plan of campaign?

This plan had two major weaknesses. Firstly, there was no effective liaison between Terry and Crook. When they started the three columns were 300–500 km away from the Indians. Secondly, there was no serious attempt to find out how many Indians they might be facing. It was wrongly assumed that the Indians would number approximately 800 warriors, which any one of the three columns could have defeated. This estimate of Indian numbers was based upon information from the Bureau of Indian Affairs, whose job it was to supervise the Sioux reservation.

WAS CUSTER RESPONSIBLE FOR THE DEFEAT OF THE US ARMY AT THE BATTLE OF THE LITTLE BIGHORN?

Things start to go wrong

The campaign went well to begin with. However, on 17 June it began to go wrong.

General Crook's column was halted for a coffee break on the Rosebud Creek. While the officers were playing a game of whist, Crazy Horse led a full-frontal attack with about 1500 warriors. By the end of the day Crook had lost 28 men killed and 63 wounded, and had fired 25,000 rounds of ammunition. He retreated southwards towards Fort Fetterman.

Meanwhile, Crazy Horse took his forces to join Sitting Bull on the Little Bighorn. His losses were 36 killed and 63 wounded. These were terribly high casualties for the Sioux. During the fighting a Cheyenne warrior, Chief Comes in Sight, was unhorsed, cut off and surrounded by Crook's Crow Scouts. His sister, Buffalo Calf Road Woman, seeing this, rode through the Crow, picked up her brother and carried him to safety. To some Indians, this Battle of the Rosebud was known as the fight 'Where the Girl Saved Her Brother'.

Four days later Gibbon and Terry joined forces on the Yellowstone River. General Terry again divided his forces. This time the infantry was to march along the Yellowstone towards the Little Bighorn. Custer was ordered to follow the Indian trail found by Major Reno – which was, in fact, the trail left by Crazy Horse – and approach the Little Bighorn from the south. He was offered 180 extra men from the Second Cavalry and Gatling guns, but refused them.

Custer rode south but then deliberately disobeyed orders. Instead of circling the Wolf Mountains he rode straight across them. By marching through the night and driving his men and horses hard he succeeded in arriving at the Little Bighorn a day early. The Indians camped there were not expecting an attack. But his men and their horses were exhausted.

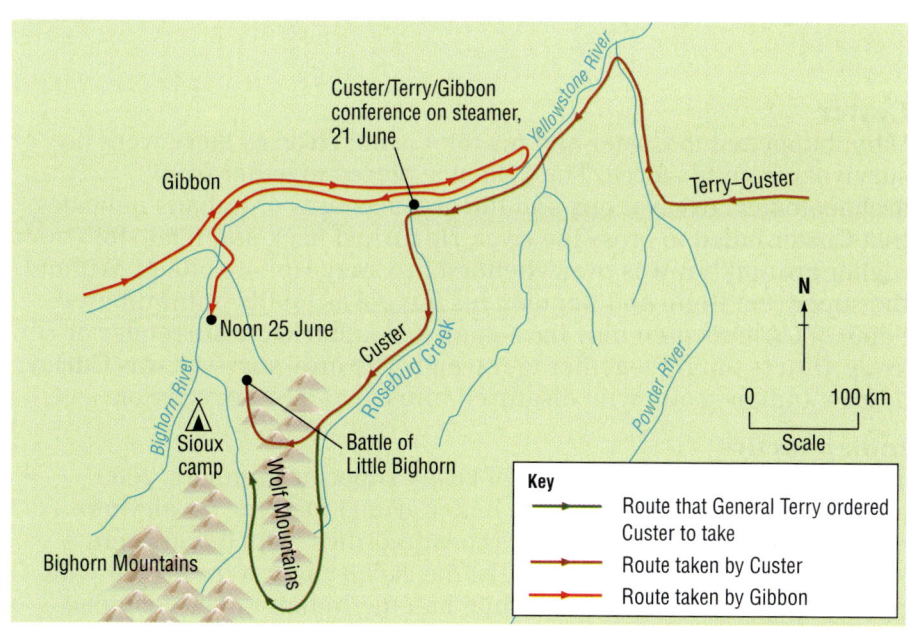

SOURCE 11 A map showing the movements of the US army before the battle

6. Who do you think was responsible for what went wrong for the US army during the campaign?

WAS CUSTER RESPONSIBLE FOR THE DEFEAT OF THE US ARMY AT THE BATTLE OF THE LITTLE BIGHORN?

The Battle of the Little Bighorn

On the afternoon of 25 June Custer reached the camp of Sitting Bull and Crazy Horse on the Little Bighorn. Despite the warnings of his scouts he decided to attack. One scout, Mitch Bouyer, warned, 'If we go in there we will never come out.' Custer may have been afraid that the Indians would escape. He wanted a glorious victory. He supposedly said, 'The largest Indian camp on the North American continent is ahead and I am going to attack it.'

Having taken the decision to attack, Custer then split his forces. This was a tactic he had used successfully at the Battle of Washita. He sent Major Reno with 125 men to attack the southern end of the Indian camp. Captain Benteen, with 125 men, was sent to the south. Captain McDougall took charge of B company and the pack train. Custer himself took 260 men further north to cross the river to attack the Indian camp.

Reno and Benteen

Major Reno's attack was stopped by the Sioux and he retreated across the river, where he took up a defensive position. Reno was then joined by Benteen and his men. For the rest of the day they were surrounded and suffered many casualties. They had received an order from Custer to support him but did not do so. In the enquiry that took place after the battle, they argued that they were unable to follow Custer's last order because they were under attack from so many Indians.

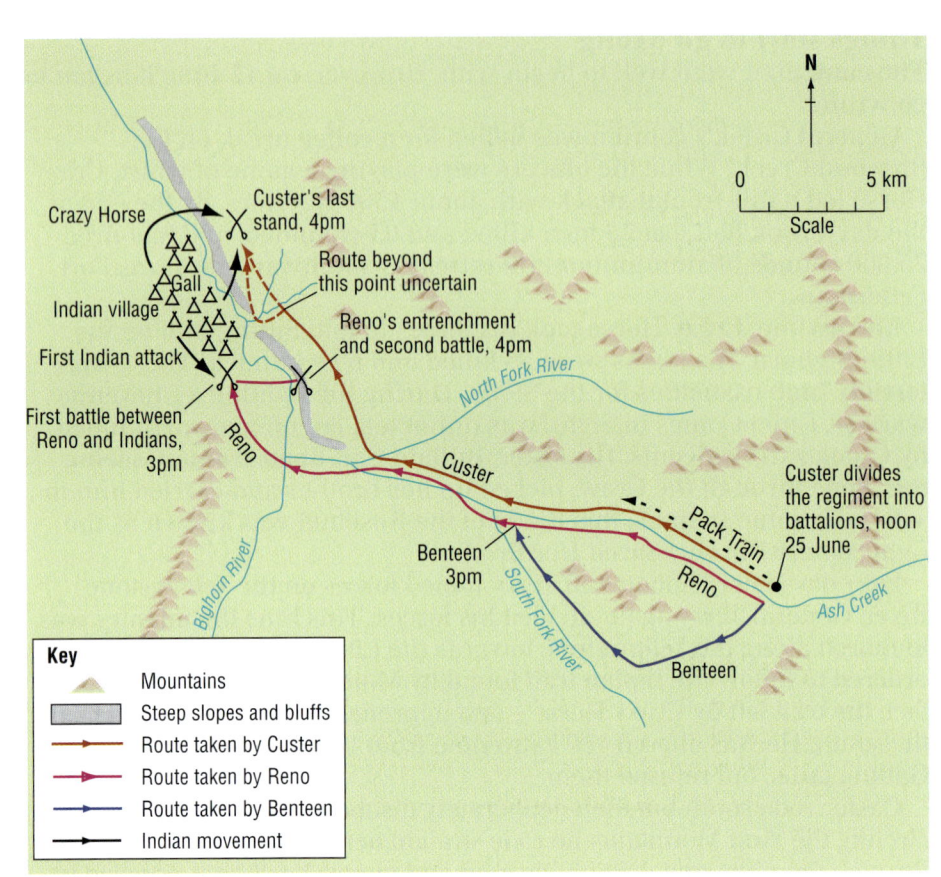

SOURCE 12 A map showing the events of the Battle of the Little Bighorn

Custer

What happened to Custer and his men is not clear as there were no survivors from his force. The evidence pieced together from archaeological excavations and the oral accounts of Indians indicates that Custer failed to cross the river. He turned back and made for higher ground but was overwhelmed by Crazy Horse's attack. Without the support of Reno and Benteen his force was totally outnumbered. Some of Custer's men may have panicked and tried to surrender or run away. Others fought together to the end. The only survivor was Curley, a Crow Indian scout, who disguised himself as a Sioux warrior.

Indian tactics

The Indians had the advantage of vastly superior numbers, 2000 against 600. Some of them were better armed than the cavalrymen. These warriors had Winchester repeating rifles, which had been supplied to them by traders, whilst the cavalrymen were armed with Springfield single-shot rifles. While half the Indian forces defended their camp, Crazy Horse led the rest to surround Custer and his men. For Indians to fight a pitched battle was entirely new. Their normal tactic was to fight a delaying action while the women and children escaped and then withdraw themselves. This change reflected the leadership qualities of Crazy Horse.

WAS CUSTER RESPONSIBLE FOR THE DEFEAT OF THE US ARMY AT THE BATTLE OF THE LITTLE BIGHORN?

■ TASK

From the evidence above who do you think was responsible for the defeat of the Seventh Cavalry on 25 June? Fill out a chart like the one below to help you analyse the evidence. In each section write your own notes about how the various actions contributed to the defeat of the US army at the Little Bighorn.

The actions of:	Custer	His subordinates (Reno and Benteen)	His superiors (Terry and Sherman)	The Sioux and their allies	Others
Planning the campaign					
During the campaign					
On the battlefield					

Was Custer a hero?

As a major defeat, this battle was subject to intense scrutiny. An enquiry was held at which many people gave evidence about what they thought went wrong. Sources 13–17 give you some evidence about Custer from the time of the enquiry:

SOURCE 13 Captain Frederick Benteen, Seventh Cavalry. Benteen had hated Custer for years

" Custer disobeyed orders because he did not want any other command ... or body to have a finger in the pie ... and thereby lost his life. "

SOURCE 14 Major Marcus Reno, Seventh Cavalry, giving evidence at the enquiry into the Little Bighorn disaster, 1879. Reno was blamed for not supporting Custer

" Well, sir, I had known General Custer a long time and I had no confidence in his ability as a soldier. "

SOURCE 15 US President Ulysses S. Grant in a newspaper interview in 1876. Custer had accused Grant's brother of corruption in 1876

" I regard Custer's massacre as a sacrifice of troops, brought on by Custer himself. "

SOURCE 16 Low Dog, a Sioux warrior present at the Battle of the Little Bighorn

" He was a brave warrior and died a brave man. "

SOURCE 17 Major General T.L. Rosser, Confederate Army, one of Custer's opponents during the Civil War, but also a close friend from West Point

" I never met a more enterprising, gallant or dangerous enemy during those four years of terrible war, or a more genial, whole-souled, chivalrous gentleman and friend in peace. "

Was Crazy Horse a great American hero?

THE LITTLE BIGHORN was a victory for the Indians, but they could not win the war. Within twelve months the reinforced US army had defeated the Sioux for good and Crazy Horse was dead. His death was very different from Custer's, but was equally violent. In August 1877 the US army was recruiting Sioux warriors from the reservation for war against the Nez Percés Indians. Crazy Horse was opposed to this. To those running the reservations he was still seen as a danger, so General Crook ordered his arrest. He was taken to Fort Robinson, escorted by Captain James Kennington, who was an Indian Agency policeman, and Private William Gentles. Seeing that they were going to lock him in a barred room in chains, Crazy Horse tried to pull away. In the struggle that followed the soldier bayoneted Crazy Horse in the back. He died later that night. Source 1 suggests that today many Americans regard him as a great American hero.

SOURCE 1 A US postal stamp of Crazy Horse, from the 1980 stamp series 'Great Americans'. Red Cloud and Sitting Bull were also depicted in this series. (See also page 161)

■ **SOURCE INVESTIGATION**

Why do you think Crazy Horse might be regarded as a great American hero? Use the biographical information in Source 2, the views of his enemies in Sources 3 and 4, the views of his friends in Sources 5 and 6, and his own words in Source 8 to help you decide. Then draw up a career chart for him like the one on Custer on page 141.

SOURCE 2 Biographical details of Crazy Horse

about 1841	Born near Bear Butte.
1858	After distinguishing himself in battle he was renamed Crazy Horse.
1861	Famous amongst the Sioux as a skilful warrior.
1865	Chosen as a 'shirt wearer', a leader of his people.
1866	Led the decoy party that lured Fetterman and his men into ambush and death outside Fort Phil Kearney.
1868	Seen as a war leader by those who refused to follow Red Cloud on to the reservation.
1871	Disgraced, and wounded, after a dispute over another man's wife.
1872	Married Black Shawl.
1873	First armed encounter with Custer and the Seventh Cavalry.
1876	Defeated General Crook at the Battle of the Rosebud.
1876	Defeated Custer at the Battle of the Greasy Grass.
6 May 1877	Surrendered at Fort Robinson.
6 September 1877	Murdered or killed resisting arrest at Fort Robinson.

SOURCE 3 An officer at Fort Robinson when Crazy Horse and his followers rode in to surrender

"By God! This is a triumphal march, not a surrender!"

SOURCE 4 Dr Valentine T. McGillycuddy, Assistant Post Surgeon, Fort Robinson

"In him everything was made second to patriotism and love of his people. Modest, fearless, a mystic, a believer in destiny, and much of a recluse, he was held in veneration and admiration by the younger warriors who would follow him anywhere ... I could not but regard him as the greatest leader of his people in modern times."

WAS CRAZY HORSE A GREAT AMERICAN HERO?

SOURCE 5 He Dog, a Sioux warrior

" He never spoke in council and attended very few. There was no special reason for this, it was just his nature. He was a very quiet man except when there was fighting. "

SOURCE 6 An Arapaho warrior present at the Battle of the Little Bighorn

" Crazy Horse, the Sioux chief, was the bravest man I ever saw. He rode closest to the soldiers, yelling to his warriors. All the soldiers were shooting at him, but he was never hit. "

SOURCE 7 The death of Crazy Horse, a pictogram by Amos Bad Heart Bull

SOURCE 8 Crazy Horse, at the start of the Battle of the Little Bighorn

" Come on Sioux! It is a good day to die. "

His dying words to his father

" Tell the people it is no use to depend on me any more now. "

SOURCE 9 Mardell Plainfeather, speaking in 1995

" Nobody knows what he looked like because he didn't want to be photographed. He did not want his image to be taken by the white man. I believe that he didn't trust anything that had to do with the white man. Total and absolute resistance even to the point of being photographed by this enemy people. "

■ ACTIVITY

Write a letter to the American Hall of Fame waxworks museum suggesting the inclusion of either Custer or Crazy Horse in their collection. Explain:

a) what Custer or Crazy Horse achieved
b) why he deserves to be honoured in this way.

chapter 8

HOW DID THE USA DESTROY THE INDIAN WAY OF LIFE?

THE US ARMY was important in the defeat of the Indians. But it was not the only factor. You are now going to look at two other factors which are arguably just as important, in that they destroyed the Indian way of life more effectively than any war could have done. These factors were:

- the destruction of the buffalo
- the reservation system.

The destruction of the buffalo herds

BETWEEN 1840 AND 1885 THE buffalo were hunted almost to extinction: their numbers fell from an estimated thirteen million in 1840 to around 200 in 1885. There were a number of related reasons for this destruction. As more and more people settled on the edge of the Great Plains and travelled across them, the killing of buffalo increased. Parts of the buffalo's habitat were destroyed, and new diseases were introduced. All of these led to a fall in numbers.

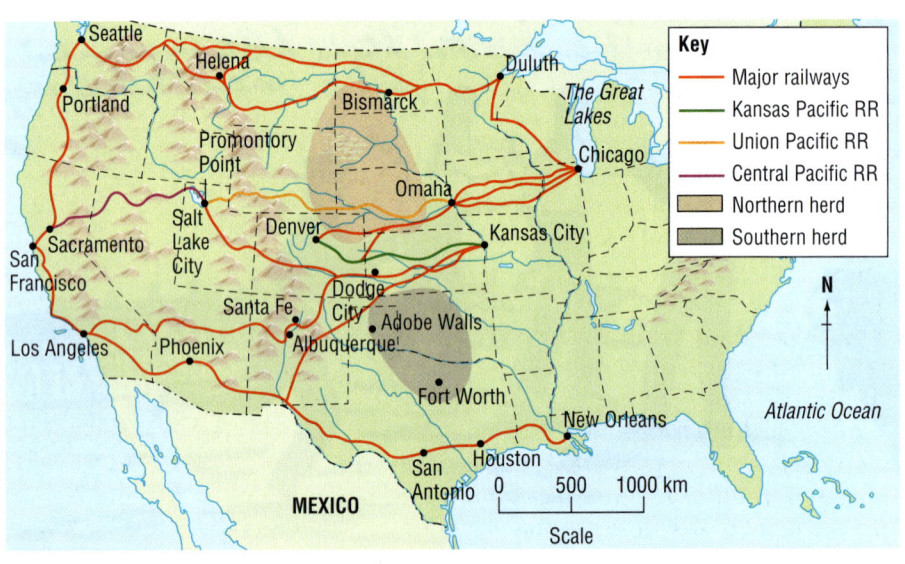

EXCURSION

on Tuesday, October 27, 1868, and return on Friday. This train will stop at the principal stations both going and coming. Ample time will be had for a grand Buffalo hunt.

Buffaloes are so numerous along the road that they are shot from the cars nearly every day. On our last excursion our party killed twenty buffaloes in a hunt of six hours.

All passengers can have refreshments on the cars at reasonable prices.

Tickets of round trip $10.00

SOURCE 1 Reconstruction of an advertisement for an excursion train, 1868

SOURCE 2 A map of the Great Plains, showing the ranges of the northern and southern buffalo herds

Hunting for sport

To begin with, the buffalo were hunted for food and for sport. Hunting increased when the railroads reached the Great Plains. Special excursion trains were run so that people could go out and shoot buffalo for sport, and the railroad builders themselves needed feeding. Buffalo hunters were employed to keep the workers on the line supplied with fresh meat. Amongst these hunters was William Cody, later nicknamed Buffalo Bill. For $500 a month he was employed by the Kansas Pacific Railroad Company to clear buffalo from the line and supply the workers with fresh meat daily, including such delicacies as buffalo tongue. Over seventeen months he killed, by his own count, 4280 buffalo. He went on to make a living from his Wild West Show, which toured America and Europe. This show helped to fuel the myth of the Wild West. He was also the subject of many 'dime novels'.

THE DESTRUCTION OF THE BUFFALO HERDS

SOURCE 3 An engraving showing people shooting buffalo 'for sport' from a train

SOURCE 4 General Custer's wife, Elizabeth

" I have been on a train when the black, moving mass of buffalos before us looked as if it stretched on to the horizon. Everyone went armed in those days, and . . . [it] was the greatest wonder that more people were not killed, as the wild rush for the windows, and the reckless discharge of rifles and pistols, put every passenger's life in danger . . . When the sharp shrieks of the train whistle announced a herd of buffalos the rifles were snatched, and in the struggle to twist around for a good aim out of the narrow window the barrel of the muzzle of the firearm passed dangerously near the ear of any scared woman who had the temerity to travel in those violent days . . . "

Why were so many buffalo killed so quickly?

Hunting for hides

Two developments led to a dramatic increase in buffalo hunting. The first, in 1871, was the discovery by an eastern tannery of a process to produce high-quality leather from buffalo hides. This meant that the price of buffalo hides shot up. The second was that the railroads had reached the Great Plains. Trains could transport the hides east to the tanning industry. The industry was centred on Dodge City and Fort Worth. Buffalo hunters now flooded on to the southern Plains, shooting buffalo for their hides.

The hunting method used could not have been more different from that of the Indians. These hunters were armed with powerful rifles with a very long range. They would take up a position at a distance from the buffalo and first shoot the leading animal. They would then shoot individual animals one at a time. If each shot killed the buffalo instantly then the rest of the group would not be alarmed and the hunter could stay in his position and continue the killing. This was known as a stand, and it was an extremely efficient method of hunting. By the end of 1875 the southern herd was destroyed.

On the northern plains the destruction of the herd did not begin until 1880. The Sioux had been defeated in 1876–77, and the Northern Pacific Railroad had reached Bismarck in 1876. By 1882 an estimated 5000 hunters and skinners were at work, and by 1883 the northern herd was destroyed.

SOURCE 5 Figures for buffalo hides shipped east by railroads, 1872–74. These figures are from Colonel Dodge's book, *Hunting Grounds of the Great West* (see page 45).

Year	Hides carried
1872	497,163
1873	754,329
1874	126,867

THE DESTRUCTION OF THE BUFFALO HERDS

Bone pickers

The hunters were only interested in hides so the rest of the buffalo was left to rot. It was not until later that the remains too were collected and sent east. Collectors were paid by the pound. Homesteaders and crews of professional 'bone pickers' collected skeletons and took them by wagon to railroad sidings. From there they were sent back east to the factories. Something like 32 million pounds of bones were sent in just over three years. In the East, the bones were ground into fertiliser, or made into buttons, combs and knife handles. The hooves were made into glue.

What was the response of the Plains Indians?

The Indians who depended upon the buffalo for their survival (see pages 22–27) were not blind to what was happening. The killing of the buffalo was one of the causes of the warfare on the Plains. In the summer of 1874, in an attempt to force the hunters from the southern plains before the last of the herds vanished, 700 Arapahos, Cheyennes, Comanches and Kiowas attacked the buffalo hunters based near Adobe Walls. The Indians launched repeated attacks against the settlement's buildings, but they were no match for the defending hunters with their powerful buffalo guns. Each time the Indians were driven back with losses. On the third day a hunter using a Sharps rifle with a telescopic sight knocked a warrior off his horse at a distance later measured at nearly a mile. At this point the Indians gave up the fight.

■ CONNECTIONS

Compare the attitudes to buffalo hunting of the buffalo hunters described in this section and the Plains Indians. How were they similar? How were they different? What do you think the two groups' opinions of each other would have been? What effect would this have had on relations between the Plains Indians and other Americans?

SOURCE 6 Buffalo skulls piled by the railroad, ready to be transported to the Michigan Carbon works, 1880s

THE DESTRUCTION OF THE BUFFALO HERDS

Was the destruction of the buffalo a deliberate government policy?

■ **SOURCE INVESTIGATION**

When the buffalo herds were destroyed the Indians had no source of food and shelter. They were forced to move on to the reservations. Some historians have argued that this was a deliberate government policy. Do you agree? Use Sources 7–13 to help you answer this question.

SOURCE 7 Tall Bull, a Cheyenne (dog soldier) chief, talking to General Winfield Scott Hancock, 1867

The buffalo are diminishing fast. The antelope, that were plenty a few years ago, they are now thin. When they shall all die we shall be hungry; we shall want something to eat, and we will be compelled to come into the fort.

SOURCE 8 Sitting Bull, Sioux chief

A cold wind blew across the prairie when the last buffalo fell ... a death wind for my people.

1. What effect did Plains Indians such as Tall Bull and Sitting Bull think the destruction of the buffalo would have on them?

SOURCE 9 General Philip H. Sheridan in a speech to the Texas legislature in 1873

These men [the buffalo hunters] have done more in the last two years, and will do more in the next year to settle the vexed Indian question, than the entire regular army has done in the last 30 years. They are destroying the Indians' food supply ... Send them powder and lead if you will; but for the sake of a lasting peace, let them kill, skin and sell until the buffalos are exterminated.

2. What effect did officers like General Sheridan think the destruction of the buffalo would have on the Indians?

SOURCE 10 Frank H. Mayer, a buffalo hunter based in Dodge City in 1873

I would ride into one of the army camps on a Sunday morning and seek audience with the commanding officer. We would sit and smoke. After a while he would ask if I could use some ammunition. Sure I could. Whereupon as much as I could carry away was all mine. I was young and callow in those days and thought it was my good looks or winning personality which was making the Army so generous with me.

Later [I] asked an officer, 'What am I expected to do with this ammunition – kill Indians?'

'Hell no, that's our job,' replied the officer. 'You just kill buffalo. We'll take care of the Indians. Mayer, either the buffalo or the Indian must go. There isn't any other way. Only when the Indian becomes absolutely dependent upon us for his every need, will we be able to handle him. Every buffalo you kill will save a white man's life. Go to it.'

SOURCE 11 Teddy 'Blue' Abbott, cowboy, in the 1880s

The buffalo slaughter was a dirty business ... All this slaughter was a put-up job on the part of the government to control Indians by getting rid of their food supply. But just the same it was a low down dirty business.

3. Did Teddy 'Blue' Abbott believe that the destruction of the buffalo was a deliberate government policy?

SOURCE 12

In 1874, Congress passed a bill protecting the buffalo, but President Ulysses S. Grant did not sign it. (This meant that it did not become law.)

SOURCE 13 Richard White, writing in the *Oxford History of the American West*, 1994

It now appears that the buffalo was in trouble by the 1840s not so much from overhunting, although this was a factor, but from a combination of drought, destruction of its habitat by white settlers, competition for grass with Indian horse herds and diseases brought by the cattle of white travellers.

4. Now write your answer to this question: was the destruction of the buffalo a deliberate government policy? Explain your answer.

How were reservations used to control the Plains Indians?

SOURCE 1 A government agent distributing food rations to the Sioux Indians

Government policy

From 1825 onwards a system of Indian reservations was developed on the Great Plains. On the reservations the Indians were supervised by government-appointed Indian agents. The reservations were intended to keep Indians apart from the homesteaders and ranchers. On them, the Indians were expected to live as farmers. To start with, the Indians were allowed to leave their reservations to hunt the buffalo. After the conflicts in the 1860s and 1870s they lost this right. From then on the government followed a policy described by General William T. Sherman as a 'double process of peace within their reservation and war without'.

Reservation conditions

By the mid-1870s the Indians were virtually prisoners on their reservations and, for many, conditions were bad. The reservations were usually on land that the settlers did not want, such as farm land of very poor quality, sometimes in unhealthy places. This made it very difficult for the Indians to feed themselves, and this in turn made them dependent upon government hand-outs of food. For a society based upon hunting and war, the life of a farmer dependent upon government hand-outs was demoralising. There was no way for a warrior to gain or maintain status.

In some cases the Indians were badly treated by dishonest Indian agents. Housing monies were stolen, food rations were inadequate and medical treatment was not available. People were punished for offences without trial and individuals were sometimes murdered. Disarmed, without their horses, poorly fed and sometimes suffering from diseases such as measles, influenza and whooping cough, the Indians were unable to resist. They could no longer even hunt the buffalo as the herds had been wiped out.

SOURCE 2 A cartoon of 1890 attacking corrupt Indian agents

1. What point is the cartoonist of Source 2 trying to make?
2. How does he do this?

HOW WERE RESERVATIONS USED TO CONTROL THE PLAINS INDIANS?

To a small number of Indians the reservation was an opportunity. Lesser chiefs could gain importance by co-operating with the Indian agent when the traditional leaders, men such as Sitting Bull, had refused to do so. For some, there was the power and prestige of being an armed member of the Indian police. Sergeant Red Tomahawk, who shot dead Sitting Bull, was a Captain of Indian Police by 1892. Some nations, such as the Pawnee, were already farmers as well as hunters. For them, the change in lifestyle was not so great as for hunters like the Sioux.

In the 1890s the management of reservations was reformed, with various Church groups such as Catholics, Methodists and Quakers being put in charge. Even then the Indian agents were not always honest.

SOURCE 3 Indian Agency Police photographed by D.F. Barry, 1890. Sergeant Red Tomahawk, the man who killed Sitting Bull, is centre

3. Why might these Sioux warriors have agreed to become policemen for the outside authorities?

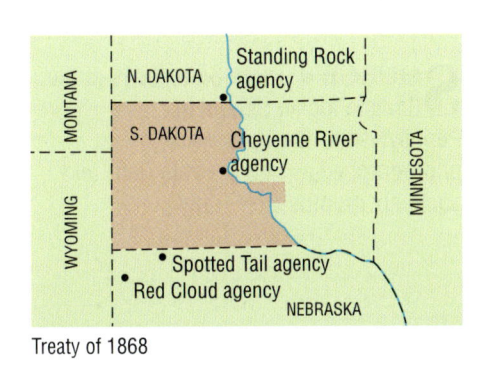

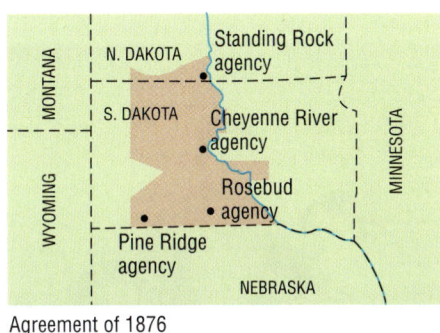

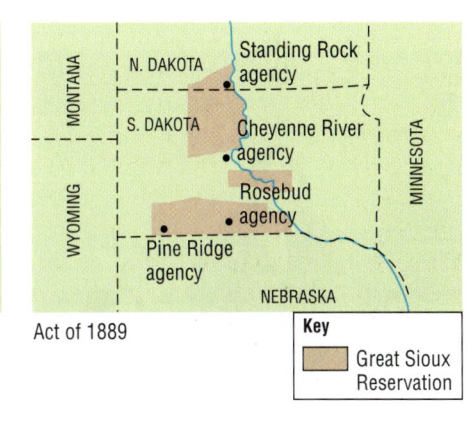

Treaty of 1868

Agreement of 1876

Act of 1889

Key: Great Sioux Reservation

SOURCE 4 Maps showing the reduction of the Great Sioux Reservation, 1868–90

The destruction of Indian culture

The government followed a deliberate policy of destroying all aspects of Indian culture. For the Sioux nation this policy had the following five strands.

1. Territorial
Through a series of laws the government reduced the size of the Sioux reservation and split up the Sioux into smaller groups.

2. Political
At first, rations on the reservations were given to the chiefs to distribute. Later, this policy was changed. Heads of families were encouraged to collect their own rations. This weakened the power and authority of chiefs. In 1885 the government took control of all legal matters. Indians had lost any power to judge and punish members of their bands.

HOW WERE RESERVATIONS USED TO CONTROL THE PLAINS INDIANS?

In 1887 the Dawes General Allotment Act was passed. This allowed the communal reservation lands to be broken up into individual plots. This was intended to completely destroy the power of chiefs and the tribal structure. Individual Indians would become land-owning farmers. They would not need to go to their chiefs, or even see them, as they became self-sufficient. The Act also allowed any land left over to be sold to non-Indian farmers. It was another opportunity for land-grabbers to make money.

> **SOURCE 5** An extract from the Presidential address of President Chester A. Arthur, 6 December 1881
>
> *"The allotment system will have a direct and powerful influence in dissolving the tribal band, which is so prominent a feature of savage life, and which tends so strongly to perpetuate [maintain] it."*

3. Economic
The ban on the Sioux leaving their reservations to hunt or make war on their enemies destroyed the economic foundations of their society. There was no buffalo meat for food, no buffalo hides for *tipis*, clothing and so on, and no chance to increase their wealth by stealing horses.

4. Religious
Feasts, dances and ceremonies, such as the Sun Dance, were banned. The power of the medicine men was undermined. There was little need for young men to seek visions to give them power in war and in the buffalo hunt. This spiritual 'gap' was then filled by the arrival of Christian missionaries.

5. Educational
Children, girls and boys, were taken from their parents and sent away to boarding school. There they were to be prepared for life in 'the white man's world'. One boarding-school founder defined his aim as to 'Kill the Indian in him and save the man'. Children in the schools were not allowed to speak their own language and were punished if they did. They lived under military conditions and were taught to have no respect for their traditional way of life. By 1887, 2020 Indian children were in the 117 boarding schools and 2500 in the 110 day schools. The Sioux were unable to prevent their children being taken. If they resisted their rations were stopped until they had to give in. When the children returned from boarding school they often found that they fitted neither the Sioux world nor the world of other Americans.

The effect of all these measures was to damage tribal structures and to weaken the Indians' self-belief.

SOURCE 6 Three Sioux boys at the Carlisle Indian School in Pennsylvania. The boys were photographed as new arrivals (left) and again six months later (right)

4. Look at the changes in the second photograph.
a) How would the boys' parents have felt?
b) How would the school principal have felt?
c) How would the boys have felt?

■ ACTIVITY

The year is 1889. You are a young Sioux man/woman who has returned from boarding school to live on the Pine Ridge Reservation. Write an article for an eastern newspaper giving your views on what the government has done to your people and your culture since the wars ended.

154

HOW WERE RESERVATIONS USED TO CONTROL THE PLAINS INDIANS?

The Ghost Dance Movement

All the problems on the reservations led to an atmosphere of despair, and it was in that atmosphere that the final tragedy was played out. Just before dawn on New Year's Day 1889, a Paiute holy man called Wovoka received a vision. An Indian Messiah was coming. If the Indians remained peaceful and danced the Ghost Dance, then a new world would come. All the whites would disappear, the buffalo would return and all the dead Indians would come back to life. This Ghost Dance religion spread rapidly across the reservations in the West and reached the Sioux in 1890. It coincided with a time of great hunger on the reservations due to two factors. Firstly, the Sioux rations had been cut by the government. Secondly, the drought in the summer of 1890 led to the failure of the Sioux's crops. In this climate of hunger and despair the Ghost Dance had a great appeal and it spread quickly amongst the Sioux.

The Indian agents were seriously worried. They tried unsuccessfully to ban the Ghost Dance. When that failed they called in the army to help. The army treated it as a war situation. An attempt was made to arrest Sitting Bull because of his involvement in the movement. This was carried out by Sioux Indian police. His followers tried to prevent his arrest, a scuffle broke out and Sitting Bull was shot dead, by one of his own people, a Sioux policeman. Many of his followers fled to join the band of Big Foot, another of the chiefs leading the dance, whom the army were also moving to arrest.

SOURCE 7 Wovoka, the originator of the Ghost Dance Movement

SOURCE 8 Ghost Dance song

*Father have pity on us
We are crying for thirst
All is gone.
We have nothing to eat
Father we are poor.
The buffalo are gone
They are all gone.
Take pity on us, Father
We are dancing as you wished
Because you commanded us.
We dance hard
We dance long
Have pity
Father help us
You are close by in the dark
Hear us and help us.
Take away the white men
Send back the buffalo.
We are poor and weak
We can do nothing alone
Help us be what we once were
Happy hunters of buffalo.*

On 28 December the army, soldiers of the Seventh Cavalry, caught up with Big Foot and his band. They were then taken under guard to camp at Wounded Knee. Next morning the soldiers obeyed orders and moved to disarm the Sioux. At least one Sioux warrior resisted and in the confusion that followed firing started. Were the Seventh Cavalry looking for a chance for revenge for the Little Bighorn? Regardless of who was to blame the soldiers were ready for trouble. They opened fire with repeating rifles and four Hotchkiss cannon. By the time the firing stopped 146 Indians and 25 soldiers were dead. The Indian dead were 102 adult men and women, 24 old men, seven old women, six boys aged between five and eight years and seven babies under the age of two. As one soldier said, 'It was a thing to melt the heart of a man, if it was not stone, to see those little children with their bodies shot to pieces.'

SOURCE 9 *Ghost Dance of the Sioux Indians*, illustrated by Amedee Forestier in the *Illustrated London News*, 1891

HOW WERE RESERVATIONS USED TO CONTROL THE PLAINS INDIANS?

Afterwards, the many Indian wounded were taken to the agency church. Thomas Tibbles, a newspaper reporter wrote, 'Nothing I have seen in my whole life ever affected, or depressed, or haunted me like the scenes I saw in that church that night.' The Indian dead were left where they had fallen for three days before being buried in a mass grave.

This awful massacre marked the end of the Plains Wars. That was not all that was ended. As one survivor, Black Elk, later recalled, 'When I look back now from this high hill of my old age, I can still see the butchered women and children lying heaped and scattered all along the crooked ditch as plain as I saw them with eyes still young. And I can see something else died there in that bloody mud, and was buried in the blizzard. A people's dream died there. It was a beautiful dream. The Nation's hoop is broken and scattered. There is no centre any longer and the sacred tree is dead.'

SOURCE 10 The frozen body of Chief Big Foot, killed in the massacre of Wounded Knee

5. The soldiers in Source 11 were happy to have their photograph taken. What does this tell you about their attitude to the massacre at Wounded Knee?

SOURCE 11 The Sioux dead being buried at Wounded Knee. They were buried in a mass grave. The work was done under contract by civilian labourers who were paid $2 a body. The army stood guard to prevent attack by Sioux warriors

Chapter 9

CONCLUSION

Review: why did the Indians lose, or the settlers gain, control of the Great Plains?

■ **TASK**

This is a very important historical question to consider now that you are almost at the end of this depth study. It is frequently asked by examiners. For example, you might be asked: 'Why were the white Americans able to destroy to a great extent the way of life and culture of the Plains Indians?'

In order for you to write your answer it is necessary to summarise much of the work that you have been doing throughout this book. As you know, no historical event has a single cause. There are a number of causes that you should consider. These are summarised on these two pages. Make your own set of cause cards using just the headings, and use them to help you think about the following questions.

1. Are all the causes relevant?
2. Can they be grouped into different types?
a) Try grouping them into economic, political and military causes. Try fitting these into a Venn diagram. What does that tell you about these causes?
b) Now try splitting the causes into short-term and long-term causes. How does this help you to understand the causes of the Indians' defeat?
c) Can the causes be grouped in other ways? Try Indian weaknesses, other people's hunger for land, the role of the US government. You might be able to think of other ideas. What does this add to your understanding?
3. Are some causes connected? If so, how are they connected? On a plain sheet of paper try drawing the connections between other causes and:
   ■ the railroads
   ■ the American Civil War.
   Now try the same with the cause that you think is most important.
4. Are these causes all equally important or are some causes more important than others?

Now decide how best to arrange your cause cards to answer the question. Each card or group of cards should provide the basis for a paragraph of your answer. Stick them down. Now you are now ready to start writing your answer.

Manifest Destiny

Americans believed that it was their Manifest Destiny to occupy the whole continent from coast to coast. This seemed to be a justification for treating badly those who stood in their way, in particular the Plains Indians, but also Mexicans. It enabled them to justify both the Indian Wars and removals and also the war against Mexico in 1846. It also lay behind the mistreatment of other ethnic groups, such as the Chinese who were brought in to build the railways.

Government policy

The US government, on the whole, supported homesteaders, miners and ranchers against the Plains Indians. There was never enough money spent either to support Plains Indians on the reservations or to allow them to live on in their traditional ways. This was inevitably going to lead to conflict. When conflicts arose the usual solution was to send in the US army to 'deal' with the Plains Indians.

The end of the American Civil War

In 1865 the American Civil War ended. This enabled the United States government to turn its attention to the West. Soldiers were available for the US Army of the West, and money was available for railroad building. Many people, such as the freed slaves from the South and former soldiers, were anxious to build a new life on the Great Plains. From this date onwards the days of the Plains Indians were numbered.

The development of homesteading

The homesteaders wanted land for farming, which they then fenced in. This land had been buffalo pasture and was part of what the Plains Indians considered to be their hunting lands. Homesteaders also scared away game. In effect, they cut down the Plains Indians' living space. Whenever there was trouble on the Great Plains they demanded protection from the US government. They wanted the US army to move the Plains Indians on to reservations.

REVIEW: WHY DID THE INDIANS LOSE, OR THE SETTLERS GAIN, CONTROL OF THE GREAT PLAINS?

The spread of cattle ranching

From the 1870s onwards ranchers wanted land to graze their cattle. This land had been buffalo pasture and was part of what the Plains Indians considered to be their hunting lands. The cattle drives of the 1860s also scared away game, including buffalo, from their routes. Again, the effect was to cut down the Plains Indians' living space. Whilst some cattlemen and ranchers lived peaceably with the Plains Indians, others did not. Those who did not demanded that the US army deal with the Plains Indians. By this they meant that the army should remove the Plains Indians from the Great Plains.

Gold

The discovery of gold in Colorado and Montana in 1858, and in the Black Hills in 1874, brought thousands of miners on to Plains Indian lands. The mining camps and towns took up land, impinged on Plains Indians' religious beliefs and led to the destruction of game in the surrounding area. The development of the mines broke existing treaties and brought miners and Plains Indians into direct conflict. Usually this led to military intervention by the US army.

The transcontinental railroads

The builders of these railroads, such as the Union Pacific Railroad Company whose lines ran along the Platte River valley, needed to finance their work by selling land grants to homesteaders. They therefore wanted to force the Indians out. The railroads brought buffalo hunters to the herds and provided a way of shipping buffalo hides back east to the tanneries. The railroads also supplied the army bases, such as Fort Abraham Lincoln, with men and supplies. While the railroads were being surveyed and built the workers killed and disturbed the game, including the buffalo, on which the Plains Indians depended. The completion of the transcontinental railroad split the great buffalo herd into two.

Reservations

The system of reservations kept the Indians away from homesteaders, miners and ranchers. It enabled the government to control the Indians. By taking away their horses and weapons and by forbidding them to leave the reservation the government made the Indians dependent on hand-outs. This took away the Indians' power to resist. Any protest could be stopped by withholding rations or by using force.

Destruction of the buffalo

The destruction of the buffalo herds took away the Indians' means of supporting life on the Plains. (Look back to pages 22–27.)

US army

The US army was too powerful for the Indians to fight. Whilst some historians argue that man for man the Indians were better fighters, there were too many soldiers. The system of forts gave the US army bases from which to control the Great Plains. The introduction of the strategies of total war and winter campaigns were decisive in defeating the Plains Indians. These last two were the work of Generals Sherman and Sheridan.

Indian organisation

The Plains Indian nations were never able to mount long campaigns against the US army as they had their families to feed and protect. For example, after the Battle of the Little Bighorn the Indian bands split up. There was not enough game in any one area to support so many people. Also they lacked the organisation for prolonged warfare. Whilst a great leader like Crazy Horse could bring warriors together for a short period of time, those warriors could not be made to do anything they did not want to do.

Indian tactics and weapons

The Plains Indians fought in a totally different way to the US army. They were unwilling to suffer heavy casualties and could not replace their losses. So they were never able to fight the army on equal terms. Usually they were less well armed. Every soldier had a rifle, and army units often had artillery and Gatling guns. Not every Indian had a rifle. For example, when Crazy Horse surrendered in 1877 his 250 warriors had 46 breech-loading rifles, 35 muzzle-loading rifles and 33 revolvers between them.

Divisions between Indian nations

The tradition of warfare on the Great Plains meant that the Plains nations never all combined to fight the US army. Some nations, such as the Crow, Shoshone and Pawnee, fought with the US army against the Sioux. Equally, while the Sioux were fighting against the US army they still continued to raid their traditional Indian enemies.

Why study the American West?

WE HAVE STUDIED the American West for four reasons.

1. What it means to be human

It has helped us to understand what it means to be human. We have concentrated upon the ideas and beliefs, values and attitudes of the men and women of the West. The one thing that all the Indians, cowboys, homesteaders, hunters, miners, outlaws, ranchers, travellers, saloon girls, soldiers, warriors and workers had in common was their humanity.

2. Refighting the Battle of the Little Bighorn

People in the United States of America today are still concerned about what took place during this period. Take the Battle of the Little Bighorn, for example. The site of the battle was originally called the Custer National Park. Then, in 1991, it was renamed the Little Bighorn National Park. This name change caused a great deal of argument, reflecting the concern of modern Americans, as Sources 1, 2 and 3 confirm.

1. What do you think the National Park should be called?

SOURCE 1 An extract from the *Guardian* newspaper, 26 April 1991

Custer's descendants lose their own last stand 115 years on

The descendants of General George A. Custer are up in arms about a Congressional decision to meet Indian objections and rename the Custer National Battlefield Park the Little Bighorn Park, site of the celebrated victory of the Sioux nation over the US Army.

Congressman Ben Nighthorse Campbell, an Indian who has been behind the renaming campaign in Congress, said yesterday that this was the only battlefield in the world named after the loser, and the only US National Park named after an individual.

"I'm just kind of wiped out today after all this", said Colonel George Armstrong Custer III, from his retirement home in Pebble Beach, Florida. "No opposition to the name change was invited at the Congressional hearing. I thought this was supposed to be a democracy.

"It is sad to see this Congress yield to a small pressure group in the Indian community and a few staffers within the National Park Service," Custer's great grand-nephew went on. "Five members of the Custer family died in the battle – so we earned the name Custer right there."

SOURCE 2 An extract from the *Guardian* newspaper, 25 June 1996

A battle has broken over a commemoration of Custer's defeat, with whites accusing the Cheyenne of triumphalism

Now the superintendent of the Little Bighorn Battlefield National Monument is a Mandan Hidatsa Indian who passionately wants to make it a more welcoming place for Indians. But he is finding that for many on both sides of the fight the wounds of the battle still go deep.

"This represents the end of the way of life for the Indian people," the superintendent, Gerard Baker, said as he gestured toward the battlefield in the rolling hills of Southern Montana. "When Indian people come here, they cry and they get mad for the loss of that way of life, that freedom. It's something we'll never get back."

Mr Baker has made big plans for the 120th anniversary of the fight, today and tomorrow. Whites and Indians from all the tribes in the battle – Cheyenne, Arapaho, Lakota, as well as the Arikira and Crow who fought on Custer's side – will go to the monument for prayers, a buffalo feast and a ceremony that is generating some outrage.

"We're going to have an Attack at Dawn ceremony," Mr Baker said. "It will be on Tuesday, the anniversary of the day that Custer and his men were all killed in the first part of the two-day battle."

Indians will ride horses to the boundary of the monument at daybreak, head for a mass grave where 200 troopers are buried, and "count coup" by using a stick to hit a stone obelisk that marks the grave. Counting coup was a battle tradition in which warriors proved their skill and courage by striking an enemy with a special stick and then returning to the tribe.

"I've told the tribes, 'This is your day,'" Mr Baker said.

Members of several groups that commemorate the cavalry, including the Custer Battlefield Historical and Museum Association, contend that Mr Baker's programme insults the troopers who died.

Mr Baker, who said he had received three death threats in his three years of working at the battlefield, said that the interpretation at the monument had always been biased and that he was merely trying to make things "more user-friendly for Indians".

WHY STUDY THE AMERICAN WEST?

SOURCE 3 An extract from the *Guardian* newspaper, 27 August 1997. The photograph shows Chief Sitting Bull, who led his warriors against Custer at Little Bighorn

Four generations after Indian warriors killed Custer and the troops under his command in the hills overlooking the Little Bighorn River in 1876, the National Park Service is going ahead with plans to build a monument to the Indians who died in the battle. A design was chosen earlier this year, but critics say the structure will detract from the granite obelisk to the 270 soldiers and Indian scouts of the 7th Cavalry killed in the battle.

About 75 Sioux and Cheyenne warriors also died in the battle. The memorial planned in their honour would be a walk-in monument expected to cost up to $2 million (about £1.25 million).

"If you want to emphasise the Indian victory, please don't do it at the mass grave of 200 soldiers," said Wayne Sarf, a New Jersey history professor and and a leading critic of the Indian memorial.

Such complaints fail to move Gerard Baker, a Mandan Hidatsa Indian from North Dakota and the superintendent of the Little Bighorn National Monument, which covers more than 700 acres. "This memorial will represent all the fallen American Indian people," he said, striding over the proposed site on Last Stand Hill, about 50 yards from the 7th Cavalry obelisk. "This wasn't the only battle the Indians won," he added.

Part of the anger of white traditionalists stems from a sense that they are losing control of history. Although six western states, including Montana, have counties named Custer, Congress voted in 1991 to strip Custer from the name of the battlefield here in Crow Agency, Montana. The same legislation authorised the construction of the memorial to the Indians killed in battle.

The battlefield itself is now part of the Crow Indian reservation. They were given as their reservation the Powder River country that the Sioux had earlier taken from them. There was controversy in 1996 when Cheyenne warriors counted coup on the memorial to the dead Seventh Cavalry. There were arguments in 1997 about the erection of a monument on the site to the memory of the Indians who were killed in the battle.

These arguments happen because the impact of these events is still important today. The Indian nations have continued to be badly treated ever since and they are still struggling for their rights. To them, the events of the past are an injustice. Their lands were stolen and their ancestors slaughtered. To this day the Sioux nation has refused to take the government money paid for the Black Hills. In 1980 the US Supreme Court awarded the Sioux $105 million as compensation for the theft of the Black Hills. The Sioux rejected this money and today it is in a bank account managed by the Bureau of Indian Affairs.

Crazy Horse

Another example is the Sioux treatment of the memory of Crazy Horse. An attempt to make a TV film of his life story in 1995 was bitterly opposed with lawsuits. No Sioux actor would agree to play the part of Crazy Horse. Meanwhile, a massive sculpture is taking shape in the Black Hills at Thunderhead Mountain, 8 km north of Custer. It was begun in 1947 by the sculptor Korczak Ziolkowski and is being completed by members of his family. The letter from Chief Standing Bear commissioning his work read, 'My fellow chiefs and I would like the white man to know the red man has great heroes too.' The finished sculpture will be 195 m long, 170 m high, and so big that the nostrils of his horse are carved 15 m deep. More than six million tonnes of granite will have been blasted out during its construction.

Crazy Horse himself refused to sit for a photograph. How do you think he would feel about this massive sculpture which has become a tourist attraction?

SOURCE 4 The sculpture of Crazy Horse at Thunderhead Mountain in the Black Hills. To check on the progress of the monument you could visit the Crazy Horse Memorial website, http://www.crazyhorse.org

WHY STUDY THE AMERICAN WEST?

Re-enacting history

It is not only the Sioux who are concerned with their history. Source 5 shows the Mormons in Weymouth, Dorset, re-enacting the journey of their fellow Mormons to Salt Lake City in 1847. Their concern for their shared history is a reminder of the intolerance and persecution that they faced then, and reflects their concerns about their place in society today.

SOURCE 5 Members of the Weymouth congregation of the Church of Jesus Christ of Latter-Day Saints walk from Bridport to Dorchester to mark the 150th anniversary of the Mormon trek to Salt Lake Valley

3. Getting better at history

This depth study has helped you to get better at doing history. In it, you have used a wide range of sources to gather evidence about the past. You have used diaries, engravings, fiction and film, graphs, maps, models, paintings, photographs, reconstructions, stories, songs and tables. You have considered how useful and reliable those sources are. This ability to use sources is a core skill in history and, you will find, in life. It is particularly important for an area of the past such as the American West, where the image portrayed by the media, particularly film and television, is so powerful.

It has also enabled you to investigate the lives of some contrasting sets of people. You have seen how the Indians and settlers lived and how their view of the world differed. You have tried to see life through their eyes in order to understand why they acted in the way they did. This is another core skill in history and in life.

It has also helped you to see that events do not always have simple explanations. Sometimes the most obvious explanation is not correct. Do you still think that the Indians were defeated solely by the might of the US army, or do you think there are more complicated reasons for the destruction of the Indian way of life? Historians need to look beyond the obvious. They need to keep asking 'why, why, why?' and not be satisfied with easy answers.

4. Learning lessons from history

Finally, there are lessons to be learnt from history, if we choose to learn them. What was done to the Plains Indians might today be called a policy of genocide. There are many recent examples of genocide. Laurence Peter, Professor of Education at the University of California, said: 'History repeats itself because nobody listens.'

So what do you think? What lessons do you think we might learn for today from the struggle for the Plains between 1840 and 1895?

Glossary

adobes buildings built with bricks made from dried earth or clay and straw

artisans craftspeople and artists

bull boats boats made from buffalo hides stretched on a willow frame

chuck wagon a wagon used for carrying food and cooking utensils on a cattle drive

circa approximately (abbreviated as c.)

claim a piece of land or a stake in a mine

claim jumping stealing someone else's land or mining stake

demobilised released from the army

forty-niners miners who took part in the Californian Gold Rush of 1849

homesteaders settlers who acquired their own land which they farmed and built their homes on

hurdy-gurdy girls dance hall girls or prostitutes

lariats lassoes, the cowboys' catch rope made from braided rawhide

lynched unlawfully killed by a mob, without a proper trial

medicine man name given by non-Indians to an Indian holy man believed to have healing powers. *See also* **shaman**

Mormons members of the Church of Jesus Christ of Latter-Day Saints founded in 1830 by Joseph Smith

nations Indian nations were made up of tribes and bands, with a structured and traditional way of life. However, these nations did not have set geographical boundaries

open range large area of unfenced land on which cattle can graze

parfleches untanned buffalo hides that are dried after being soaked in water and lye to remove the hair

pioneers settlers of a new country or region

polygamy having more than one wife at the same time

Presbyterian mission Protestants who hoped to persuade the Indians to convert to Christianity

prospectors people who searched for sites where gold could be found

ranchers people who own or manage a ranch

rawhide untanned buffalo or cattle hide

reservations areas of land set aside for the Indians by the US government. The Indians were forced to live on reservations after settlers had taken over most of their land and the buffalo herds had been wiped out

saloons places where alcohol was sold and consumed. Usually there were gambling tables too

shaman a man who the Indians believed could cure sickness by using the power of the spirits

stampede a sudden rush of large numbers of animals caused by them being frightened or startled

subsistence survival – in the sense of being able to produce enough food to live

sweat lodge a low hut made from a willow frame covered with hides. Water thrown on the fire turned to steam. Sweating was used for purification and to cure illness

tanned made into leather

vigilante a group or person who claimed to uphold law and order, and deal with suspected wrongdoers. Vigilante activity often resulted in violent attacks on other settlers, particularly those of a different race or religion

Index

Abbott, Teddy 'Blue' 97, 104, 151
Abilene 95, 120–21
American Fur Company 25, 54
Arapaho Indians 131, 132, 138, 150, 159
Arikira 15, 159
Arizona Rangers 114
army
   'buffalo soldiers' 134
   conditions in 134
   defeat of Indians, role in 126, 127, 129, 131, 132, 133, 135, 136, 137
   enlisted men 135
   forts 131, 132, 134, 135, 158
   Indian scouts 136, 143
   strategies against the Indians 158
Army of the West 134, 137, 157
Arthur, President Chester A. 154
Ashley, General William Henry 54
Averill, Jim 106

Badlands 12
Baker, Gerard 159, 160
banks 58, 73, 111
barbed wire 88, 99, 100, 105, 111
Battle of the Greasy Grass see Battle of the Little Bighorn
Battle of the Little Bighorn 35, 132, 134, 136, 137, 138–45, 158
Battle of the Rosebud 136, 143
Battle of Washita 140, 141, 144
Beadle and Adams 108
Benteen, Major Frederick 144, 145
Bentley family 82
Big Foot 155, 156
Billy the Kid (Henry McCarty, William H. Bonney) 116–19
Black Elk 34, 156
Blackfoot Indians 17, 38, 49, 56
Black Hills 12, 34, 35, 126, 133, 140, 160, 161
   and mining 48, 132, 158
Bodmer, Karl, paintings by 36, 43
Bonney, William H. see Billy the Kid
The Book of Mormon 72
Bozeman Trail 131
brand marks 99, 100, 111
Brannan, Sam 68, 77
Bridger, Jim 57, 77
Buffalo Bill (William Cody) 108, 148
Buffalo Bill's Wild West Show 132, 148
Buffalo Dance 24, 36
   buffalo herds 98
   carcass, uses of 26–7, 150
   destruction of 7, 148–51, 158
   hides, uses of 16, 18, 19, 26–7, 134
   hunts 24–5
Bureau of Indian Affairs 126, 142, 160
Butch Cassidy and the Sun Dance Kid 109
Butch Cassidy and the Wild Bunch 113

California 51, 58
   Gold Rush 68–9
cannibalism 56, 67
Canton, Frank 106
Catlin, George 17, 19, 27, 33, 35, 44, 45
   paintings of 9, 21, 24, 25, 31, 32, 36, 38, 42, 44, 46–7
cattle barons 106–7, 111, 116
cattle breeding 99

cattle drives 94–5, 96–7, 120, 121
cattle ranches 98, 116, 158
   and barbed wire 105
   and homesteaders 94, 104
   and Indians 97
Cayuse Indians 63
ceremonies 27, 36
Champion, Nate 107
Cherokee Indians 14
Cheyenne Indians 15, 21, 29, 92, 131, 132, 136, 138, 140, 150, 159
Chivington, Colonel J. M. 126, 136
cholera 15, 69
Christianity 51, 58, 153, 154
Church of Jesus Christ of the Latter-Day Saints see Mormons
Civil War 83, 84, 94, 95, 110, 111, 120, 136–7, 157
claim jumping 71, 111
Chinese Exclusion Act (1882) 112
Cody, William (Buffalo Bill) 108, 148
Coe, Phil 121
Colorado, ranching in 98
Comanche Indians 9, 33, 45, 96, 98, 150
counting coup 30, 159, 160
cowboys 8, 83, 88, 96–7, 99, 100–3, 120, 121, 151
cow towns 95, 96, 110
   Abilene 95, 120–23
Crazy Horse 20, 30, 35, 131, 132, 140, 143, 144, 146–7, 158, 161
Crook, General George 132, 136, 142, 143, 146
Crow Indians 19, 29, 48, 136, 143, 158, 159
Curley (Crow scout) 48, 136, 144
Custer, Elizabeth 141, 149
Custer, George Armstrong 132, 138, 140–41, 142, 143–4
Custer, Colonel George Armstrong, III 159
Custer National Park 159
Custer, Tom 120

dances 24, 36, 37, 154
Dawes General Allotment Act (1887) 154
Deere, John 88
Delaware Indians 50
depression, economic 58, 73
Desert Land Act (1877) 83
dime novels 108, 117, 118, 148
disease 15, 62, 70, 71, 77, 86, 152: see also cholera; measles; smallpox
Dodge, Colonel Richard 18, 21, 45, 149
Donner party 66–7
drinking 55, 70, 71, 101, 120, 121, 135
Duley, Captain William J. 130
Dykstra, Robert 112

Eastman, Seth 21
education 126
   Indians 19, 154
   migrants 80, 92
The Emigrant's Guide to Oregon and California 59
farming on the Great Plains 87–9
fence cutting 111
Fetterman, Captain William 131, 146
Flathead Indians 55
Flying Hawk 18
Fort Laramie Treaty 131, 132

forts 60, 131, 132, 134, 135, 158
forty-niners 68–71
fur trade 54–5

Galbraith, Thomas 129
gambling 55, 70, 71, 101, 120, 121
Garrett, Sheriff Pat 116, 117, 118
Gentles, Private William 146
Ghost Dance Movement 133, 155
Gibbon, Colonel 142, 143
Glidden, Joseph 88
gold mining 48, 68–71, 131, 132, 140, 141, 158
   claim jumping 71, 111
   legal code 71
   towns 8, 70, 71
Goodnight, Charles 95, 98
Gould family 64–5
grain prices, collapse of 58
Grant, President Ulysses S. 145, 151
Great American Desert see Great Plains
Great Emigration 58
Great Plains 3, 58, 74
   farming on 87–9
   Indian tribes, distribution of 14
   physical geography 12–13
Great Sioux War 132–3
Greeley, Horace 50, 80
guns, Indians and 15, 30, 56, 158

Halliday, Daniel 88
Hardin, John Wesley 121
Hastings, Lansford W. 66
Hickok, James Butler (Wild Bill) 7, 108, 120–21
Hidatsa Indians 34, 43, 159, 160
Homestead Act (1862) 83
homesteaders 3, 9, 82, 157, 158
   and barbed wire 105
   and cattle ranchers 94, 104
   farming conditions 87
      improvements in 88–9
   and Indians 90, 92, 127
   living conditions 86
   migration, reasons for 83–5
   women, role of 90–93
horse stealing 111
   Plains Indians and 29, 30, 32, 111

Iliff, John W. 98
Indian Agencies 129
   Police 133, 146, 153, 155
Indian Problem 126, 127

James–Younger Gang 111, 114
Johnson County War 99, 106–7
judges 114

Kansas Pacific Railroad 120, 148
Kennington, Captain James 146
Kiowa Indians 41, 98, 150
Kit Foxes 21, 30

Lakota Sioux Indians 37, 159
land
   Indian view of 35, 48–9
   settlers' view of 49
law and order
   in Abilene 120–21
   enforcement agents 114
   lack of 110–13
   vigilantes 114–15

164

INDEX

Lincoln County War 116
Lincoln, President Abraham 129
Little Bighorn National Park 159
Little Crow 30, 129
Little Crow's War 128–9
Long, Major Stephen 13
Loving, Oliver 95, 96, 98
Lowe, Sergeant Percival 135
lynching 106, 114, 115

Mandan Indians 43, 159, 160
Manifest Destiny 50–51, 157
Marshall, James 68
marshalls 114, 120
McCall, Jack 121
McCarty, Henry see Billy the Kid
McCoy, Joseph 95, 101, 120
McDougall, Captain 144
measles 63, 152
medicine men 20, 37, 38–9
Mennonites 84, 88
migration 51, 60–67,
    reasons for 58, 83–5
miners 49, 83: see also gold mining
missionaries 72
    Mormon 74, 79
Mississippi River 12, 43
Missouri River 54, 59, 60
Missouri state 58
    Mormons in 73
Mormon Diggings 68
Mormons 68, 72, 161
    and Indians 80
    in Kirtland 73
    in Missouri 72, 73
    in Nauvoo 74–6
    and polygamy 74–5, 76, 81
    in Utah 79, 81
    wagon trains 76–7, 79
Mormon War 80
Mountain Meadow Massacre 80
mountain men (fur trappers) 54–7, 58
Myrick, Andrew 129

Navaho Indians 104
Nez Percés Indians 55, 146
Northern Pacific Railroad 149

Ohio and Mississippi Railroad 113
Ojibwa Indians 15, 30
Olinger, Deputy Robert 118
Oregon 51, 58
Oregon Trail 54, 131
O'Sullivan, John L. 50

Paiute Indians 66, 155
Parkman, Francis 19, 38, 45
Pawnee Indians 29, 43, 45, 158
pemmican 26, 27
Perpetual Emigrating Fund 79
Peter, Laurence 162
Pinkerton Detective Agency 114
Plains Indians
    buffalo, uses of 26–7
    buffalo hunts 24–5
    and cattle ranchers 97
    chiefs 20
    children 19, 47
    and Christianity 153, 154

councils 20–21
culture, destruction of 153–4
education 19, 154
exposure, death by 19
family life 18–19
and fur trappers 56
and homesteaders 90, 92, 127
horses 15, 19, 24, 30, 32–3
and horse stealing 29, 30, 32, 111
and land, relationship to 35
medicine 38–9
and Mormons 80
organisation of society 20
religion 26, 34–5, 38, 49, 154, 155
reservations 3, 98, 128, 133, 136, 152–3, 158
tipis 16–18
warfare 29–30
warrior societies 21, 24, 30
Plummer, Henry 114
polygamy 19, 47, 74–5, 76, 81
Potawatomie Indians 50
Powder River country 29, 136, 160
Prairie Schooners 59: see also wagon trains
Pre-emption Bill 58
prostitutes 70, 120, 121
Pueblo Indians 15

racism 71, 104, 112, 114, 121
railroads 3, 83, 84, 85, 95, 158
    and buffalo herds, destruction of 7, 148–9
    refrigerated rail cars 98
    robbery on 113
ranching, open range 94, 99, 104
Red Cloud 20, 127, 131, 132, 136
Red Cloud's War 29
Red Tomahawk, Sergeant 153
Reed, James 66, 67
Remington, Frederic 139
    paintings by 6–7, 57, 109, 127, 155
Reno, Major Marcus 143, 144, 145
reservations 50, 98, 128, 133, 136, 158
    conditions in 129, 152–3
    government policy on 152
robbery 113
Rocky Mountains 12, 54, 56, 60, 131
Russell, Charles 102–3
rustling 100, 106, 109, 111, 116

Sagar family 60, 62–3
Salt Lake City 72, 78, 79, 80, 87
    plan of 78
Sand Creek Massacre 126, 136
Santee Sioux 30, 128–9, 132
Sarf, Wayne 160
Scalp Dance 36
scalps 6, 16, 30, 31, 56, 129
Scott, John 74
settlers
    view of Indians 46–7
    view of land 49, 51
shaman see medicine men
sheep farming 104
Sheridan, General Philip 132, 137, 142, 151, 158
sheriffs 71, 114, 116
Sherman, General William Tecumeseh 127, 135, 137, 151, 158
Shoshone Indians 136, 158

Sibley, General 129
Sioux 15, 16, 19, 29, 48
    buffalo hunts 25
    daily life 16–21
    Lakota 37, 159
    religion 34–5: see also spirit world
    Santee 30, 128–9, 132
    warfare 29–30
Sioux Indian Police 133, 155
Sitting Bull 20, 30, 35, 36, 126, 129, 131, 132, 143, 153, 155
slavery 83, 84
slaves and ex-slaves 71, 73, 84
smallpox 15, 57
Smith, Jed 54, 56
Smith, Joseph 72, 73, 74, 75, 81
South Pass 54, 60, 77
spirit world 20, 24, 33, 34–5, 36, 38, 41, 45, 46
Sun Dance 36, 37, 154
Swift, Gustavus 98
Terry, General 136, 142, 143
Texas 51
    ranching in 94, 98
Texas longhorns 94, 98, 99
Texas Rangers 114
Tibbles, Thomas 156
Tilghman, Bill 114
Timber Culture Act (1873) 83
timelines
    American West 1840–1895 4–5
    cattle ranching 107
    Great Plains conflict 124–5
tipis (lodge; tepee) 16–18, 31, 34, 46, 47
trade with Indians 15, 25, 43, 64
trappers (mountain men) 54–7, 58
travois 16, 17, 27
Tunstall, John 116
Tutt, Davis 120

unemployment 58
Union Pacific Railroad Company 106, 158
Ute Indians 14

vigilantes 7, 114–15, 118
The Virginian 108
visions 35

wagon trains 6, 51, 54, 57, 60–67, 69
    Indians and 64, 65
    Mormon 76–7, 79
Warner, Luna E. 90
warrior societies 21, 24, 30
water supply 78, 86, 87, 88, 90, 99, 104
Watson, Ella 106
wheat 79, 88, 89
Whitman Massacre 63
Wild Bill Hickok see Hickok, James Butler
Williams, Mike 121
windmills, pumps driven by 88, 99
Wister, Owen 108, 109
Wolcott, Major Frank 106
Wounded Knee 155–6
Wovoka 155
Wyoming Stock Growers Association 106

Young, Brigham 76–7, 78, 79, 80, 81

Ziolkowski, Korczak 161

165

Acknowledgements

Photographs reproduced by kind permission of:

Cover: *top* Private Collection/Bridgeman Art Library, London, *bottom* Solomon D. Butcher Collection, Nebraska State Historical Society; **p.6** *tl* Robert Hale Ltd, *tr* Peter Newark's Western Americana, *bl* Corbis-Bettmann; **pp.6-7** *b* Amon Carter Museum, Fort Worth, Texas (1961.381); **p.7** *tl* Peter Newark's Western Americana, *tr* Moviestore Collection, *br* Kansas State Historical Society, Topeka, Kansas; **p.8** *tl* American Adventure World, Ventureworld Limited, *tr* Montana Historical Society, Helena, *bl* Peter Newark's Western Americana, *br* Reproduced by permission of the American Museum in Britain, Bath ©; **p.9** *t* Solomon D. Butcher Collection/Nebraska State Historical Society, *c* Peter Newark's Western Americana, *b* Peter Newark's American Pictures; **pp.10-11** Private Collection/Bridgeman Art Library, London; **p.13** Tom Bean/Corbis; **p.17** Museum of the Plains Indian, Browning, Montana, Photo Courtesy of the U.S. Department of the Interior, Indian Arts and Crafts Board; **p.21** *t* Peter Newark's Western Americana, *b* © Gilcrease Museum, Tulsa, Oklahoma; **p.24** *t & b* Peter Newark's Western Americana; **p.25** *t* National Museum of American Art, Washington D.C./Art Resource, New York, *bl* The Gerald Peters Gallery, Santa Fe, New Mexico, *br* Moviestore Collection; **pp.31-32** Peter Newark's Western Americana; **p.36** *t* Joslyn Art Museum, Omaha, Nebraska; Gift of Enron Art Foundation, *b* Peter Newark's Western Americana; **p.37** Neg./Transparency nos. 1901(4) & 1902(4) (photo by Logan) Courtesy Department of Library Services, American Museum of Natural History; **p.38** Peter Newark's Western Americana; **p.39** *t* Neg./Transparency nos. 1901(4) & 1902(4) (photo by Lynton Gardiner) Courtesy Department of Library Services, American Museum of Natural History, *bl* Buffalo Bill Historical Center, Cody, Wyoming, Chandler-Pohrt Collection, *br* Buffalo Bill Historical Center, *z* Cody, Wyoming, Gift of Irving H. "Larry" Larom Estate; **p.41** Courtesy of Phoebe Apperson Hearst Museum of Anthropology and the Regents of the University of California; **p.42** National Museum of American Art, Washington D.C./Art Resource, New York; **p.43** *t & b* Joslyn Art Museum, Omaha, Nebraska; Gift of Enron Art Foundation; **p.44** National Museum of American Art, Washington, D.C./Art Resource, New York; **pp.46-47** Peter Newark's Western Americana; **p.48** Mary Evans Picture Library; **p.50** Museum of the City of New York/Bridgeman Art Library, London; **p.51** *t* National Cowboy Hall of Fame and Western Heritage Center, Oklahoma City, *b* National Museum of American Art, Washington D.C./Art Resource, New York; **p.53** *t & b* The National Archives/Corbis; **p.54** Walters Art Gallery, Baltimore; **p.55** Beinecke Rare Book and Manuscript Library, Yale University; **p.56** Joslyn Art Museum, Omaha, Nebraska; **p.57** Peter Newark's Western Americana; **p.59** Corbis-Bettmann; **p.61** *t* The Denver Public Library, Western History Collection, *b* Peter Newark's Western Americana; **p.62** University of Michigan Museum of Art, Bequest of Henry C. Lewis (photo: Partrick Young); **p.63** Oregon Historical Society (OrHi637); **p.64** The Denver Public Library, Western History Collection; **p.65** *t* Peter Newark's Western Americana, *b* Utah State Historical Society; **p.66** Peter Newark's Western Americana; **p.67** Culver Pictures; **p.68** *t* The Bancroft Library, *b* The Oakland Museum of California, Gift of the Museum Founder's Fund (A68.90.2); **p.69** Hulton Getty; **p.70** Peter Newark's Western Americana; **p.74** *t* Church of Jesus Christ of Latter Day Saints, Archives Division, *b* The Denver Public Library, Western History Collection; **p.75** *t* Church of Jesus Christ of Latter Day Saints, Museum of Church History & Art, *b* National Portrait Gallery, Smithsonian Institution/Art Resource, New York; **p.76** Church of Jesus Christ of Latter Day Saints, Archives Division; **p.77** © Courtesy Museum of Art, Brigham Young University, Provo, Utah. All Rights Reserved (photo: David W. Hawkinson); **p.79** Amon Carter Museum, Fort Worth, Texas (1965.168); **p.81** *l* Corbis-Bettmann, *r* Peter Newark's Western Americana; **p.82** Solomon D. Butcher Collection, Nebraska State Historical Society; **p.83** Peter Newark's Western Americana; **p.85** *t* Kansas Collection, University of Kansas Libraries, *bl* The Kansas State Historical Society, Topeka, Kansas, *br* Solomon D. Butcher Collection, Nebraska State Historical Society; **p.86** Corbis-Bettmann; **p.88** Peter Newark's Western Americana; **p.89** Nebraska State Historical Society, Solomon D. Butcher Collection; **p.90** The Kansas State Historical Society, Topeka, Kansas; **p.92** *t* Peter Newark's Western Americana, *b* Corbis-Bettmann; **p.93** *t* Library of Congress/Corbis, *b* Fort Collins Public Library; **p.95** Peter Newark's Western Americana; **p.97** Reproduced by permission of the American Museum in Britain, Bath ©; **p.99** The Montana Historical Society, Helena; **p.102** *t* Peter Newark's Western Americana, *b* Courtesy of the Montana Historical Society, Mackay Collection; **p.103** *t* Courtesy of the Montana Historical Society, Mackay Collection *b* Peter Newark's Western Americana; **p.104** The Moorhouse Collection, University of Oregon Library, Eugene; **p.105** Solomon D. Butcher Collection, Nebraska State Historical Society; **p.106** American Heritage Center, University of Wyoming, Laramie; **p.108** Peter Newark's Western Americana; **p.109** *t* The Moviestore Collection, *c* The Kobal Collection, *b* Mary Evans Picture Library; **p.111** Minnesota Historical Society, St. Paul; **p.112** Peter Newark's Western Americana; **p.113** *t* American Heritage Center, University of Wyoming, Laramie, *b* Peter Newark's Western Americana; **p.115** Kansas State Historical Society, Topeka, Kansas; **p.117** *l & tr* Peter Newark's Western Americana, *br* Beinecke Rare Book and Manuscript Library, Yale University; **p.118** *t* Beinecke Rare Book and Manuscript Library, Yale University, *br* Peter Newark's Western Americana; **p.119** *tl* University of Nebraska Press, Lincoln, *tr* Peter Newark's Western Americana, *b* Moviestore Collection; **p.120** The Kansas State Historical Society, Topeka, Kansas; **p.121** Peter Newark's Western Americana; **p.123** Mary Evans Picture Library; **p.127** *t* Peter Newark's Western Americana, *b* The Denver Public Library/Western History Collection; **p.129** Peter Newark's Western Americana; **p.130** *t* Minnesota Historical Society, St. Paul, *b* Peter Newark's Western Americana; **p.131** Peter Newark's Western Americana; **p.132** © Smithsonian Institution, neg. no. 3195-G; **p.133** *l* Bismark Tribune, *r* Peter Newark's Western Americana; **p.134** *t* Beinecke Rare Book & Manuscript Library, Yale University, *b* University of Arizona Special Collections, Tucson, Arizona; **pp.135-7** Peter Newark's Western Americana; **p.138** Buffalo Bill Historical Center, Cody, Wyoming; **p.139** © Smithsonian Institution, neg. no. 55299; **p.140** Peter Newark's Military Pictures; **p.147** University of Nebraska Press, Lincoln, Copyright 1967. Used by special permission; **p.149** Peter Newark's Western Americana; **p.150** Burton Historical Collection, Detroit Public Library; **p.152** *t* © Smithsonian Institution, neg. no. 56630, *b* Prints and Photographs Division, Library of Congress; **p.153** Denver Public Library; **p.154** *l & r* © Smithsonian Institution, neg. nos. 57489 and 57490; **p.155** *t* Peter Newark's Western Americana, *b* Mary Evans Picture Library; **p.156** *t* Peter Newark's Western Americana, *b* Nebraska State Historical Society; **p.159** Peter Newark's Western Americana; **p.160** Corbis-Bettmann; **p.161** *t* photo: Robb Dewall; **p.162** © Dave Penman.

(*t* = top, *b* = bottom, *r* = right, *l* = left, *c* = centre)